BLOOD
SWEAT
TEARS

For all of us.

Letter from the Editor

When I hiked the Appalachian Trail, I didn't bleed. I was getting "the shot" and hadn't had a period in over a year. When I perused the hiking forums searching for information about mail drops and gear and shuttles and hostels and hitchhiking, I skipped the threads where women discussed bleeding on the trail with a smug thought to myself: *Not me. I am period-free.*

A few years later, while working in the natural food industry, I learned a lot of disturbing things about the effects of hormonal birth control on women's bodies and minds. So, I made the decision to return to the land of the bleeding. By then I was an experienced hiker, quite familiar with shitting in holes and peeing on my shoes. The first time I dug a cathole, I was in tears by the time all was said and done. I am grateful that I got to experience a graduated easing into bodily functions on the trail. I shudder to think how I would have handled bleeding for four straight days as a baby backpacker.

These days, I often see prospective thru-hikers in online forums and at live events riddled with anxiety and desperate for guidance on how to manage the finer aspects of existing in a body that will continue through its monthly cycles regardless of the environment.

Society has convinced 50% of the population to downplay the fact that 50% OF THE POPULATION is bleeding in their pants for four to seven days every month. I have actually said out loud, "It's just your period, but you're in the woods. It's really no big thing. You do the same thing you do every month, but in the woods. *You're overthinking it.*"

I don't know why I've said this. To seem cool? Nonchalant? To try to keep these rightfully panicking, uterus-having comrades of mine from forgoing their thru-hiking dreams because they're going to bleed a little?

The truth is . . . hiking while bleeding is often a terrible, no-good, not fun, bad time. And we should all get a gold star for doing it when it happens. I have often planned my adventures around my monthly cycle, but that can only be done with so much accuracy and intention.

Sometimes the body just decides to bleed early. Or sometimes you have permits for a certain day. Or are meeting a friend on their one day off. Sometimes you just have to keep living your life, even as blood gushes between your legs. Because you had the luck of the draw, being born with a functional uterus.

This book is an acknowledgment that being on trail while existing in an assigned-female-at-birth body comes with a specific set of challenges. Some physical, some societal, and many mental. And we aren't doing ourselves or each other a service by minimizing and acting like nothing is happening when we slog up and down mountains wondering whether that's our tampon leaking or swamp ass soaking our underwear.

Sharing these stories and speaking our truth is a powerful form of connection. It is also the key that sets us free.

—Christine Reed

BLOOD

the red bibler tent

BEHIND A LARGE ROCK, I SQUATTED AND BENT MY HEAD TO observe the color of my pee. A red drop fell.

"What?" I quickly did the math. My period was a week early.

"Fuck," I muttered and, while peeing, reached into the top of my day pack for a wad of toilet paper. I tore off a piece, folded it in my hand, and cupped it into place. Then I hitched up my underwear and trekking pants.

At that moment, my period supplies were zipped into a blue duffel bag, strapped on the back of a mule, trotting their way to Aconcagua base camp. The toilet paper would have to suffice until I could catch up with them. Under the midday Argentina sun, I returned to where the other members of my climbing team, all men, were taking a short break alongside the beaten trail, and said nothing about this new development. It's not like any of them would have had a pad or tampon. Instead, I clipped my pack around my waist and told our expedition leader, Tim, that I would go ahead to base camp to scout for some tent sites.

I wanted to retrieve my pads as soon as possible.

"Okay," he said. "Just take your time adjusting to the altitude."

"I will," I promised, before heading toward the snow-covered massif of Aconcagua, the highest mountain in the Americas, measuring in at 22,837 feet. Our team of seven was self-organized by Tim, who had an impressive mountain resume with summits of Everest, Kanchenjunga, Denali, and Aconcagua and expeditions to K2 and Lhotse. Tim and I had grown up in the same small town in central New York, on neighboring family farms, which shared a property line. Since he was fifteen years older, we didn't really get to know each other until I was in my twenties and pursuing a life with mountains as the focus.

After completing an undergraduate degree in environmental studies, I had taken on a job as a wilderness therapy instructor in the rugged Adirondack Mountains, living out of my backpack every other week. When I completed my master's degree, I became a college instructor, leading students on immersive backcountry experiences.

Through the hometown grapevine, Tim had heard about some of my adventures and asked me to be his strong second on Aconcagua. I took the responsibility to help him guide one of the Seven Summits seriously because I wanted to expand my own climbing resume before leading a team to Denali the following year. My expedition skills were strong, but I'd never been to extreme altitude, which is classified as anything over 18,000 feet. I wanted to experience that on a less technical mountain before journeying to the deep crevasses and sheer slopes of Denali.

I'd been to high and very high altitude multiple times on expeditions to Ecuador, Nepal, the Cascades, and the Sierra Nevada and had never had any issues within that range of 5,000 to 15,000 feet, so I felt pretty confident coming into Aconcagua. Even with that confidence, I took the acclimatization process seriously. The night before we started our expedition, I abstained from drinking wine in Mendoza with the rest of the team and focused only on water and electrolytes. Competitive by nature, I wanted to show my teammates just how capable I was. It didn't help that I was the only woman on my team and felt it was my responsibility to make a physical statement for an often underrepresented and misunderstood gender on mountain expeditions. My acclimatization strategy paid off, and the previous night at Camp Confluencia, located at 11,122 feet, my oxygen levels were the highest of those in the group: 100 percent when measured with a pulse oximeter.

As I trekked alone to base camp, I felt the warm gush of blood every now and then and hoped it was hitting the toilet paper wad instead of my underwear. My lower back ached slightly, from period pain and from hiking with a pack. I clapped my hands with excitement when the yellow expedition tents of Plaza de Mulas base camp came into view. My pace quickened and I passed a sign announcing the elevation of 14,400 feet, almost the same as Mount Whitney, the highest point in the contiguous United States.

In base camp, international climbers nodded their heads as they passed me. All were men. I returned their nods and tossed back my shoulders, to give my five-foot-eight frame another inch. It stoked my competitive flames to know that I was the only person on my team, or it seemed on any of the teams on the mountain, who would have to navigate the logistics of bleeding for four days at altitude. I could have my period and still be the first into base camp. Now I just had to find my bag.

At the cook tents, I was directed by a young man to a nearby dome shelter that housed all the duffel bags brought to camp by the mules.

"There you are!" I cheered when I found it amid the pile of mostly yellow North Face ones and hoisted it over my shoulder. At an open tent site, I unzipped the side compartment in search of a heavy-flow maxi pad. My system for periods in the backcountry was simple: I used pads. With a regular cycle, I packed a total of eight—one for each day, one for each night. It was during my years as a wilderness therapy instructor that I began wearing pads consistently instead of tampons. The students in the program were provided a plastic bag full of pads of various sizes, referred to as a "fem kit." I began using the same system so that when my students complained about not being able to have tampons, I could say, "I use the fem kit too and it's safer to use pads on long expeditions because we don't always have reliable ways to wash our hands."

After my wilderness instructor days, I continued using the fem kit. There was something about shedding my blood upon the ground that felt symbolic, ceremonial, and incredibly natural. To me, red blood on red leaves, white snow, or palomino-colored desert sand was beautiful.

The latrine at base camp was a large structure made of sheet metal with a front door that rattled when opened. Inside, I found a clean and luxurious pit toilet, fully stocked with toilet paper and hand sanitizer. It helped that the climbing season on Aconcagua was about to end so the population of base camp was low. Our expedition was one of the last that would be on the mountain. Still, I raised my neck gaiter up around my nostrils, sat over the oval hole, and tossed the wad of bloody toilet paper down into the abyss.

My bowels grumbled and the period diarrhea began. Over the years of expedition life, I had observed that my bowels were looser at altitude and when I got my period. Now, I had the lovely combination of the two. In addition, I'd been diagnosed with ulcerative colitis, a chronic disease of the large intestines, when I was ten. The whole host of gastrointestinal issues that came along with my diagnosis had ironically been a major factor in why I felt so at home in the outdoor field. Everyone had poop stories from bad water or bad food and had more than likely shit their pants at some point on an expedition. Though ulcerative colitis was much more complicated than awkward poop stories, in the mountains it could be something to bond over, rather than something wrong with me. And that had been healing for my younger self.

After my trip to the latrine, I washed my hands at a faucet near the mess tents and popped two Imodium. As I returned to my tent site, my teammates entered base camp.

"Hey!" I waved them over to where our bags were, so we could begin the process of setting up camp. My teammates broke off into pairs and found empty tent sites close to mine. I challenged myself to be the first one set up. Working solo, I moved swiftly to unroll my one-person Bibler tent. With my trail runners, I pushed rocks aside to make space for the tent. Then I snapped the poles into place and inched them through the fabric. Once the tent was erected, I attempted to drive the stakes into the ground, but it was so hard that even using a rock as a hammer hardly made a dent. I was forced to tie the stakes to strands of paracord and secure large rocks atop them.

When I was done arranging gear inside my tent, I glanced around to see if I had won my secret game. I had. Everyone else was still looking for rocks to fasten their stakes. Inwardly congratulating myself, I sat down on a large rock. The landscape before me was jagged and dry with hues of green and gray. The opening of my tent faced east and to the west the sun blazed over the imposing summit of Aconcagua.

"Bethany, can you help me set up our mess tent?" Tim asked.

"Sure," I said. When I stood up, my vision blurred, and I felt a hot pain in my abdomen. "Uh, I have to go to the bathroom first," I called to Tim. I made it back to the latrine just in time for another bout of diarrhea to unleash its fury.

My head throbbed and I cradled it between my hands. It unnerved me that I was losing blood and liquids at the same time. Ten minutes crawled by before I found enough strength to lift myself off the pit latrine and return to my tent.

Tim came over to ask if I was okay.

"Yeah," I lied.

"Why don't you lie down in your tent, and I'll send Paul over? You probably have a bit of altitude sickness," Tim said.

I agreed, then crawled into my tent. For one person, the Bibler was spacious. My sleeping pad and bag lay on one side and my clothes were folded on the other. My body started to cool from the lack of movement, so I zipped a fleece over my green polypro top. I lay on top of my sleeping bag with my eyes closed. Paul, our team doctor, arrived a few minutes later and knelt near my head at the entrance of the tent.

"Hey, Bethany, I heard you weren't feeling too good," he said.

"Yep," I said, still wearing my sun hat and sunglasses.

"What's going on?" he asked.

"I'm having diarrhea," I slurred. Each word was hard to enunciate, and I felt drunk.

"When did it start?" he asked.

"When I got my period," I said. Which I knew wasn't entirely true. I got my period first, then I hiked to base camp, rushed around, and got hit with some harsh diarrhea and altitude sickness.

"Oh, I'm sorry about that," he said.

I pried one of my eyes open beneath my sunglasses to see that Paul's face was forlorn. He looked at me like I had just lost a beloved pet or something. If I hadn't felt so miserable, I would have laughed. Okay, I had my period, but wasn't it obvious that I was suffering from altitude sickness? And that was the much more serious issue?

While Paul assessed my vitals, I wanted to say: *You see, Paul, sometimes high altitude brings on menstruation cycles early and I got my period today, a whole week before it was scheduled to arrive. And it's too bad that we as a society don't talk more openly about periods or I might have actually remembered to carry a pad on me. Instead, I packed all my pads in the duffel bag that the mules carried. Then, I hiked into camp too quickly because I needed my pads. Now, I have diarrhea and mild altitude sickness. And I'm concerned about getting dehydrated. Oh, and I have ulcerative colitis that I'm afraid will flare up. On top of that, I want to appear strong and capable and have a hard time asking for help.*

But I had no energy to string together that many words, so I summed it up as, "I get bad diarrhea with my period."

"Okay, I have some pills for that"—his voice perked up—"the diarrhea part."

Paul dug into his medicine kit, placed a full water bottle with electrolytes by my head, and dropped two small white pills in my hand. I curled over onto my side and popped them into my mouth. I tasted their bitter coating as soon as they made contact with my tongue. I took a swig of water. The whole process of rolling over and swallowing liquid sent waves of nausea through me. I groaned, lay back down, and closed my eyes.

"That should help slow the diarrhea," he said. "Keep hydrating, that will help too."

"Okay," I said and held up my thumb. The sound of his boots crunching against the gravel as he walked away hurt my hair. The afternoon dragged on in small repetitive movements. I'd open my eyes and look at the ceiling of my tent. Then I'd close them. I'd have to use the latrine. Then I'd wash my hands and lie back down. I'd drink from my water bottle. Then I'd do it all over again. Hours went by and the brightness of the sun softened. Amber light fell upon my sleeping bag.

By the end of the day, the temperature had started to fall. I wrapped my sleeping bag around my shoulders. Then I traded my sun hat and sunglasses for a knit cap and headlamp. My headache subsided and I didn't feel the urge to use the bathroom anymore. In the entrance of my tent, I placed my journal upon my knee and wrote, *Day 3, I got my period.*

My pencil tapped against the paper as I looked out at the horizon line of jagged peaks illuminated by pink light. I felt an empty homesickness. Maybe that's why I had told Paul earlier that I had my period —I wanted to share those words with someone, even if it was a man. I wanted someone to know what I was going through. Even if Paul had never had a period, perhaps I could explain it to him. Not only the blood that flows out, but the emotions too. To my teammates, I wanted to appear strong, confident, and capable. But smoldering underneath my competitive nature was a fire to represent women who had been left off mountain expeditions simply because of their menstrual cycles. Though what really stoked the flames was knowing how some women were still mistreated around the world for simply being women.

I thought of a book I had read in high school called *The Red Tent*, by Anita Diamant. In the book, which takes place during biblical times, the red tent is a place where women are sent when they have their periods or are about to give birth. Away from men, in the privacy of the tent, they learn what it means to be in a woman's body and the responsibilities that come from that. It's where they gossip, laugh, and pass down the secrets of womanhood to the next generation. Two decades later, I still recalled one of the scenes quite vividly, where a young girl experiences her period for the first time and sees the blood drip upon the desert sand. I felt like that girl today.

I also remembered a time in 2018, when I led a group of American students to Nepal to study environmental and social justice issues with a college in Kathmandu. Before we left the country, I met with my female students to brief them about having their periods in Nepal. It was like our own red tent meeting.

"Bring your own products and keep them concealed. Make sure anything you throw away is securely wrapped in toilet paper," I'd said.

Once in Nepal, we trekked to Ghorepani, a remote mountain village around 9,000 feet with panoramic views of the Annapurna range. Early one morning, I stopped on a walk to sit on a concrete step to stretch and take in the sunrise. Before sitting down, I surveyed the ground for leeches, which were prevalent in May right before the monsoon season. When I returned to the teahouse where we were staying, an older Nepali woman grabbed my arm and pulled me aside. She didn't speak any English, so she just pointed to the blood on the back of my trekking pants.

"Oh, leeches," I groaned. She continued to scowl at me. I realized there was no point trying to communicate what had really happened, so I went to my room and changed my pants. Any sort of blood on the butt cheek would be viewed as period blood and that was highly taboo. While we were in Nepal, three young girls died from exposure in menstruation huts. Though not a common practice anymore in most Nepali communities, menstruation huts stemmed from the same principle as the red tent—secluding women while they bled.

I heard a pair of boots approach my tent.

"Come try to eat something," Tim said.

"I'm not hungry," I said.

"It will help you recover."

"Okay." I set my journal aside and walked over to the small kitchen tent. There I sat with my teammates on rolled-out ground pads.

"Feeling better?" Paul asked.

"Yes, much better." I sipped on a cup of salty chicken broth.

"You know," Paul leaned in to whisper, "you're much tougher than all of us because you are a woman."

"Oh, I know," I agreed.

After another helping of chicken broth and ramen noodles, I excused myself from the circle of expedition stories and returned to the privacy of my red tent. I usually enjoyed adventurous mountain stories, but today I longed for a woman to laugh with and commiserate about period stories.

That night, a full, red-tinted moon rose over the Andes Mountains. Under the moonlit summit of Aconcagua, I peed on the hard ground and unashamedly left a red stain. I appreciated that my body was tied to one of the most reliable cycles of nature. Not only would I climb this mountain, I'd do it with my period. I would dedicate that to all the women who'd gone before me, who were just as strong and capable as I, but who didn't get invited on the expedition. And to all the women around the world who were still sitting in their own red tents for four days and nights without the proper care and support they needed. How I wished I could share my Bibler tent with them.

———

ON THE SECOND day of my menstrual cycle, I rested and read books in base camp. On the third, the team and I did a carry to camp one. Then on the fourth, we relocated to camp one. With that, the latrine and garbage cans were left behind. Now I had a black plastic bag to poop in. The Bibler tent also remained at base camp, and I had to give up the privacy and sanctity of my red tent. Now I'd be sharing a tent with Tim and his teenage son, Henry. It wasn't ideal, but as we progressed up the mountain, we needed to live in a more compact space to stay warm and ease camp duties. Tim and I had discussed this during one of our expedition preparation phone calls, and because he was a friend of the family, I felt the most comfortable tenting with him and Henry.

Statistically speaking, it would have been hard to find another woman to share a tent with on a high-mountain expedition. Believe me, I had tried my hardest to recruit another female, with no luck. Women's participation in the sport was much less than men's. I'd been on the Aconcagua expedition for six days now and had spoken to only one other woman—a member of a British team I met in base camp. Unfortunately, sharing a tent with men is another taboo that has kept women off mountain expeditions, and consequently the first summits of every 8,000-meter peak in the world were made by teams of men. Because of the self-care needed inside the protective walls of a tent, men and women sharing that space can be perceived as scandalous if they are not in a romantic relationship. Changing clothing and going to the bathroom become all the more difficult when privacy from tentmates is required.

Camp one, around 16,000 feet, was much colder and more exposed than base camp. The first night we were there, the wind barreled down from the upper mountain and rattled our tent. I put in earbuds so that I could fall asleep. Midway through the night, I awoke with the urge to urinate. While the men on my expedition could stay in their sleeping bags and use their pee bottles during the night, I could not. Nor did I feel comfortable squatting over a Nalgene in the corner of the tent while two people slept beside me. Reluctantly, I unzipped my sleeping bag and bit my lip in envy for the ease male bodies have on mountain expeditions. The cold absorbed me as soon as I emerged from my sleeping bag. I yanked my puffy jacket over my polypro top. From the bottom of my sleeping bag, I grabbed my inner boots, hat, and gloves, which I slept with to keep them warm.

I was met with a howling gust of wind as I scrambled out of the tent and clicked on my headlamp. With my head down, I made my way to one of the large rocks that I'd been using as a pee area. Suddenly, the wind stopped and the night was completely still. I pulled back my hood, clicked off my headlamp, and looked up into the night sky. Any anger, envy, or resentment toward the men warm in their sleeping bags dissipated. Above me, the stars were like none I had ever seen before. The edges of the mountains formed dark silhouettes against a sky of glittery light. It seemed every night that the waning gibbous moon lost more of its illumination, another layer of stars emerged.

My bleeding was complete, and I removed the last pad from my underwear lining, rolled it up, and disposed of it in my fem kit bag. When the next full moon appeared in the sky, I would bleed again. Just as I clicked on my headlamp to return to my tent, another urge hit me. This one sharp and forceful. The diarrhea that had begun in base camp had not slowed, even with a steady dose of Imodium. Unable to retrieve my black poop bag in time, I squatted, and a liquid stream of mostly dehydrated meals screamed out of me. If having explosive diarrhea wasn't bad enough, the very moment I began pooping, the wind picked back up.

"Fuck!" I tried to move my foot before a spray of diarrhea landed against it. But it was too late.

"Ugh."

This was a first for me in my adult life. Never before had I actually shit on myself. Yes, I had shit my pants, but this was a different feeling altogether. I could move forward one of two ways. I could be super pissed, or I could laugh about it. I decided to laugh about it and actually muttered aloud, "Bethany, I can't believe you just shit on your foot."

With my wipes, toilet paper, and hand sanitizer, I cleaned myself up to the best of my ability. At the entrance of the tent, I took off my poop-stained booties and stashed them under a pile of rocks so that they wouldn't stink up our dwelling or blow away in the middle of the night. Zipped back into the warmth of my sleeping bag, I shook my head and giggled. It's funny how the universe provides exactly what we need in very strange ways. For the last four days, I'd felt disconnected from my teammates because of my female body. But tonight, my body gave me a poop story. And I'd be sharing that with my teammates over breakfast. At least that was something they'd understand.

———

BETHANY ADAMS (SHE/HER)

Wilmington, New York—ancestral Mohawk land and traditional territory of the Haudenosaunee peoples

Bethany is a writer, mountain athlete, guide and outdoor instructor. She holds a master's degree in community development and has been published in *Trail Runner* and *Outside* magazines. She is the first woman to achieve 100 fastest known times (FKTs), and in 2020, she and Katie Rhodes became the first women to climb all forty-six High Peaks in the Adirondacks unsupported. She is thrilled to share stories of the healing she has found in nature and the strength of the female athlete.

She can be found on Instagram @bethany.climbs.

a period of transition

SHIT. I WATCHED REDDISH-BROWN LIQUID SPILL FROM THE
plastic tube. *Shit.* It was day fifty-two, just over the halfway point of
my run across the country. I had stopped to pee, using the fancy
funnel contraption I'd purchased at REI the week before the start of
the run. It was a device that helped level the playing field, or in this
case, the running field, allowing me the incredibly useful ability to pee
standing up. After some trial and error, and a few wet shorts, I had
mastered my new tool and by this point, it was second nature.

Mid-September on the outskirts of Oklahoma City, where the
rolling plains transitioned into row houses, I stood peeing, and now
bleeding. The last few days had been spent running between expansive
fields of wheat and corn, each stalk waving as I passed. I was in my
unofficial running uniform—a sweat-stained blue T-shirt promoting
one of the nonprofits I was supporting and orange Soffe shorts, the
really short and thin kind worn by both Hooters girls and Marines.
Faded to a light dusty orange from the hours spent beaten by the late-
summer sun, they were the only shorts that didn't leave my sweaty,
salt-caked inner thighs rubbed raw.

I watched as the stream grew darker, wondering if I should tell my
support driver. After the first time I discovered blood in my urine,
seven weeks ago, I had promised myself that if it happened again, I

would take a few days off, see a doctor, and even consider stopping this madness. Only a week into the California desert, I had been questioning whether I could really make it across the country on foot. I had watched bloody urine run down my leg in the shower that night, mixing with the dirt, sweat, and tears, fearing that my body would give out before my already shaky spirit. I had cautiously kept going, threatening to drown myself with more fluids and more electrolytes—"super hydration," a friend had called it. That initial bout of blood cleared after a day or two and I had been running strong since.

This whole thing started as part of my transition from active-duty military service. Having spent my entire young adult life serving as an intelligence officer in the Marine Corps, I had a strong sense of identity—after all, that's what the Marine Corps promises: "We Make Marines," the recruiting posters proudly boasted. When people asked what I did for work, I told them I was a Marine. Not that I worked for the Marines or that I was in the Marine Corps—but that I *was* a Marine. I had started to realize that there was little room for anything else, any other facet or face. But that wasn't the only thing I was, or the only thing I wanted to be. Leaving the organization meant that would change—that it would *have* to change. I needed to rediscover, or perhaps even re-create, an identity for myself outside of the uniform.

While my physical finish line for the run was clear (the Atlantic Ocean, or more specifically, Virginia Beach), the personal and professional endpoints were ambiguous. I had no job lined up; I didn't even have an address for the Marine Corps to send my stuff. During my exit interview with the transition assistance officer, I laughed when he asked, "Where will you be living when you leave active duty? We need something in this box." I offered all I could: "Um, I have a 1995 EuroVan that I'm going to sleep in as I run across the country." For a minute I thought the counselor might refer me to housing services. Luckily, he was a friend of mine, and he only chuckled as he signed off on the form. "Living in a van in America. Check."

I was sure the answers would be found on the other side of the country, on the other side of the run. I had gotten the idea years prior from another woman, Anna, who had "crossed" (as it is called among those who undertake the endeavor). In the months leading up to my start date, I could think of little else. My obsession centered on the discovery that awaited me along my beloved home country's back roads and highways. Whenever people asked me why I was doing this, I always gave the same stock answer. I was running to raise funds and awareness for the communities that had welcomed me during my active-duty service. Joining the Marine Corps was a discomfiting transformation. Having grown up in a rural midwestern town, I found myself chronically homesick and lonely amid the constant change. I often felt like I stuck out among the strangers who wore the same clothes as me. I had found support and connection through the special needs, veteran, and gold star communities, and I wanted to punctuate my service by dedicating this grand, inspiring gesture to them.

Secretly, I had a more selfish goal. I couldn't quite put it into words, but I knew I wanted to be the woman on the other side of the miles. I didn't know who she was or what was so appealing about her, only that I needed to become her.

I had expected the transformation to be painful, but I hadn't anticipated how much of that pain would come from the mundanity of the task. The mental brutality of the whole thing was outpacing the physical endurance challenge I had eagerly sought out. My running resume was impressive: a couple hundred-mile races, a series of six back-to-back marathons, long rucks, an Ironman, and something called the "Death Race." I wasn't new to the demons that pop up during long stretches, but their persistence, the unrelenting nature of running thirty-plus miles a day for ninety-nine days, called for energy and willpower I had never before required. Along with blisters and shin splints, I managed feelings of isolation, loss, guilt, and regret.

I continued to dig deeper with every passing day. I was a woman after all. I had spent my entire life watching women beat against the relentless, so I knew how it was done. The never-ending cycles of work, of violence, of endurance.

Standing over the puddle of urine and blood, I shot a text to my nurse and doctor friends. They all said the same thing: *Get to a doctor. Stop running.* They told me blood in the urine is a telltale sign of rhabdomyolysis, a process in which the body starts breaking down muscles for fuel—an ever-present threat for someone trying to run a 50K every day for weeks.

I was googling every variation of "blood in urine" and "bleeding while running" when I felt the familiar rush of warm liquid pooling in my shorts. I shoved my hands to my vulva with altogether too much enthusiasm for the Oklahoma City side street and pulled up my fingers to reveal blood. Thick, bright, welcomed blood.

My period.

Of course. It was my period. It had been twenty-eight days to the hour since it had last started. It hadn't even occurred to me that the blood could be something as normal and regular as my menstrual cycle, rather than a warning sign of disaster. I was on a once-in-a-lifetime journey of strength and endurance, where everything felt foreign and chaotic, but here this constant marker of biological time was somehow unexpected.

I laughed as I searched for the baggy of emergency toilet paper in my running vest.

Ha! False alarm, it was my period, I responded to my concerned friends.

You're still getting your period on this thing?

You can take the girl out of the Midwest, but you can't take the Midwest out of the girl—as fertile as a cornfield.

I had always had very regular cycles, my biology running like clockwork, and an assumption of strong fertility. *My mom had her period until she was, like, fifty-five*, I followed up to my friends—a revelation that my mother would perhaps prefer not be made public. But I was encouraged by that knowledge. I had always wanted kids. At thirty, just in the initial "maybes" of my first healthy long-term relationship, I knew the clock was ticking. I had donated my eggs a few times already and had been encouraged by the follicle counts, but even the most advantageous biology has an expiration date.

Can you grab some tampons? I quickly texted my support driver, then thought, *Shit, did I just do that?* I was a feminist, but the kind who had grown up in a society in which all things feminine were hidden away, decidedly in the private domestic sphere. Years ago, the request would have been impossible for me to type out to any man, particularly a man with a face like Jordan's. Out here on the run, everything seemed stripped away—pride, modesty, and best of all, shame. Out here a tampon was survival. I couldn't spare the energy to hide the blood or sweat or tears of my working body.

Blood that, as a tween, I had waited for, had wanted so desperately to arrive.

Back then, it felt like everyone else was ahead, getting their periods before me. In reality, I was well within the normal ranges of development, but to an overachiever, normal felt like falling behind. I had been so anxious about "becoming a woman" that I begged my mom to let me wear panty liners "just in case." It was that same desire to become the next version of myself that drove me to overload my schedule and enroll in college at fifteen. To sign up for longer and harder races the morning after I finished the last one. To commit to running across the country. I have always wanted to be the woman on the other side.

The morning I finally discovered the first rusty brown stain on my days-of-the-week underwear, I nearly pumped my thirteen-year-old fist in the air. I had been checking every time I used the bathroom for signs: squinting at the discharge, wondering if it was maybe a little reddish, inserting my fingers in my vagina to see if maybe I was just minutes away from "my time." Every stomachache for months was a false promise of cramps. I even bought a pair of white jeans—remembering all the "I got my period in white shorts" stories I'd read in *CosmoGirl*. My mom was not the type to turn it into a celebration, but secretly I wished she were. As a brand-new teenager, I was so enamored with this mile marker of adulthood that I barely cared about skipping the hotel pool that week. *Sorry, can't, I'm on the rag,* I thought to myself. *Just the sacrifices a woman has to make.*

Just the sacrifices a support driver has to make, I teased Jordan as he texted me a picture from the feminine care aisle at the local CVS.

Pearl, sport, heavy, light, pads, cups, napkins—a smorgasbord of options for the menstruators among us. I texted him my preferred brand, weight, and quantity. *Got 'em*, he wrote back. I hoped that he had looked at grabbing tampons much like grabbing another pack of deli cheese (I was on a swiss kick) or Epsom salt. I hoped he saw the tampons as nothing more than supplies for a feminine body running across the country. I met up with him at an ad hoc stopping point, careful to push away any of that lingering shame. He asked if I needed him to drive me to a bathroom. "Nope, I'll do it right here," I responded, searching his face for any bit of disgust or repulsion. I found none.

I'd met Jordan on my last deployment. He was quiet, mysterious in his seriousness, and shockingly good-looking with a swoop of salt-and-pepper hair and a light dash of freckles across his nose—the kind of looks that draw comments from strangers. He was everything that was my opposite, but we had formed an unlikely friendship. I had been looking forward to spending time with him on this adventure. Even more, I was curious if that friendship had the roots of something more. He was unlike the men I was usually drawn to—and maybe that was the point. I had seen glimpses of his goofy humor, his soft heart when he spoke of his daughter, and his kindness when he mentioned a loyal friend. He was redefining my ideas of men and the masculine at the same time that I was challenging my ideas of my own feminine.

I was raised to believe in the strength of women, as long as that strength didn't challenge a man's, as long as it didn't encroach on the masculine. The feminine was to be honored, but privately and within pre-established bounds. Femininity was a complement to masculinity, a supporting role. Femininity was vaunted, but masculinity was valued.

I stepped behind the door, as I often did to pee or change clothes throughout the days, squatted slightly, and as I had done hundreds of times before, swiftly swapped out the wad of blood-saturated toilet paper for a fresh tampon. I wrapped the applicator in some tissue and stuffed it in a bag, handing it to him to toss in the mini trash can tucked behind the driver's seat. "It's around four miles till we meet up with the Marines," he told me. "Need anything else?"

It was as if my body had subconsciously created this test. And he passed with flying colors.

In the years since my run and that unexpected blood, my period's presence or absence is something Jordan and I have shared joyfully in, its arrival each month signaling another cycle of fertility, the start of a countdown to attempt pregnancy. Its absence signaling my first, second, and third pregnancies—one of the first indications that a new life would soon be on its way.

As I picked up the pace through Oklahoma City, I was joined by a band of Marines from the local recruiting station. Surrounded by men in their issued fitness uniforms, I sensed old ideas of femininity creeping in. The Marine Corps is a place of "fitting in." The discipline hinges on uniformity, or so we're told, and that uniformity is masculine. I subconsciously touched my front vest pocket, the one with the emergency tampon tucked in it. I remembered how I used to hide my tampons in the bottom of a magazine pouch when I packed for the field, careful not to let any pink flowers break up the green and brown of my issued gear. I remembered how some of the women in my training unit used to duct-tape the plastic bags carrying their menstrual items, camouflaging their femininity along with their faces. I remembered when, just minutes after a conversation regarding how women shouldn't be allowed in infantry units because of their "sensitivity," another Marine mentioned that the pearly purple tampon applicator (mine) he'd spotted in the porta john was "just disgusting." When a man bleeds, his blood is noble, masculine, a symbol of strength, endurance, and sacrifice. But a woman's rhythmic blood is considered a weakness, and a disgusting one at that.

I remembered often making the subtle, subconscious decision to brush off misogynistic comments like that one, opting to "fit in" or "go with the flow" in a male-dominated environment. Over my time in the Marines, I grew more cognizant of the damage such comments cause. I'd occasionally respond by mentioning how I ran my first hundred-miler while bleeding. Or that they should try completing Officer Candidate School with a three-week period.

The responses were often a mixture of "don't be so sensitive" and "ew, gross." Somehow, I was simultaneously offended and offensive.

This lack of understanding and respect was a big reason I left active duty. In my final months of service, I started to feel the freedom of release from prescribed uniformity. I grew brash in my feminism—swapping out "fitting in" with speaking up. Occasionally a new Marine would check into a unit and make what I'm sure he thought was an innocuous remark, expecting no response from his peers. Those who had worked with me long enough would look over at my desk, anticipating the long "discussion" that was sure to follow. "Tell me more about that, Corporal," I'd start, ready to launch into a dozen reasons why the comment was problematic, inaccurate, or simply unfunny. Before I had taken my first step eastward, I was being pulled by the woman on the other side.

And yet there I was, some 1,500 miles closer to her, nervously tucking my tampon into my running vest, calculating how long until I would need to change it, to avoid the horror of letting a fellow human know that I, too, was human. I caught a glimpse of the men over my left shoulder as I pushed the tampon back down into obscurity. I picked up the pace, pushing beyond what was smart. I couldn't let them think I was weak. I needed to represent not just myself, but all female Marines—hell, all women. I needed to show them I was tough. I needed to keep up. *Don't be a pussy.* I would have never stood for those words to be spoken in my presence, but there they were, in my own mind.

I thought of the monologue I'd launch into on behalf of the vulva. A defense of the entire female reproductive system, which, honestly, is nothing short of magic. It creates, nourishes, holds, and delivers human beings. Real, full human beings. The trauma that it must be willing to undergo in order to bring forth that life is unadulterated sacrifice, the biological pinnacle of altruism. No other body part does that. Legs, as useful as they are, particularly for runners, don't produce cells that multiply and divide rapidly until a new leg is formed.

A brain, arguably the most important piece of the human body both to the individual and to the collective, cannot think another being into existence. But since the beginning of time, the uterus and fallopian tubes and ovaries have done what the brain cannot, taken the contribution of sperm and, without much further intervention from their owner, gotten to work. Real, hard work.

Then, when it is time, that collective of meat and blood and tissue moves, expands, contracts, and births human beings.

Then, for the majority of the time, it repairs itself. *It repairs itself.*

Maybe we should all aspire to be more like a pussy.

From somewhere deep within my thoughts, I snapped back to the run. I looked over to my left for the leader. "Where's the captain?" I asked one of the Marines, a face I didn't recognize. "Oh, we swapped out a couple miles back," the Marine huffed and gestured behind us. *Swapped out?* I glanced over my shoulder to see a hulk of a pickup truck—mounted on unnecessarily aggressive, overtly masculine tires and wrapped in Marine Corps recruiting images and slogans—chugging behind us down the Oklahoma highway. Its oversized cab carried the men I had been so desperately trying to keep up with. I looked around at the three Marines running just a half a step behind me and realized they were the ones trying to keep up. I realized that they had been swapping out every few miles, grabbing a break in the support truck as I tried to outrun only my shame and fear of inadequacy. I slowed the pace, remembering that I had to show up tomorrow, and the next day, and the next day. As we finished the last few miles together, I joked with the Marines, laughing at their boot camp stories and learning about their families. I didn't tuck that tampon back again, although I felt my hand moving up to do so at least once more. With the pace slowed, I could take the time to talk about the run so far, sharing my favorite stories and feeling the support and admiration of the men I was so desperate to impress. "Here's where we leave you, ma'am," one of them said as we rounded the corner heading out of the city. The rest of the men hopped out of the truck for a picture. Some tried to hide limps as we lined up together. Some shook my hand with just a little more force than they had that morning. I waved goodbye as I turned to grab my newly refilled hydration pack from Jordan. "Just under ten miles to go, feeling okay?" he asked. "That was a pretty quick leg, some of those young devil dogs look to be hurting a little bit."

"I'm good." I smiled back at him. "See you in a couple hours."

I finished the day's run at my own pace, with my period and my future partner. As I rounded the corner to the cemetery where we had planned to meet again, I caught the moon rising in the late-afternoon sky.

The moon whose power so often stands in the shadow of the power of the sun. The moon who commands the oceans, pulls them crashing against the sands, shaping the earth. The moon who pulls at the oceans within us—who cycles and sheds and reappears, just as we do. The moon is both ever changing and ever present. It stands for all that it is to be feminine. To be alive.

I remember Anna telling me that by the end of her crossing she had craved the return of her femininity. Her body had leaned out, dropping the softness of her hips—her womanly shape. She began to see her body as more than just a beautiful object or vessel. This newfound utility had struck her as masculine.

Which made sense. Men's bodies are celebrated for what they can do; women, for what they look like.

But I felt incredibly feminine during my crossing. The repetitive grittiness of the work, rest, and reflection cycle of the cross-country run spoke to my feminine nature. I'm not alone in this. Women excel in ultra-endurance distances, closing the gender gaps in thru-hiking and ultrarunning. Our ability to settle into pain, to block out or endure suffering with humility and a sense of purpose—an evolutionary advantage for the childbearing sex. Perhaps I was just one of hundreds of millions of women over the years who were able to move forward despite persistent resistance.

Perhaps the femininity of my run came from the fact that for the first time in ten years, I did not put on a uniform that represents so much to so many, but to me, always the masculine. Maybe it was because I never lost my hips, the extra body fat around my middle, the reserves that my body knows to conserve to support me and my unborn fetus in times of famine. My breasts, large since the very first of hundreds of periods, certainly reduced over the miles, but perhaps less than the rest of my body. I retained so many feminine physical aspects and embraced more of the feminine spirit. I cultivated kindness and patience with myself and my growth—I had to.

Perhaps it was more poetic than that. Maybe it was because I sank my toes in the western tides before heading toward the eastern ones. Maybe it was that I started with the moon. Maybe it is because this run was so much about shedding, about cycles, about transformation —and about the pain that comes with them.

My cycle came and went in Oklahoma. It would arrive and depart once more on this adventure. Then again along the trails and trials of my future, prompting me to wash out a menstrual cup with water from an alpine stream or hastily tear cheap, thin squares of tissue in a bayou bathroom in rural Louisiana. It was steadfast, always reminding me of my strength, my femininity, and my potential—not only along back roads and mountain ridges, but in delivery rooms and nurseries. Years later it still connects me to my children, fellow women, and the divinely feminine, a connection bonded in blood. I had wanted to be the woman on the other side of the run. Not the person, the woman. For years in the Marine Corps, I had tucked that femininity away, stuffing it into the corners of cargo pockets and into magazine pouches. I had traded it for aggression and a masculine version of power. I'd traded my ability to withstand pain and to comfort those in pain for the ability to inflict it.

The Marines subscribe to a different kind of power than the woman I have become. I no longer hide my femininity, for that is where my endurance, my true power, lies.

———

Maggie Seymour (she/her)

Beaufort, South Carolina—traditional territory of the Yamasee and Kusso peoples

Maggie is a midwesterner, a runner, a diplomat, and a Marine. She completed a transcontinental run from San Diego to Virginia in 2017 and is currently attempting to cross all fifty states on foot. She holds a BS in political science; MAs in military history, journalism, and sociology; and a PhD in international studies. As an occasional trail runner, she slowed down and hiked the northern half of the Pacific Crest Trail with her partner in 2017. She's now focused on passing along that love of camping, running, and trails to her growing family. She is eager to see some of her favorite things combined—the outdoors, human bodies covering long distances, and the power of the feminine.

She can be found on Instagram, Twitter, and Facebook @runfreerunner and at www.runfreerun.com.

out of order

I CRIED WHEN MY PARENTS DROPPED ME OFF AT THE SAN Francisco International Airport. Though to be fair I think most people would have cried after staying up all night frantically packing, then being forced awake at 4:30 a.m. to jump in the car, just to artfully miss the turn to the airport drop-off—not once, but twice. However, this information was not known to the passersby nor to the security officer checking my passport. No, by the looks of my tears, one certainly never would have guessed that I was going on a trip I had been dreaming of for months.

"Date of birth," demanded the TSA agent.

Date of birth? Date of BIRTH? When was I born? September? Yes, September!

"S-September," I responded.

He raised his eyebrow, and I remembered that birthdays include more than just the month.

"September eleventh . . . 2003."

He gave me the knowing nod all TSA agents give upon hearing my birthday.

"Flying alone?"

"Yes." At least this I was sure of.

Once through, I made my way to the gate to check that it existed and then headed to a nearby cafe to grab a chai. My mind raced with gleeful excitement . . . and then with less-than-gleeful excitement. *I bet the gate changed . . . it absolutely positively must have changed since I last saw it . . . I must hurry or it will be gone!* Drink in hand, I begrudgingly returned to the gate, which was, not surprisingly, in the exact spot I had left it. But alas, that knowledge was not enough to soothe my anxious mind. *I bet my plane left yesterday . . . I bet there never was a plane . . . I bet the nonexistent plane is gonna crash . . . oh no, don't think the plane will crash, then it's definitely gonna crash . . . or maybe it won't because what's the chance of me predicting a plane crash . . . okay, well now I need to knock on wood . . . crap, there's no wood here . . . okay, well, my old babysitter told me I could knock on my head instead . . . okay, okay, i'll do that . . . ahh, i'm going to die . . . crap, now I need to knock on my head again . . . how many times can I knock on my head before they escort me out . . .*

"Now boarding Group C," a woman's voice announced over the speaker.

ON THE PLANE I sat in the window seat next to a young couple from Florida. We exchanged pleasantries. They mentioned that they were on their way to a family cabin for a fishing trip, then asked why I was headed to Anchorage.

I thought for a moment. I've never felt particularly skilled at this style of small talk, always wondering how much I should or shouldn't say.

I'm not too sure even I knew all the reasons I was on that flight.

I could have mentioned the chilly mornings growing up, when my mother used to joke, "When your dad and I lived in Alaska this would've been T-shirt weather!" She'd always follow it up with some Alaskan adventure story and say, "We'll just have to take you there someday." One of many "somedays" I thought I might have had by now. I had been a junior in high school when COVID arrived and derailed every future I'd envisioned.

I could have mentioned the feeling of apathy I'd had after

opening my acceptance letter from UC Berkeley. How my friend and I had sat under a cherry tree in the park over open containers of take-out, staring numbly at digitized confetti on our phone screens. I should have been thrilled—I'd worked so hard for this. *Why am I not excited?* I looked at my friend, who wore a similar expression of numbness—she had been accepted too. *Why aren't we excited?* Then fear. *I'm not ready. I'm not ready for college. I can't go to college. I'm still a child. Children don't go to college, especially not so close to home.*

I could have mentioned my breakdown the following week, my "unprecedented" graduation speech on the unpredictableness of life, and the resulting agreement I'd made with my mom.

"If I don't do something with my gap year, you have to promise to kick me out of the house, okay?"

How she had laughed, saying, "If for the first time in your life you somehow manage to do nothing, I promise I will kick you out. Okay?"

But in the end, I told them none of this.

"I'm going backpacking," I answered simply. They laughed and told me to watch out for bears. Sure, they probably meant it as a joke, but it was true that grizzlies were of utmost concern to me—second to moose.

AFTER TWO FLIGHTS in ten grueling hours, I arrived at the National Outdoor Leadership School (NOLS) base, known as "the farm"—a series of small buildings clustered on a large grassy lot surrounded by forest. Cottonwood fluff floated through the air, almost giving the appearance of light snow to my Californian eyes. It was nearly 6 p.m., but you wouldn't have known it, since an Alaskan summer means that the sun never truly sets.

The rest of the group, nearly all young guys, and I spent a couple of days introducing ourselves and getting acquainted with the gear that we'd be spending the next month with. We rationed out our food, learned to pack our bags, and practiced making bear calls. I noticed how easily the rest of the group slung their loaded packs onto their backs. Meanwhile, I thought I might dislocate my shoulder just trying to get it off the ground.

We were even given step-by-step instructions for how to use the bathroom, something I'd been doing for nearly seventeen years without issue. Not since toddlerdom had I been made to stop and consider how to do that.

The Fourteen Steps to the Backcountry Bathroom (Alaska Version):

1. Gather three people to accompany you (for bear safety).
2. Find a good spot away from camp, trail, and water.
3. Dig a six-to-eight-inch-deep hole, then pass the trowel to the next person.
4. Open water bottle and soap container.
5. Squat and use the loo.
6. Clean crotch with water.
7. Wipe butt with hand.
8. Wipe hand on dirt.
9. Rinse hand with water.
10. Repeat steps 7–10 until clean.
11. Clean hands with dirt and water.
12. Wash hands with soap and water.
13. Cover hole.
14. Celebrate.

"If you think about it, toilet paper is pretty weird anyway," reasoned one of the instructors. "I mean, if you've got poop on your arm, you wouldn't just wipe it off with paper. No, you would scrub with soap and water and soap and water and soap and water, and then finally with more soap and water."

His argument was sensible, but I can't say that it made me any more enthusiastic about having to wipe myself with my hand.

ON THE THIRD DAY, we boarded the bus. The Talkeetna Mountains in the distance were a brilliant green with snowy tips. Puffy white clouds filled the sky. At times I couldn't tell my anxiety from my excitement. *Am I going to be able to keep up?*

The road began to snake as we made our way through the base of the Talkeetnas, much to the dismay of my stomach, who protested the continuous jostling of the road. I doubled over in my seat. *I'm going to throw up I'm going to throw up I'm going to throw up no don't think that don't think that don't think that think about something else look up.* I forced myself to take in the scenery. In the time that my head had been down, the flat farmland had morphed into a densely wooded pine forest. Shafts of warm light wove through the trees, which occasionally gave way to shiny creeks and rivers.

Around us the mountains continued to grow, their steep snow-capped peaks loomed high in the sky. It dawned on me that *that* was where we were headed. *Into the mountains.* I had somehow led myself to believe that we would be backpacking near the mountains rather than in them. *I'm gonna get hypothermia. I'm gonna get hypothermia and die.*

THANKFULLY, at the trailhead we were told that since it was the first day, it would only be a short hike. We would need the extra time to learn how to set up camp.

We set off, following ATV trails toward the base of the larger mountains in the distance. The group was fast, as expected of young guys. Within only a handful of minutes my body was begging for a break, but I refused to stop the group. Instead I pushed on, carefully controlling my breath so as not to let the others hear the straining of my lungs. It's not that I was weak; I wasn't. In fact, in any other form of exercise—pull-ups, sit-ups, push-ups—I would have fared just fine. But this was cardio, and I'd always struggled with cardio.

As the first hour slipped into the second, and then the third, we realized the promise of a short hike may have been a lie. In total we covered nearly eight miles. Maybe a "short hike" for experienced hikers, but far too much for a group of inexperienced teens carrying fifty-pound packs, let alone one with an undiagnosed nervous system disorder (me). By the time we arrived at camp, the sunny skies had been covered by a thick overcoat of gray clouds and chilling winds, or as my mom would say, "T-shirt weather."

I watched as the guys in the group collapsed, dropping their backpacks in the bushes to the side of the trail. I felt justified in following suit, tossing first my backpack and then myself to the ground. Unfortunately for me this break was short-lived, as our instructors told us to put on more layers to conserve heat. Hurriedly I stripped down to my underwear—acutely aware of how naked I was—to add thermal pants and fleece pants under my hiking pants. I finished off the look with stiff, old, semi-waterproof rain pants. Last, I added two jackets, a raincoat, and a hat.

Yet all these layers did little to warm me against the growing storm. *What had I gotten myself into?*

Suddenly, I felt an alarmingly urgent call from my bowels. Despite the detailed instructions, and my trepidation toward the "backcountry bidet," I figured this might still be the easiest part of my day. With an excess of confidence, I grabbed my toiletry bag from my backpack and embarked on my first journey to the backcountry bathroom.

One: *Assemble the poo-train.* There really is no tasteful way to ask someone you just met to join you to poo in the woods. "Hey, hot stuff, wanna go find a nice quiet spot behind a bush where we can defecate?" I managed to convince three of the guys (including the cute one) to accompany me with only mild embarrassment.

Two: *Scout.* Together we walked a hundred or so meters away from camp through the thick Alaskan brush before running into a river and being forced to backpedal. I searched around for a good patch of bear-free shrubbery to hide me from the other members of this poop train.

Three: *Dig a crappy hole.* Frantically I began digging my hole. The ground was rockier than it had been at the NOLS farm; I dug for about a minute before my body declared I was out of time and I was forced to accept my less-than-adequate pit.

Five: *Do your business.* No sooner had I gotten my four layers of pants down, exposing my behind to the mosquitos, than my bottom exploded. I leaned back, resting on my left arm. A river of urine cascaded over the walls of my shallow pit and flooded the surrounding ground, spraying the backs of my hiking boots. As I took in the chaos, I noticed that my poo was resting half in and half out of the barely there hole. Wonderful.

Six: *Begin backcountry bidet.* I wiped my crotch with my hand— brown . . . and red.

Fuck.

The hand I was propped up on was covered in mud; my other hand was now covered in blood. I looked at the water bottle that I had brought for washing my hands and realized that I had forgotten step four, *open the water bottle and soap container.* As a result, the lid to my water bottle remained securely attached: a two-handed issue, for which I had zero clean hands.

There I squatted, caked in my own blood and shit. Mosquitos buzzed around my still-bare ass. My eyes scanned for the exit, like this was some play gone tragically wrong and I was about to be whisked away backstage, my bits hidden from the world's view. But alas, I was not so lucky.

Why did I even come here? Desperate tears spilled down my cheeks. *Is this the beautiful Alaska my parents wanted me to see?* I could have spent the summer with my friends, gone to school in the fall, done all the right things, and had a quote-unquote *good* life. But instead I had declined my college offer in favor of, what? Having to wipe uterine lining and feces with my bare, frozen hands, mourning my now-wasted potential? I could practically hear my younger self scolding, *Weren't we gonna be a lawyer, didn't you want to "speak for the trees"?*

And then, with poetic irony, I felt the first raindrops land upon my face. *Just. Keep. Moving*, they said.

Four: *De-lid your bottles.* Angrily, I scraped my hand through the dirt, wiping off the blood as well as I could. Then I picked up my water bottle with my wrists and positioned it between my arms and my body, using the inside of my forearm to twist the lid off.

Nine: *Conservatively rinse your hands.* Still squatting, I leaned forward until the cold water gushed out and over my hands, rinsing the majority of the dirt off—and wasting half of the water.

Seven: *Wash your vulva, your hoo-ha, your lady canoe, your x-marks-the-spot-treasure-box.* Once my hands were free of dirt, I poured water into my cupped hand and then wiped until clean. I repeated this process on my behind, this time making sure to wipe my hand off in the dirt between rinses.

Twelve: *Clean those bloody hands.* I uncapped the soap and squeezed out a few drops to wash my hands with. Once my water bottle was empty and my fingertips were white, I was confident enough that I could insert a menstrual cup without giving myself an infection.

I DUG AROUND in my drawstring toiletry bag looking for a cup and liner. I removed the paper backing from a panty liner and adhered it to my underwear. My hand instinctively crumpled the wrapper and I searched for a trash can. Except this was the wilderness, and there were no trash cans. *Great.* I shoved the wrapper into the pocket of my now-soaked raincoat, where it would live for the next month.

Next, I folded the silicone menstrual cup between my fingers, the same as I had always done at home, and inserted it. Normally it would pop open, creating a neat seal against the walls of my body. But today, it didn't. I pinched at the bottom of the cup and ran my finger around the upper edge, trying desperately to get it to open.

Maybe my position is wrong? I was squatted lower than I would be on a toilet, so perhaps it would help if I stood. I went to stand, but as I lifted my behind into the air, I quickly discovered two truths. One: my legs were far more tired from the day's hike than I had known. Two: multiple layers of pants around one's ankles are practically handcuffs.

The combination of these facts resulted in my sudden and unexpected descent to the freshly muddied ground.

A long moment passed as I sat. Shivering. In the rain. Sobbing. And pantless.

I could hear the guys' voices around the bushes. *They must be done already. They must be waiting for me. They must not have gotten their periods yet—late bloomers.* I couldn't help but roll my eyes and laugh at the ridiculousness of the situation. *I bet they think I'm taking the world's largest dump right now. If only they knew I finished that about five minutes ago.*

Nine: *Thoroughly rinse, again.* With an empty water bottle I threw my hands up in defeat before wiping them on some wet leaves. I wiped the tears from my cheeks just for the rain to rewet them, then the mud from my still-bare butt. *Just. Keep. Moving*, I told myself.

Seven and Three-Quarters: *Recognize women have extra work.* I wiggled my way back onto my feet, careful not to get my hands dirty again, and continued trying to get my cup in. Once again I folded it into a U shape before inserting it. Then I ran my finger around the outside edge, giving it room to pop open. Success.

IN TOTAL, my bathroom expedition couldn't have lasted more than ten minutes, but it felt as if an eternity had passed by the time I saw the faces of the comrades who'd accompanied me. We walked back to camp together, taking turns to make polite comments on our experiences, not yet comfortable enough to share the dirtier reality.

"Tough ground, huh?"

"Oh my god, wasn't it?"

"Dude, the *ROOTS*."

I thought about the blood stuck under my fingernails, about the mosquito bites on my ass, about the urine on the backs of my hiking boots. Defeat hung heavy in the damp air.

Twenty-nine days later we made our return to civilization by bus. At times the endless road was obscured by fog so thick that even the mountains disappeared. I rested my head on the window, skull rattling against the glass. It was peaceful.

I could have spent the summer with my friends, gone to school in the fall, done all the right things, and had a quote-unquote *good* life. But maybe this is a better one.

———

Saryn B. Schwartz (she/her)

Oakland, California—Ohlone land and traditional territory of the Bay Miwok

Saryn grew up camping, hiking, and exploring the redwoods near her home. More recently she has spent time backpacking in Europe and Southeast Asia. She is a current student at UCLA with a strong interest in environmental policy. She is passionate about the outdoors and has taken courses with NOLS; she also spent four months in Bhutan with the School for Field Studies, where she conducted biodiversity survey research. Now, amid learning to navigate chronic illness, she has continued to find her peace in nature.

She can be found on Instagram @saryn.schwartz.

unstoppable flow

ONE MONTH AFTER MY FIRST ULTRAMARATHON, I SAT WITH my laptop open atop the rolling container of dog food in my bathroom. The metallic smell of blood clots the size of my fist rapidly exiting my body melded with that of low-grade kibble. I typed away on my latest client article while the splotches and drips painted the inside of the toilet bowl like a red Jackson Pollock. Tiny flecks of blood found their way around my body to the fresh white paint on my walls and the aging laminate floor.

What a terribly inconvenient way to go about my workday.

A sane person might ask: *How did I let things get this bad?* But it didn't happen all at once.

My body, more specifically my reproductive system, has been a challenge since the very beginning. Since my first period, at eleven years old, it'd been on a rampage of ruined clothes, embarrassing social situations, and doctors' assurances that nothing was, in fact, "wrong" with me. Back then, I was the only menstruator in a house with two brothers and a mom who had long since had her uterus removed. My mom quietly stocked pads and tampons under my sink, but information about my cycle was distributed on a need-to-know basis, and it was strongly implied that I was the only one who needed that information. Over the years, I grew accustomed to symptoms that any other person would likely consider alarming. I learned not to ask questions that had no answers, and to deal with my body as best I could. Hormonal IUDs had offered some relief through my twenties, but no explanation.

In January 2020, I picked up running. I'd had an on-and-off relationship with the sport throughout my life, and I wanted to approach it differently this time. In the past my running had been motivated by "signed up for a race, gotta run it, don't want to waste the entry fee," or "those people are running, I want to be friends with them, I should run." This time I wanted to learn to enjoy it. No mileage goals, no pace goals, no race goals, no trying-to-impress-others goals. Just learn to enjoy the thing. Running also fulfilled my desire to stay active while living full-time on the road, without needing partners or gyms.

By the end of 2021, I was running a minimum of six miles three or four days a week. I was proud of my physical abilities as well as how much I actually *enjoyed* running. I felt strong and capable in my body, though my period had begun to falter. I could mostly ignore the near-constant spotting, as things were going so well otherwise. And I'd spent more than twenty years practicing at various degrees of this particular pretending, so it was easy enough to do.

With some high-pressure encouragement from my ultra-athlete dad, I decided to sign up for my first ultramarathon in January 2022. After scouring the online registration pages, I picked the 50K Pine Trail Run and officially began training for the distance. I moved into a cute little house in Bisbee, Arizona, down the street from my parents after three years of vanlife. And I scheduled a little doctor's appointment, just to get things checked out.

I started exploring the open desert behind my house in accordance with my training schedule. I learned the trail network and the unofficial bypasses that allowed me to circumvent those pesky No Trespassing signs and access larger swaths of the desert landscape where nobody would see me for miles. I loved my solitude and the time and space to explore new things. My smile grew wider every time I found a new road, a path I hadn't seen before, some relic of mining history, new animal tracks, or something different blooming. And each time I reached a new mileage threshold, I was lifted up by soaring feelings of accomplishment and reaffirmed in my abilities. Running is addictive, haven't you heard?

When my dad joined me for the first time on a long run, I led him around my special routes and shared the rocky, prickly, dry terrain with him. He let me set the pace, though he certainly could have gone much faster. The pad I wore in addition to my ultra tampon began rubbing a burning hot spot in the crease at the top of my thigh within the first few miles. I slowed my pace and adjusted my gait in a full-body attempt to relieve the friction but hesitated to reach down and readjust my underwear in my dad's presence. He'd already made his discomfort surrounding the acknowledgement of what he referred to as "administrative issues" quite clear when I'd mentioned my upcoming doctor's appointment to my mom at their house the week before. I ignored the searing chafe in my groin as my dad doled out useful information about managing one's body while distance running. We talked about fueling for long runs, debating the merits (or lack thereof) of running-specific foods versus gummy bears. He coached me on electrolytes and hydration—imperative details for desert runners especially. He told me about his training regimen when my brothers and I were kids—basically that there was none and you ate whatever you wanted the rest of the day after a long run. I listened and took copious mental notes; he'd been running since before the internet and science, he'd done it all a thousand times before. Just as when I was a little kid, I believed my dad knew everything I would ever need to know.

A few weeks later, my blood work came back normal and my doctor found "nothing of note" in my physical exam. She smiled and nodded as I explained my concerns, then gave me permission to act as though nothing was out of the ordinary, unless things got worse.

As my weekly mileage increased and my long runs got progressively longer, my period kept pace. I learned to plan for what went into my body on a run; I also learned to account for what would come out. On shorter runs, I could get by with water, a handful of gummy bears, and a single super tampon. Over ten miles, and I added a second water bottle with electrolyte drink mix, supplemented my handful of gummy bears with whatever other snack I was experimenting with—stroopwafels, chewable electrolytes, even more gummy bears—and backed up my tampon with a pad, no matter what week of the month it was. My menstrual arsenal grew to battle the inevitable leakage. I endeavored to make it through my run, no matter how long, without having to acknowledge that what was happening in my body could be an obstacle in the pursuit of my goal. The training program had brought with it a mixed bag of emotions, the pressure to be ready for the race often overtaking the joy I had only recently found for the first time in running. Each time I ran a new longest distance for the first time, I found myself torn between some sense of pride and one of skepticism at my own abilities. Had I really run fourteen miles? And sixteen? And twenty? Was that me? This body? Surely not.

A month after my first appointment, I was back in the doctor's office being referred for an ultrasound. Her tone remained one of casual procedure, never revealing even a modicum of urgency or concern. As much as I tried to ignore the ever-increasing deluge of blood and pieces of my insides, my body never allowed me even a moment's peace. It had almost become easier to ignore it while running than at any other time of the day. At least then I could focus on the sweat beading on my upper lip, the tight flexion of my calves and quads, and the hard contact between the soles of my feet and the old mining roads and desert trails I'd come to love. The rest of my day had devolved into a period-centric dance. I was forced to constantly wear multiple feminine hygiene products, I slept on a towel every night, and I often got up in the middle of the night to change pads. I never left the house without my purse looking like a diaper bag and always thought twice about how a leak would impact my outfit. At this point, I was spending at least a hundred dollars a month on menstrual products.

In late March, I geared up for my second twenty-mile run. I packed my vest with water, electrolytes, and snacks. I pulled on the toe socks I wore for runs over fourteen miles, to avoid annoying blisters between my toes. I inserted a fresh super plus tampon and affixed an overnight pad to my first pair of underwear, then pulled on a pair of period undies over the top. A third pair of underwear held the whole thing together since the elastic in period undies is an absolute joke. The tampon would hold for the first three miles, maybe, spilling over to the pad by mile five, and if I was lucky, whatever made it all the way through wouldn't be any more obvious than the fact that I was wearing three pairs of undies under my purple leggings.

I ran the first ten-mile loop alone, beginning at the edge of town and winding up the old streets until the pavement dissolved into gravel and then single-track trail. The gradual elevation gain steepened and small rocks gave way to larger, sharper ones, which required me to watch my step more often than the ever-expanding view. The climb peaked at the base of humming cell phone towers, before an easy descent back down the road to where my van was parked.

By the time my friend Robert joined me for the second loop, I was lighter in both hydration and blood cell count. Sweat and blood ran out of me as fast as my belief in my ability to do what I'd set out to do. Emotions were running high. Though I was appropriately trained for the distance, it was taking all I had to keep moving. Frustration swirled inside me and I had to let it out—my internal monologue became external and Robert was a captive audience.

"I can't believe I thought I could do this. I'm so friggin' slow. I can't even run right now. Who do I think I am? I shouldn't be doing this. I can't do this. I'm never going to finish this race. I'll never be a runner. I'm always going to be slow. How have I been training for this long and am still this incapable? I can't do this. Shouldn't this be easier by now? I'm not built to be a runner. It's not this hard for everyone else, there's something wrong with me. I can't do this."

After I'd run my legs and mouth into the ground, Robert quietly ventured to point out that he was surprised by how negative my self-talk was. I wondered about this. Perhaps somebody who shows up for their first run since high school PE in jeans, with a bookbag full of granola bars, and casually crushes ten miles, as Robert had recently done, wouldn't have anything negative to say about their own performance. What must it be like to come at something like running with no expectations beyond showing up? In the two years before signing up for this race, I had found joy in running, but never that level of freedom from self-judgment.

I drove straight home afterward and peeled off my bloody armor to reveal the wounded body beneath. I would not, could not, give up. I would keep running. Because I had to. I had to prove to myself and everyone else that blood was no reason to quit. That my womanness was not my weakness. I stepped into the shower and washed the blood away.

My ultrasound revealed an extra-thick uterine lining, one large fibroid, and a tilted uterus. My doctor asked me what I thought we should do about it. I told her that I'd like a hysterectomy. I knew my mom, and her mother before her, had had one around my age—but she'd had three children by then. We had rarely spoken of it and I was too young to even remember her having it. Even in that moment, I struggled to relate what I was going through to her experience, and the thought of bringing it up with her in any detail made me uncomfortable. These just weren't the kinds of things we talked about.

The morning of race day I felt a familiar excited static in the predawn desert air. Runners and crews milled about, preparing to begin. I'd been to plenty of ultramarathon starting lines as a kid to see my dad off. This time, he and my mom, and our combined three dogs, were supportively present to see me off. I handed them the last of the layers I wouldn't need once I started running and joined the herd of nervous runners.

The gun went off and we all politely made our way up the single-track to find our place in the pack. I fit in somewhere in the mushy middle and kept my pace purposefully slow so I wouldn't let my excitement get the better of me.

The first ten miles were cruisy and glorious. Sunrise painted the rolling hills through the high desert landscape, which were decorated with scrub brush and aspen trees. The first aid station was eleven miles in. My folks were there with my prepacked gear bag—extra clothes, extra tampons and pads, extra food. We took a picture, I loved the pups, re-upped my gummy bear and water supply, and found that the aid station surprisingly wasn't stocked with Gatorade. A third of the way into the race, I left the aid station still feeling fresh and capable, bolstered by the lack of blood in my pants. The next stretch would be the hardest, though—this is where the route would climb a few thousand feet to the top of the Mogollon Rim.

As expected, the next ten miles were, in a word, awful.

The ecosystem quickly shifted from dry high desert to fern-covered forest, which did provide some privacy when I needed to find a place off-trail for an urgent pee. The lush foliage disguised the sharp ascent of the trail. Within a few miles, the gradual upward tilt evolved into a full-on straight-up wall passable only by an endless series of switchbacks. I stopped to breathe every three or four steps, until even that was not sufficient. I sat down beside the trail to rest, trying to steady my heart and lungs. When another runner asked if everything was okay, I nodded him on and stood back up before I was ready. I had to keep pushing.

Getting close to the top of the mesa, I could see the glorious blue of an aid station tent through the trees. I'd almost made it! I was so close! A chair and some sustenance were in sight! I crawled and clawed my way up the trail. The tent never materialized. What I had seen was only the bright blue of the sky. My pounding heart sank into my stomach, weighing me down as I crested the top of the rim. Unbeknownst to me, the race organizers had moved the aid station even farther down the road than was planned, due to some nesting endangered birds.

Where the trail met the main road, I could see that the mile ahead was flat. I willed my legs to run, that's what you do on flat terrain. After two steps they refused, and my body would not kick itself out of first gear. We would not be running for a while.

The second aid station didn't allow crew members, so it was a quiet respite of soda and snacks, but again, no Gatorade. I walked in, grabbed a few sips of ginger ale, and stuck some snack packs into my vest pockets before hitting the road again.

The flat, dusty terrain was shaded by tall, skinny pine trees that stretched toward the sky. Between the second and third aid stations, the only breaks from walking came in the form of failed attempts to run. I knew that my folks would be at the third aid station, and there I would be able to call it quits, take the DNF, and escape this misery. I wasn't capable of completing the race. I pulled into a crowd of celebratory runners, their families, and a flurry of cowbells. My parents were there with everything I needed. After a few bloody trips to the porta-potties and a precooked frozen pizza, my stomach settled. The atmosphere was exuberant and overly stimulating. The aid station volunteers and support crews cheered incoming and outgoing runners. I got caught up in the energy of the moment and left the aid station alongside my fellow runners, forgetting all about my plans to DNF.

It wasn't until a few miles down the trail that I realized what I'd done—that aid station was the last chance for a graceful exit. Now I would have to actually finish the race. Fuck.

The next segment descended from the dusty high desert into another canyon teeming with life, this one holding a soft, padded trail for my weary feet to plod along. I felt a creeping sense of my own capability returning. With a sharp left turn, the trail abandoned the cool, green shade for exposed red rock desert complete with yucca, cacti, and hydration-sucking temps. My legs struggled again to move, my urgent bladder needs became more frequent, and I wondered how I would make it to the end. There was one more aid station, but crew members were not allowed; a DNF there would be inconvenient, a burden to the race organizers, and I couldn't be one of those. But I also couldn't possibly finish this race.

Stumbling upon a single person with a stack of sodas, I'd found the last attempt at an aid station. There were no vehicles to remove me from the course. There was still no Gatorade. But that soda gave me enough life to push through and continue on. The last few miles would have been beautiful had I not just spent the last ten hours pushing my body and mind beyond their limits. Rolling hills, exposed views, red dirt with sage-green bushes. The closer I got to the other side of the never-ending hills, the closer I knew I was to finishing this race. When I thought about it, tears flooded my eyes and blurred the trail in front of me. I pushed them away.

The finish line cowbell was the sweetest song I'd ever heard. The last quarter mile was downhill on an easy slope and my legs found fresh momentum. I cruised through the finishing arch on less than fumes, but I finished.

I hugged my parents. I knew I'd made my dad proud. He understood what it was to run an ultramarathon, especially one with such challenging terrain, but he didn't know the uniquely female suffering I'd endured to stand there, sweat-soaked and bleeding.

I took two full days of rest and recovery after the race, then eased back into running. I had worked so hard for this level of fitness; I wasn't about to sit on the couch and lose my endurance. As my weekly miles took a significant cut, my daily flow continued to increase. Enough to cause alarm, maybe, but I was more concerned with the money I was spending on hygiene products and the fact that I couldn't confidently leave the house without fear of bleeding through my clothes.

I wasn't worried for my health, I was in the best shape of my life. I'd just run an ultramarathon. And the doctor had told me to continue on like normal unless things got worse. Was more blood worse? Or just more of the same?

On the day I sat working from my laptop on the toilet, I didn't decide to go to the ER. I was told to. By a good friend, who had experienced something similar. Someone I felt comfortable talking to about my body because she had talked to me about hers. I had reached out hoping to commiserate. I just wanted to feel heard. To have somebody know what a relatively crap day I was having.

She convinced me to drive myself to the hospital. By the time I walked through the sliding doors to a nearly empty waiting room, I was sweaty and lightheaded, and wearing clothes I would never want to be seen wearing in public.

I only waited a few minutes before being taken to a more private vestibule in the back. The nurses drew blood from my arm even though I had plenty making a voluntary exit elsewhere. During the three hours I was there, I spent perhaps ten collective minutes with staff. Hook up to blood pressure machines, wait. Draw blood, wait. Pee in a cup, wait. Didn't draw the blood properly, draw it again, wait. Wait. Wait. Wait. Machines beeped. Staff scuttled about a few inches from my vestibule. No one paid me any mind.

After a few hours, a doctor came in and told me that, although my hemoglobin was at a 7, it needed to be at a 6 for me to be given a transfusion. He gave me a pamphlet about "uterine disorder," including a page listing the twelve symptoms a patient should go to the closest emergency room for. I had every single symptom.

I was discharged from the hospital at 1 a.m. with an expensive bill, no answers, no medicine, no guidance, and a heavy feeling of hopelessness.

The next day I went to my brother's wedding. Even though I was bleeding out, I spent the weekend acting as if I was only tired and nothing else was out of the ordinary. I danced and laughed with my family, walked all over the city, and went out for meals—all while keeping an eye on the nearest bathroom and taking breaks to visit it every thirty minutes.

After the wedding, I dove headfirst into researching my condition and what, if anything, I could do to tourniquet my uterus. By piecing together information from research papers and anecdotal articles, I began a supplement regimen that I hoped would keep me alive until my next doctor's visit. I started slathering on progesterone lotion in the parking lot of the shop I bought it in. I would have bathed in it if I could have. My receipt also listed B vitamins, iron, and zinc. Another hundred dollars.

Within forty-eight hours, the bleeding stopped.

For the first time in six months, I wasn't bleeding. Every time I went to the bathroom, I was in disbelief at my unstained underwear. It wasn't all sunshine and clean undies, though. My ability to run seemed to disappear as soon as the bleeding ceased. On my next run, I made it only a block from home. I found myself with an excruciating headache, hold-on-to-the-ground dizziness, and debilitating fatigue. I pushed a little farther and a little farther and eventually gave up because I was in danger of losing consciousness. I didn't know how to feel, but broken and devastated were high on the list.

I had found a Band-Aid for my unending bleeding, but I had also reached the limit of my ability to continue pushing through. I do not believe that training for the race exacerbated my condition; on the contrary, I believe that training for the 50K had kept the worst of my symptoms at bay for a few months.

It was as if my body had said, *One thing at a time, this training is a lot so we can't bleed out right now.* And then, as soon as the race was over, the red dams broke.

It took a few weeks before I attempted to run again. My body demanded time to rest, to heal, to produce new red blood cells. That first mile back was on a dirt road near my house with my dad and our dogs. Scraggly creosote and acacia bushes lined the edges. The dogs picked up smells from the local wildlife; they didn't mind how slow I was, they were just happy to be out and about. My body could move only a few feet at a time between breaks to stop and catch my breath. There was concrete wrapped around my ankles and crushing my lungs. My head felt floaty and detached from the rest of my body.

It almost felt like it wasn't worth it. I walked and struggled through a single mile, having just run thirty-two a month before. It wreaked havoc on my mind. But then I remembered how running had made me feel. Even when my body was falling apart from the inside, the desert, the trails, the feeling of movement in my body, my connection with nature—it had all kept me going.

And I still have a long way to go. I'm still taking my self-prescribed regimen of supplements. I still haven't gotten any answers from a doctor. More difficult appointments where my experience has been discounted and minimized have dissuaded me from pursuing the hysterectomy that would relieve my symptoms. Just as my body needs rest from the ordeal it's been through, so does my mind, so do I.

———

HOLLY PRIESTLEY (SHE/HER)

Wherever the van is parked—always on native land

Holly is a freelance writer who was fortunate to have been raised in an outdoorsy family who took her camping and hiking from the time she was weeks old. As an adult, she thrives with her pups in a nomadic lifestyle. She loves getting out into nature and away from humans, seeing the seasons change, watching flowers bloom, and witnessing how nature works symbiotically to nurture life in all its forms, all while seeing what adventures her body is capable of. After growing up in a house and society where women's menstrual realities were not discussed, she wants women to advocate for themselves and to not be ashamed of this super-human thing that we go through.

She can be found on Instagram @hollycpriestley and at www.hollycpriestley.com.

trails for my daughter

Week 5—Prospector Trail

MY BELLY IS FIRM UNDER ITS TYPICAL HALF-INCH LAYER OF fat. I have the start of six-pack abs with the top two divots carved out just below my breasts. I don't yet know I'm pregnant. Hormones make my energy levels surge. Early in the morning before work, I run a long, rocky trail named after men who searched for silver in the tilted ridges of a red-and-gold sandstone sea. This is the Red Cliffs National Conservation Area, a preserve of canyons, benches, and round "sugar-loaf" formations where the threatened Mojave desert tortoise lives in southwest Utah. Just up the street from my house, this is my second home. It is the place that will witness my transformation.

April in the Mojave Desert means that purple blooms of desert four o'clock and cheerful desert marigolds light up the trail on both sides of my shoes. Inside my body, estrogen levels rise, thickening the lining of my uterus so that the embryo can implant. Side effects include increased serotonin and endorphins. I fly over stream cross-ings, boulders, and green-eyed tortoises emerging from their burrows. After my run, I head to work at a small conservation organization dedicated to keeping this land permanently protected.

Week 6—Coachwhip Trail

I jump off the trail and jog up a dry creek bed into a blood-red alcove. Walls of Navajo Sandstone conceal me. I pull my shorts down and squat low over the red pebbles while controlling the flow so that it doesn't spray my running shoes—a move I've learned over hundreds of trail pees. When I'm done, I stay in my squat and hop around to shake the drops off. The wind gets rid of the rest. I love peeing outside, and I'm proud that I never leave toilet paper behind. The sun on my ass and the wind whistling below feels taboo and exhilarating.

I look at the wet ground for clots of dark blood, but don't see any. My period is late, and I'm also peeing more than normal. My diabetic body is trying to get rid of the excess sugar associated with pregnancy, but I don't know this yet. I've lived with type 1 diabetes for thirty years. When I was diagnosed at age two, doctors told my parents that poor blood sugar control would lead to the loss of my eyes, my feet, and my ability to have children. I run and hike to ensure that I remain whole.

Week 7—Mill Creek Trail

I learn that I'm pregnant on Mother's Day. I didn't believe a baby could make a home in this body with diabetes. So I had never considered whether I wanted to be a mother. I thought the whole thing was impossible.

Holding the positive test in my hand, my mind travels first to the red rock. I'm an outdoorswoman and conservationist who finds purpose and sustenance in wild places. Will having a baby erase my essence or distill it?

My husband and I take a night hike to let the news sink in. Bats flit across an indigo sky silhouetted by jagged basalt mesas and domes of sandstone etched by ancient winds. The slender arms of creosote weave in and out of the dark. Clusters of yucca spikes offer their ivory blossoms up to the moon. We walk up a wash rippled with silky waves of sand and sit down. He's quiet but excited about the baby. I'm scared of the changes that will come. My uterus is still the size of my fist. Placenta is an organ that has never before existed in my body.

Week 10—Grapevine Trail

Earlier today, I saw my baby's fluttering heartbeat. With one prod of an ultrasound wand, she became *so real*. Now, I see her heart in the cottonwood leaves rustling in the breeze. I see her everywhere.

Holding the grainy black-and-white picture of her ten-week-old body, I promise to show her that women can do hard things. We can hike, run, and work while growing life. Pregnancy is not a disease. It's a transformation as dynamic and earthshaking as the uplift of the Colorado Plateau along whose edge I now run.

I want my daughter to know that she can find comfort in nature. I hope she feels me searching for it now. This morning, my obstetrician labeled my pregnancy as high-risk and told me to deliver by C-section. I shared my excellent blood sugar control and exercise habits, but she didn't listen. Leaving her office, I cried, and I'm still crying on the trail now. I want to give birth the way my female ancestors did, not cut open and vulnerable on a surgical table.

My feet follow an old two-track that rises slowly through sandstone benches and coral hills quilted in yellow snakeweed and mint-green sagebrush. I jog for one- and two-minute stretches, then walk with my hand on my belly, breathing deeply to ease the nausea. I make it to the edge of the Cottonwood Canyon Wilderness and do the turn-around ritual I created as a teenager. I kiss the tips of my fingers and then touch them to the brown carsonite marking the wilderness boundary. The worries trickle out of my head. I tell them to stay put in the gathering of basalt boulders at the base of a wrinkled sandstone mountain.

Week 12—Babylon

A nurse draws eight tubes of my blood for genetic testing to screen for conditions like cystic fibrosis and Down syndrome in my baby. The dark red spurting from the crook of my arm is the same color as my favorite sandstone alcoves—the shady ones dripping with ferns and figworts.

This blood will offer insight into the baby's health because her cells have crossed the placenta into my bloodstream. At this moment, up to 6 percent of the free-floating DNA in my blood plasma is from my daughter. She will remain with me for decades, her fetal cells lingering for thirty years or more.

After the appointment, I drive to Babylon in Red Cliffs to walk in the Virgin River. I won't get the test results back for weeks, and I'm left with big questions. A river of genes flows forward; I can feel it in my growing belly. While I can't change the river's course, I can plan for what may surface. Type 1 diabetes, breast cancer, depression, alcoholism, long legs, ski jump nose, fine hair, otherworldly stubbornness, introspectiveness, and logophilia swirl in the currents.

Orange cliffs hem the river where I walk, and water gathers in waist-deep pools against the rock. Scarlet monkey flowers and ferns tumble down from the cliffs, trailing their fringed stems in the milky green water. I walk slowly, looking for spiny soft-shelled turtles under the ripples and Mojave desert tortoises among the rocks onshore.

The tortoises here have been transplanted, pulled from their burrows before bulldozers arrived and then resettled in a strange land where they're often unable to enter the breeding pool. Their bloodlines have been disrupted. I see a set of tortoise tracks leading toward the water's edge. Their scaled feet leave little cloudlike tracks floating on the sand. Heron, mule deer, coyote, lizard, and antelope ground squirrel feet pattern the bank where the tortoise comes to drink.

I inherited my love of wild places and wild creatures and my sense of stewardship from my father. He took me hiking from the time I could fit into a backpack. My childhood unfolded on weekend adventures to caves, streams, and canyons. But it was more than nurture that made me feel at home in the natural world. It was also in my blood.

We all carry wild maps in our blood: maps of lands that our ancestors knew intimately, and loved, and newer maps born from even a single generation of dedicated observation and reverent appreciation of place. I wish to pass on a wild map of red canyons, sand dunes, and juniper-studded plateaus to my daughter. She will be able to orient herself among the cliffs and washes of southwest Utah because of the topography lines drawn in our blood.

Week 20—Hell Hole Trail

Today was another rough day at the OB. I learned that I have placenta previa, a condition where the placenta covers the cervix. Life-threatening bleeding can happen if the vessels connecting the placenta to the uterus tear during exertion. My OB told me to stop running. "What about hiking?" I asked. "No," she said.

My instincts tell me she is wrong. My instincts say, *You should make a decision about caring for a healthy pregnancy while walking in the sunlight, not while being examined in a tiny room under fluorescent lights.* My instincts say, *While you're at it, you should see a waterfall. Waterfalls are good places to think.*

So I start slogging through the deep sand of a wash called Hell Hole that leads to the base of Red Mountain. My stressed joints carry an extra twenty pounds. My thoughts percolate. *Keeping my daughter safe is my top priority.* Rounding a bend, I see an old desert oak with hundreds of glossy acorns on the ground around its roots. *I will not be strong enough to give birth if I give up wild places.* Purple and scarlet pebbles crunch beneath my feet. *I believe in myself and my ability to keep us safe outdoors.*

I stop often to drink water and rest with my tiny daughter, who is the length of a banana, according to the baby app. Eventually, I make it to the back of the wash, where 1,500-foot sandstone cliffs tower over the desert floor. The high country above sometimes sends snowmelt down the cliffs in ropes of thundering water. Today, small trickles spill down like threads of silk. I unlace my shoes and free my swollen feet. I step into one of the pools. The cool liquid is delicious on my skin and the rich funk of water in the desert is pungent in the air. I press my palms into the water sliding down the cliff. Nobody's around, so I lift up my T-shirt and press my belly against the cliff, too. The water slides over me like a silver gown. She kicks for the first time. I decide to trust my instincts.

Week 33—Red Reef Trail

My belly gets in the way when I bend to lace up my boots and my old T-shirts don't fit anymore. Linea nigra, the pregnancy line running vertically down my stomach, is peeking out. I'm thirty pounds heavier now, but I'm happy to move my new body through a valley hemmed in by soaring red cliffs and filled with fragrant sumac, cholla cactus, and rabbitbrush. My dad joins me on the trail and points out spots where my brother and I played as kids: a huge, hollowed-out cottonwood trunk we'd slip inside to hide; an alcove whose shadowed walls dance with pictographs; a cut in the sandstone where Quail Creek flows cold and swift. We used to ride through the narrow chute and then scream and laugh when we got spit out the other side into a churning pool.

My body remembers these places, and I yearn to share them with my daughter. I feel her dancing in my belly and in my blood as I hike. About a mile down the trail is a beautiful plunge pool the color of dark jade that is fed by a slow-flowing waterfall. Ten or twelve little round holes are carved into the sandstone beside the waterfall. They provide foot- and handholds to help a person climb to the top. Before my pregnancy, I would have zipped up without a second thought, but now I think for two. If I fell, it would be a long drop onto hard stone. I ease my swollen feet into the bottom two holes. Immediately, I feel off-kilter. My belly doesn't allow me to hug the rock like a lizard anymore.

Clinging to the cliff, I realize that I am creating trails for my daughter to walk in the future. By not erasing myself from wild places right now, by not giving in to fear, I am shaping a trail for the two of us to follow once she is born. We are strong and capable women, and we are not afraid. I climb the waterfall inch by inch while my dad waits below.

It's a little victory, but it feels huge. From the top of the waterfall, I can see to the east for at least fifty miles. The open land is melodious. Red ridges and cliffs crash like waves onto the shore of Sand Mountain and then fizzle away. The Hurricane Fault crackles and hums, carrying seismic energy from north to south. The temples and towers of Zion peek out in the distance, murmuring sweetly. I hold my belly and speak the names of everything I see to my daughter. I am building her blood map of this place. I believe that people are extensions of the land that nurtures them. "This is us," I tell her, "and this is our home."

Week 35—Spanish Wash Trail

Today we search for carvings in sandstone made by Spanish traders in the 1700s. I leave a note for my husband: "We're on the Spanish Wash Trail, back by 6 p.m." The "we" pops out automatically. She's not earthside yet, but every swish and swirl inside my stomach says *soon*. I wrap a length of patterned turquoise cloth, called a rebozo, around my belly for support. We trudge down a trail that's been ground by mountain bikers into powder over slickrock. Danger arithmetic sometimes fills my brain when I'm solo-hiking with my daughter. *What if I fell down this hill? What if I started bleeding from between my legs?*

It would be so easy to turn around, go back to the house, and lie on the couch. But my dream of hiking with my daughter once she's born is stronger than my fear. I can see us under trees, winding through canyons, climbing mountains. This hike is practice for those future adventures.

We reach a sandy wash the color of rose quartz. A star on the map says the carvings are here. I search for the crosses and quartered circles I've seen in pictures. My feet are hot and swollen. Puffy tissue rolls over the edges of my shoes. It irks me that I can't find the carvings. I envisioned their discovery as something I could share with her, a story I'd tell her someday that would start, "You went hiking with me before you were born, and together we found . . ."

With only an hour of light left and four miles to hobble back to the car, I start to feel anxious. Each step is agony with all the extra weight on my frame. I can walk an eighth of a mile at a time before I need to rest. *What if I get lost in the dark? What if I have to spend the night in freezing temperatures?*

Two miles to the car, and I can't even find a rock to sit on. I lower myself to the ground in the middle of the trail. Pale blue light drains from the cold sky. My feet throb. Potent emotions that have piled up for months escape from my eyes and throat. My fury at the medical establishment for disbelieving in me, my anxiety about hurting my daughter if I climb a mountain, my fear about losing my familiar body, my familiar life—it all comes out now. I weep and blow snot out of my nose until there is no more liquid. No more grief. Nothing left to do but take out my headlamp, get up, step back into my body, and keep walking.

39 Weeks and 5 Days—Bone Wash Trail

I've resisted immense pressure from the doctors to have a C-section, but agreed to schedule an induction. This is my last hike before my daughter is born. My brother and husband join me on the trek down Bone Wash. On this last day of my old life, I travel with the boy I hiked with throughout my childhood and the man who will hike with my daughter through hers.

It's overcast, and frost clings to the sandstone. Rain-drunk lichens sparkle in hues of emerald, mint, and red-orange. Rock lace covers the walls like a shawl. Hundreds of small holes are carved out of the stone in intricate, crochet-like patterns.

Hiking in a heavily pregnant body is dreamy and slow. I move deliberately. My belly creates its own gravity, drawing into its orbit little leaves on the wind, grains of sand, bees, and out-of-season damselflies. The hormone soup coursing through my body makes me happy and sleepy. I think of my daughter constantly, picturing her in the land with me. I tell her the Latin names of the plants and trees I know.

About one mile in, the wash tightens dramatically, and the floor changes from sand to stone. I struggle to climb up the slick pour-overs. We come to a canyon narrow enough that you can place your feet on one wall and your hands on the other. I take pictures of my brother spanning the gap. Then I give it a try. For a second, I support my weight between the walls and hover over the canyon floor with my giant belly hanging down, like I am flying.

39 Weeks and 6 Days—St. George Regional Hospital

This morning, I wear my backpack to the hospital instead of the trail. I arrive at labor and delivery at 7 a.m, and my daughter is born twenty-eight hours later. Small and large traumas to my flesh and psyche accumulate during those hours. I am hooked up to IVs and monitors that prevent me from honoring my body's wisdom. I have powerful quadriceps, hamstrings, and glutes. I have steady, nimble feet. I've been squatting for months, practicing slow breathing. But I am not allowed to use these resources to birth my daughter.

My uterus is physically not ready to deliver her, so my body is subjected to mechanical and chemical interventions meant to force birth. A foley catheter, a rubber tube with a balloon on one end, is shoved through my cervix into my uterus, and the balloon is filled with water. It places pressure on my cervix, causing dilation. Every half hour, a nurse reaches between my legs and yanks on the end of the tube to increase the pressure.

An IV pumps Pitocin, a synthetic version of oxytocin, into my veins. It makes my uterus contract powerfully and without rhythm or respite. When I can't handle the pain anymore, I get an epidural. The catheter in my spine brings relief, but now I can't move my legs. I feel disconnected from my body, like the line between my consciousness and my flesh has been severed. A nurse places a urinary catheter and I listen to my pee drain into a bucket.

When it's time to push, I'm not a person anymore. I'm a husk. I'm rolled onto my back and my legs are held up and spread wide in front of a parade of strangers. I'm coached to curl up around my baby like I'm doing a sit-up, while holding my breath and pushing for ten seconds at a time. I repeat this pattern for more than five hours. Eventually a doctor comes in and pulls the baby out with forceps.

Finally, she's on my chest, skin to skin. I should be glowing, but I'm not. I'm not happy. I'm not sad. I'm not really *anything*, and simultaneously, I'm *everything*. I'm a mother to a baby girl with black hair, blue eyes, a powerful voice, and insatiable hunger.

Later that night, I dream another birth . . .

When my contractions begin, I start walking the trail, slow and steady. I drape myself over boulders to rest when the pain gets intense. I wrap my arms around cottonwood trees, lean into their strong trunks, and listen to the music of their translucent green leaves. I watch the clouds change shape. I take my time with every movement. No rush. No timeline. I walk until I can't anymore, and then I crawl, but eventually I make it to the pool at the base of the waterfall. Between the womanly walls of the canyon, I labor in the wild green water. I pour cups of it down my head. When I get cold, I lie in the warm sand. I push on all fours and howl like a coyote. I hang from tree branches to stretch my spine. I stick my fingers into the holes carved into the sandstone, hold on for dear life, squat, and push. I reach into the red rock for the strength I need, and I find it.

1 Week Postpartum—One Block From Home

I am raw. I am swollen. I am bleeding. I am adult diapers. I am cracked nipples. I am engorged breasts. I am forty-eight stitches in the perineum. These realities of the female body—I cannot bring onto the trail.

I am exhausted. I am a screaming baby choking on hot tears. There's no separation between me and her. When she wails, I feel it in my guts. So I slide her tiny body into a front pack and walk out the door. I want to calm her by walking up my street toward Red Cliffs. Inside the pack, she quiets down and snuggles into my chest, but my quads start burning only one block up the street.

I can't push my legs up the hill. It feels like I'm moving through quicksand. The skin around my stitches burns. My breasts are rock hard, ready to burst with milk, rubbing against my shirt. Everything hurts. I turn around and tears roll down my cheeks and fall into her dark hair. I never thought I'd lose the ability to walk up the block. Back at home, I do some googling and learn that I have an open wound the size of a dinner plate inside my uterus from where the placenta detached.

3 Weeks Postpartum—Dino Cliffs Trail

I can walk up the street now, so I hike the two of us to the dinosaur tracks at the bottom of a sandy hill. Mindfully, I walk, waiting a moment between steps so that I know I'm stable and won't slide. I hold my daughter's little hands, which dangle from the sides of the carrier.

On the trail, I run into women who tell me that I'm brave to be hiking alone with a baby. I'm not brave, I'm just healing. I'm looking for a feeling of familiarity in this new life that's split me apart. I'm returning to the wild to return home to my body.

We stop at the *Eubrontes* tracks, big three-toed tracks left behind by *Dilophosaurus*. Two parallel sets of tracks cut a diagonal line across the sandstone, one adult and one juvenile traveling side by side. They sparkle in the sun, filled with water from last night's rain. The sweet, spicy smell of creosote lingers in the air. For a minute, I feel like myself again.

10 Weeks Postpartum—Edge of the Desert

My stitches have healed, and I've been wondering what it would feel like to run again. I walk past houses with xeriscaped yards and decorative flags that read "Welcome Spring" to the edge of the desert, where I break into a slow jog over the red sand. With each stride, it feels like a five-pound weight is bouncing up and down inside my vagina. Everything feels haphazardly thrown together. The extra skin on my belly moves up and down with each step.

My new body has loose flesh, lots of it. It has unexpected dimples and puckers. It has bigger breasts, but also a bigger stomach and hips. I see a lithe jackrabbit bounding over the slickrock, and a pang of jealousy hits. I laugh at the ridiculousness of it all, but soon tears squeeze out of my crinkled eyes. I cry alone in the desert until my milk lets down and I have to return home.

Later, a pelvic floor physical therapist gives me a regimen of breathing exercises, core work, and kegels that I practice during evening walks with the baby. I hold kegels while climbing up and down red shale hills. To keep myself motivated, I play games with the scenery. *Hold the kegel for the distance it takes to walk between those two creosote bushes. Keep your abs zipped up until you pass the alcove.* Big boulders covered in lichen, extra-tall creosote bushes, and flowering cacti become my cheerleaders.

12 Weeks Postpartum—Chuckwalla Trail

My daughter is three months old when my plans unravel. She won't let me carry her in the front pack anymore. She screams, flails her hands, and kicks her feet. Throughout my pregnancy, I had looked at framed photos of my dad packing me as a baby up Mount Charleston, through Valley of Fire, and into Red Rock Canyon. I had imagined the adventures I would take *my* daughter on and had dreamed of sharing my reverence for wild places with her.

And now, here she is, having a meltdown on a busy trail. The Chuckwalla Trail hugs chalked sandstone walls popular with climbers. Typically, I like to watch them scamper like lizards up and down the rock, but today I rush down the sandy path, searching for a private spot. I find a slab of rock screened by brittlebush and chocolate flowers. I sit down and take my daughter out of the pack to nurse her. I look around carefully to see if anyone is coming. I don't want to be bare-breasted with a baby if a group of men passes by.

Over my years of solo-hiking, I've been made to feel unsafe on the trail. I've been followed for short distances, propositioned, and asked by one man to help him read a map in a way that made the hair on my arms stand up. Remembering these incidents infuriates me. Women and girls deserve to be on the trail in peace, and we need to see each other in wild places to know that we belong here.

The long history of women being seen as prey by predatory men means that we must choose to be outdoors judiciously and with the ability to defend ourselves. Knife, bear spray, and pistol are some tools I've carried to make myself feel safe on the trail. I will teach my daughter to safely use any tool that expands her horizons outside.

I lift my T-shirt up and unsnap my bra cup. I latch the baby to my nipple, and she starts to suck. I feel my milk let down with a fiery sensation. It's coming too fast, and she rips her mouth away. My nipple sprays five or six streams across her face. My milk lands in tiny opals on the red sandstone. I have to aim my breast at the rock until my milk stops spraying. Then I relatch my daughter and let her drink until she's drowsy.

I put her back in the pack and begin walking home. She's calm for five minutes before she starts screaming again. I don't know what to do. Climbers look down at us from their perches on the walls. Someone yells, "Is she okay?" We won't go back for three months, partly because of the Mojave summer heat and partly because it feels too challenging, too uncertain, taking a baby on the trail.

24 Weeks Postpartum—Santa Clara River Trail

We travel north to the Pine Valley Mountains, a 10,000-foot range clad in ponderosa pine and Engelmann spruce. These are the indigo mountains we gaze up at from our home in the desert. The snowmelt that runs down their sides erodes the sandstone of Red Cliffs, carving the canyons I visited during my pregnancy.

I bring a baby wrap for my daughter, a new method of carry that I hope will allow us to hike around Pine Valley Reservoir. I put her legs on either side of my hip and then fiddle around with the twenty feet of fabric until I feel like pulling my hair out. The wrap tails flop on the ground, picking up long ponderosa pine needles and flakes of bark. Barely holding on to my squirming baby, I cross the fabric over my shoulders like a samurai and then wrap it around my waist twice.

Finally, I get her tied to my hip and we walk across a rock dam to a paved trail that hugs the side of a round, sapphire-blue lake. Giant ponderosa pines sway in the wind, catching pieces of fluffy cloud. Their sun-warmed sap makes the air smell like butterscotch. It's serene, but my daughter is fussing.

At only six months old, she already wants to be moving her own body through nature. This is probably why we struggled hiking in the front pack. She didn't want to be pinned to my chest. She wanted to be in the middle of everything.

At the lakeshore, I take her out of the wrap and put her bare feet in the dark mud. She squeals and reaches down to slap the mud with her hands. Soon we're both covered in chocolate speckles. I hold her up under her armpits and follow her tiny feet. She guides us to a thick patch of horsetails and runs their slender green bodies through her fingers. Then she walks into the lake and starts babbling like she's talking to an old friend. She's up to her thighs in freezing water and wants to keep going, but I redirect, and now we're following the shore to the mouth of the Santa Clara River.

It hurts my back to hunch over like this, helping her walk, but she's elated. She is connecting with nature. Every rock, leaf, and tree receives her generous attention, and mine too, since we're traveling together. We gaze at every spiderweb, worship every waterfall, and dance around every wildflower like drunken bees. It's true and full immersion in the world.

One day, she will love the natural world as passionately as I do. Maybe, like me, she'll work to conserve wild lands and creatures for future generations. As we wade down the creek under the alders, I think about the difficulties of working in conservation and choosing to have a child. There's an unspoken attitude that if you truly care about conservation, you won't bring children into the world to gobble up its resources, or to suffer under climate change.

And yet, here is this baby of mine who is jubilant in creeks and forests. Here is this baby who will be a gift to the earth if I nurture her love of it, and if I show her how to turn her love into action. We defend what we love. I've spent much of my adult life defending endangered plants, watersheds, wildflower meadows, and desert tortoises because I grew up on the land. I learned to love and see the land as an extension of my human family. Maybe the most important thing I can do as a mother is to help my daughter fall in love with nature.

30 Weeks Postpartum—Quail Creek Trail

My daughter is big enough to ride in a traditional baby backpack. The kickstand on the outside of the pack holds it upright on the ground while I place her inside and tinker with the impressive array of straps and buckles. When she's finally strapped in, and all the snacks and baby items are stowed, I can't figure out how to get her onto my back. Lifting up by the shoulder strap makes the pack and her body swing out at an unnerving diagonal.

I think about perching the backpack on top of a boulder and backing into it, but that seems even riskier. Taking a deep breath, I let my biceps do the thinking. I lift and shoulder the pack quickly, and it works. Peering over my shoulder, I see her smiling face. I cinch the hip belt down. She yanks my braid and laughs.

I've been waiting for this moment. We've got each other and plenty of supplies, and now we can adventure. She looks out at the ivory trumpets of datura flowers and the distant red cliffs with their shadowed alcoves. I look down at the aggressive fire ants on the trail, so many that it looks like a conveyor belt is moving under my feet. I high-step in my sandals to avoid being bitten and try not to fall over and feed the baby to the ants.

A little wooden footbridge spans the first crossing of Quail Creek. In the shade of coyote willows just up from the bridge is a beautiful brown sandbar ribboned with gold and mocha sediments. I take her out of the pack to walk, and she drags her bare feet through the luscious mud, caressing it with her toes. She loves the feel of it, and when I sit her down on the stream bank, she holds herself up for the first time. She keeps herself upright to grab handfuls of mud to taste. I jump up and down in the creek, yelling, "You did it! You did it!" Some hikers walk by and ask, "What did she do?" I exclaim, "She sat up for the first time!"

On the map, I mark the spot on Quail Creek where she sat for the first time by drawing a tiny chair. Then I draw my own "baby key" in the bottom left-hand corner. *What will come next, and where will I mark it on the map?* The anticipation is a warm feeling in my chest. I realize, now, that I always wanted to be a mom.

I think back to all the time that my dad spent with me building rock dams in creeks, rescuing frogs, searching for horned lizards, hiking to ancient bristlecone pines. In those moments, there was a gentle spiraling feeling tugging me into the future, the inkling of an idea too big yet to be expressed, that one day I would get to do these same things with my child.

Now we walk down the creek together, with me holding her up beneath her armpits. In the deepest spots, the green water goes up to her chubby thighs. She's a confident walker, kicking her feet out from her hips in giant steps. When she sees something that excites her, she pants like a dog, flails her arms, and speed walks, splashing both of us. Horsetails wave mesmerizingly in the breeze on the banks of the creek. Water striders and tadpoles flicker in the shadows. Every few feet, she stops to bend over the skin of the water and go fishing for stones.

Inch by inch, we walk downstream, the baby backpack and any specific destination forgotten. We move slowly and joyfully, not missing a thing. Crayfish whiz across the stream bottom with their pincers snapping. Sapphire dragonflies land on the willow branches above our heads. Raccoon and bird tracks greet us from the banks. I press Rhiannon's hands into the mud so that she can leave her calling card too.

THE TRAILS TRAVELED in this essay (except for the Santa Clara River Trail) are found inside the Red Cliffs National Conservation Area. This land is home to the densest remaining population of threatened Mojave desert tortoises found anywhere on earth. It also encompasses cultural heritage sites belonging to the Southern Paiute, two designated wilderness areas, a dozen sensitive wildlife species, and 130 miles of trail—all protected from the rapid development occurring in Washington County, Utah. Even so, Red Cliffs is currently under threat from a proposed high-speed, four-lane highway called the Northern Corridor. Local governments want to route the highway through land they promised to permanently protect in 1996, even though better-performing alternatives have been studied and vetted. If it is allowed to proceed, the Northern Corridor would set a dangerous precedent for the destruction of other protected public lands. For more information, and to join the fight to save Red Cliffs and keep protected lands protected, visit the website of Conserve Southwest Utah at www.conserveswu.org.

———

SARAH THOMAS-CLAYBURN (SHE/HER)

St. George, Utah—Shivwits Band, Southern Paiute homelands

Sarah fell in love with the natural world as a child hiking short distances and exploring natural features slowly with her dad and brother. She holds a BA in English and creative writing, and recent poetry of hers can be found in the gorgeous zine *Protect Red Cliffs: Art and Narratives of a Threatened Place.* She believes that the earth is as animate and embodied as any person, and that wild places enjoy receiving the loving attention of people. She is passionately working to entice the next generation of wild women onto the trail with stories of confident adventure and raw honesty about the experience of being in a female body outside.

She can be found at https://ladymuir.wordpress.com/.

una ofrenda de sangre para la montaña

MI PRIMER ASCENSO CON PERIODO MENSTRUAL FUE EN LOS Andes, en la región de San Pedro de Atacama ubicada en Chile, donde vivo. Realizaba un curso de montañismo en el que era necesario completar en una semana el ascenso a cuatro cimas, con un aumento progresivo en dificultad y desnivel. Decidí participar para certificarme y aprender las rutas como parte de mi preparación en mi trabajo como guía de montaña. Al atardecer, en el día que se tenía previsto el tercer ascenso, llegó mi "lunita" (como llamo a mi menstruación). Había ascendido al volcán Sairecabur en dos oportunidades y sabía que era capaz de hacerlo de nuevo, pero le dejé saber a mis instructores que ese día no iba a poder para no exponer ni al grupo ni a mí. Sabía que el primer día de la menstruación era el más difícil, pero que era pasajero y que iba a poder continuar al siguiente día.

Me quedé en el campamento base.

Tres días después, el grupo estaba programado para hacer el cuarto y último ascenso al volcán Cerro Colorado, a 5748 metros sobre el nivel del mar (msnm). Me sentía mucho mejor, así que le pregunté a los instructores si podía unirme de nuevo, ya que quería que supieran que estaba comprometida con el curso y que era capaz de hacer el último ascenso con éxito. Al principio dudaron, pero al final accedieron.

Revisé el informe del clima y preparé mi mochila con mi equipo de montañismo. Metí un botiquín de primeros auxilios, tres litros de agua, un termo con una infusión de plantas locales para la altura (hojas de coca y "rica-rica"), casco, abrigo extra, barritas de cereal, algo de fruta y chocolate. En uno de mis bolsillos guardé mis ofrendas y amuletos para hacer el pago a la Pachamama. Éramos un grupo de 8 personas, siete hombres y yo.

Ocupé mi lugar al final del grupo, moviéndome a un ritmo lento y constante. Llegamos al Altiplano, una inmensa llanura a 4000 msnm, rodeado de una vegetación amarilla llamada "paja brava" o "coirón". Había oído, como todo el mundo, que no es aconsejable escalar montañas sangrando. Nuestro cuerpo necesita más glóbulos rojos en la altitud, y la eliminación de ellos durante la menstruación nos hace más vulnerables al mal de altura. Caminé deliberadamente, chequeando mi cuerpo a lo largo del camino, preguntándome cómo se sentía.

No pasó mucho tiempo antes de que mi instructor viniera a decirme que iba demasiado lento. Me sugirió que me quedara en la base esperando al equipo. Le recordé que esto era un curso, una experiencia de aprendizaje, no debería decirme que me apurara o que me quedara, debería estar enseñando, animando, guiando a todos por igual. Hubo un momento de tensión en el grupo, pero me mantuve firme. Ni una sola persona se puso de mi lado; me hicieron sentir rechazada por algo que no puedo controlar, mi cuerpo. Mi condición de mujer no era bienvenida en este grupo de hombres. Hay mucho sexismo en Sudamérica. Sentía que había mejorado un poco por nuestras conexiones con otras culturas, pero en esta expedición me sorprendió haberlo vivido en carne propia.

En mi enojo, le dije al resto del equipo que no me hablaran y me dejaran tranquila durante el ascenso. Seguí en silencio detrás de mis compañeros. Llegamos al paisaje de la puna, a 5000 msnm donde ya desaparece la vegetación y las montañas volcánicas se asoman en todas las direcciones. Me sentí bien físicamente, tan fuerte como cualquier otro día en la montaña. Finalmente llegamos a la cumbre a tiempo. Pensé en la creencia de que las mujeres son débiles en este estado, pero sabía de primera mano y de mi propia experiencia que esto no era así.

Seguí entrenando y desarrollando nuevas habilidades hasta que eventualmente me convertí en guía de montaña. Hubo una época en la que cada vez que planificaba un ascenso tenía la menstruación, por lo que decidí investigar y ver qué información había disponible acerca del tema. Busqué historias acerca de mujeres que practican el montañismo con la menstruación y encontré muy pocas. Incluso, llegué a cuestionarme si era cierto que las mujeres somos más propensas a sufrir mal de altura mientras menstruamos. Comencé a analizar mis sensaciones. El experimento comenzó con el Cerro Toco, a 5600 msnm —hago ascensos frecuentes a esa montaña y sé exactamente cómo me siento cuando voy—.

Para los antiguos habitantes y las poblaciones indígenas actuales, los picos más altos de los Andes representan a los apus sagrados (dioses y divinidades). Es una práctica común entregar alguna ofrenda a los apus cuando ascendemos. Los indígenas le rezan a los apus por el bienestar de las personas, piden que haya una buena cosecha en el año o que llueva en abundancia. El "pago a la Pachamama" se hace con hojas de coca, alcohol, fruta, quinoa y madera. Algunos de los que trabajamos como guías de montaña seguimos honrando estas tradiciones: invitamos a los clientes a participar en la ofrenda para que también entiendan que hacer montañismo en los Andes no es solo una actividad deportiva, sino que está rodeada de ciertos rituales y magia, sobre todo en los picos más altos y los volcanes.

La primera vez que entregué la sangre de mi periodo menstrual como ofrenda a las montañas fue por casualidad. Me encontraba en la cima del volcán Saciel, sin ningún tipo de ofrenda para el apu. Inmediatamente pensé: "¿Por qué no?". Cavé un hoyo en la tierra y vertí la sangre desde mi pequeña copa de silicona. En ese momento entregué lo más profundo de mi ser. Con esa ofrenda me sentí incluso más conectada con la montaña. A partir de ese ascenso, decidí que siempre que estuviera en ese estado de mi ciclo menstrual, mi ofrenda iba a ser esa para la montaña. Cada vez que lo hago me siento más fuerte, más conectada con lo que hago y mi capacidad de hacerlo como mujer. Practicar montañismo es más que un deporte para mí: es un viaje de autoconocimiento. He aprendido muchísimas cosas con esta práctica y quisiera regresarle ese regalo a las montañas cada vez que vuelva.

a blood offering to the mountain

MY FIRST ASCENT WITH MY MENSTRUAL PERIOD WAS IN THE Andes Mountains in the San Pedro de Atacama region of Chile, where I live. I was attending a multiday mountaineering course, summiting four mountains in a week, increasing in elevation and difficulty with each ascent. I was training to learn the routes in preparation for my job as a guide. On the day of the third summit, my "moonlight" (as I refer to menstruation) arrived at dawn. I had climbed the Sairecabur Volcano twice before and knew that I was capable of the ascent, but I let my instructors know that I would not be able to go that day. The first day is often painful and difficult for me, but I knew that I would be able to climb the next day.

Instead, I stayed back at base camp.

Three days later, when the group was scheduled to make our fourth and final ascent—of the Cerro Colorado volcano, 5,748 meters above sea level—I was feeling much better. I asked the instructors if I could make the climb. I wanted them to know that I was invested in the course and was capable of completing the most difficult climb. At first, they expressed doubt about bringing me along, but in the end they agreed.

I checked the weather and donned my mountaineering gear to leave with the rest of the team. In my pack, I loaded up my first aid kit, three liters of water, a thermos with an infusion of coca leaves and rica-rica for the altitude, my helmet, an extra coat, cereal bars, fruit, and chocolate. Into one pocket I tucked my amulets to make payment to the Pachamama. We were a group of eight—seven men and I.

I took my place at the back of the group, moving at a slow and steady pace. We hauled up to the Altiplano, an immense plain 4,000 meters above sea level, surrounded by yellow vegetation called *paja brava* or *coiron*. I'd heard, like everyone else, that it is not advisable to climb mountains while bleeding. Our bodies need red blood cells the most at altitude, and the elimination of them during menstruation makes us more vulnerable to altitude sickness. I walked deliberately, checking in with my body along the way, asking how it felt.

It wasn't long before my instructor came to tell me that I was going too slowly. He suggested that I stay at the base and wait for the team. I reminded him that this was a course, a learning experience; he shouldn't be telling me to hurry up or to stay, he should be teaching, encouraging, guiding all of us the same. A moment of tension passed through the group, but I stood my ground. Not a single person stood by my side, leaving me feeling rejected because of something I have no control over, my body—my very womanness was not welcome in this group of men. There is a long history of sexism in South America, but it has gotten better over time, because of our connection with other cultures. I was surprised, then, to experience it on this expedition.

In my anger, I told the rest of them to continue on and not talk to me. I followed along in silence behind my teammates. We reached the puna, at 5,000 meters above sea level, where vegetation disappears and volcanoes can be seen in all directions. Physically, I felt good, as strong as on any other day in the mountains. We ultimately reached the summit in good time. I thought about the belief that women are weak in this state, but I knew from my own experience that it wasn't true.

I continued to learn skills and eventually became a moun-taineering guide. Somehow, I kept being scheduled to climb mountains when I would be on my period, and I began to wonder what information was available. I searched for stories or studies regarding women's experiences mountaineering while menstruating and found very little. I wondered if it was even true that women were more prone to altitude sickness while menstruating, as I had heard. So I began to analyze myself. The experiment began with Cerro Toco, at 5,600 meters above sea level. I make frequent ascents there and know exactly how I feel on this mountain.

After many ascents, I began to understand how my body felt. I found the truth, which is that I feel like the daughter of the volcano. I have the same inner power, the force that comes from the uterus, from the entrails. This internal force, the magmatic chamber that burns at the insides of the volcanoes, keeping them alive, is the same force that pushes me to overcome hours on the hill and reach the summit with my heart pumping blood through the muscles that brought me there.

For the ancient inhabitants and current Indigenous population, the high peaks of the Andes are recognized as sacred *apus* (gods or divinities). It is a common practice to give some offering to the *apus* when making an ascent. Indigenous peoples ask the *apu* for the life of the inhabitants—praying for good harvest or plenty of rain. The "payment to the Pachamama" is made in coca leaves, alcohol, fruit, quinoa, and wood. To this day, some of us who climb or work in the mountains carry out this practice to honor this tradition. As a climbing guide, I invite my clients to be part of this place, bringing an offering to the summit, so that they understand that mountaineering in the Andes is not just something sporty, but that there is a certain ritual and magic when being on these high peaks, especially the volcanoes.

The first time I offered my blood to the mountains was by chance. I found myself at the summit of Saciel Volcano with no offering for the *apu*. Immediately, I thought, *Wow, why not?* I made a little hole in the earth and left the blood from my little silicone cup. At that moment, I gave of my innermost being. I became even more connected with the mountain in my offering. Since that ascent, I have made this offering whenever I go into the mountains in this state. Each time, I feel stronger and more connected to what I do, and to my ability to do it as a woman. Mountaineering is more than a sport to me: it is a journey of self-knowledge. I have learned so much and I want to return that gift to the mountains.

Cecilia Castillo Saldivar (she/her)

San Pedro de Atacama, Antofagasta, Chile—traditional territory of the Quechua, Diaguita, Uru, Chichas, and Lickanantay peoples

Ceci is an adventure tourism guide in the Andes Mountains who always knew she wanted to live her life outdoors. After college, she sought certification in first aid, mountaineering, geology, flora and fauna, astronomy, and Leave No Trace. She lives her life boldly and confidently, and she feels that the key to making this a better world is to share our experiences. She loves to travel and experience new places and cultures and is interested in creating a community among women.

She can be found on Instagram @cecilia.csaldivar.

bleeding thru

As a kid, I participated in a local nonprofit with the goal of getting kids outdoors: paddling on the New River, exploring cave systems, and backpacking a few nights on the Appalachian Trail. It was there that the seed of thru-hiking first took root. As my dream of thru-hiking the AT became a reality after college, my parents and Gram tried everything they could to hold it off. My dad attempted to "forbid" me to go alone, even suggesting he'd tag along for the journey.

Between holding several jobs, consistently tackling over twenty credit hours at school, and being a practicing polyamorous woman deeply connected to the Asheville dancing scene, you could say I fully embraced every moment as if it were my last. Due to what I now understand was undiagnosed ADHD, I could be impulsive, distracted, and disorganized. I was having fun and staying busy, but I wasn't sure what I was working toward. The AT felt like an opportunity to work through questions of who I wanted to be and how I might get there. Post-college, the chance to keep the "real world" at bay a little longer was one I couldn't pass up.

As I planned and prepared for the trail, my dad began to understand that digging in his heels was wasted effort; his twenty-one-year-old daughter would be tackling the AT solo. All that was left for my family was to offer their begrudging support and trust me to take care of myself more than they'd ever had to before.

In February 2019, I wrapped up working six eighty-hour weeks at a gem and mineral show in Tucson, Arizona, and headed back to Asheville. Being on my feet ten hours a day at the shows was unconventional training for the trail, but better than nothing. I'd only given myself four days at home to snag the remainder of what I'd need for my hike and say my goodbyes.

As a result, I sloppily threw my gear together, tallied what was missing, massaged my already sore calves, loved on my two partners I was leaving behind, shopped for said missing gear, spent quality time with my family without letting their anxiety rub off on me, and shopped for the food I'd need to get me to Neels Gap from Springer Mountain. By that time, I'd had a birth control implant for nearly two years and had not had a period in over eight months, but I knew enough about birth control to throw my menstrual cup in my itty-bitty ditty bag just in case. I was going to have thirty-two pounds on my back, what was one more ounce?

Then, rather suddenly, four days had passed, and it was time to go.

I started the Appalachian Trail on February 24, a few weeks ahead of the usual northbound window. You could say I was overeager to a fault, but that could be said of most things I'm passionate about. I knew I would face nights below zero degrees, but it was worth it to avoid the northbound bubble. The thirty-pound pack on my back and several layers of warm clothing were my confidence in the face of the frigid cold.

At Amicalola Falls, the ranger handed me the 321st red thru-hiker identification hangtag and had me sign the registry. He then convinced me to pour out the two liters of extra water I'd planned on carrying. I smiled for a photo, purple hair blowing in the breeze, and waved goodbye to my dad as I walked through the arch and onto the trail.

The first hour or so was a blur of emotions, smiles, and giggling to myself about the absurdity of the journey I'd just begun. Kids ran past me on the Devil's Staircase up Amicalola Falls as I struggled under the weight of my pack. I stopped every few minutes to catch my breath. The freedom I felt was unparalleled to anything else I'd ever experienced. That first day with no deadline, no timeline, and nothing but miles in front of me, I wondered how I could ever go back to the routines and systems of the "real world" again.

Without all the background noise, the stream of consciousness I had grown used to slowed. I stewed over words, untangling them between the trees, forming full sentences and deeper thoughts. I delved internally into things I normally avoided. I let my imagination run wild.

I'd gone on plenty of two-to-four-day backpacking trips before, and I was confident that with a trusty guidebook in my hand, I could take care of myself. This was the first long-distance trail I'd attempted, and I'd intentionally avoided every book on thru-hiking the AT in order to have my own experience and learn from my own mistakes. I've always been a "hands-on learner," one to fully embrace adventure and failure in equal measure.

My first two weeks on the trail were an absolute dream, even as my own impatience sabotaged me at every turn. Temperatures were scarcely above freezing during the day and dipped into the single digits at night. It wasn't worth waiting around for the sun to melt the frost off my tent each morning. My lack of patience left me with frozen hands and a waterlogged tent in my pack for the rest of the day.

On several occasions, I collapsed in a sun spot off-trail to sob and blow warm air into my throbbing hands, my thirty-pound pack still strapped to my back, fingers too numb to work the buckles. Hikers would pass me as I cried, sometimes stopping to make sure I was okay. I'd smile through the tears, comment on the cold, and reassure them I'd be fine as soon as the feeling returned to my hands. It always did, and I'd wipe away my tears and soon enough be on my way.

I'd been warned against pushing big miles too soon and with too much weight on my back, but anything other than hiking or cocooning in my sleeping bag was far too cold, so I kept putting one foot in front of the other from sunup to sundown. Eventually this would lead to severe Achilles tendinitis that would take me off the trail for three weeks and cause me to seriously reevaluate my hiking style.

After my first week, my body began to rebel—and not just in the well-earned hiker hobble that accompanied me everywhere I went. I also began spotting. I'd gone to the privy, which I dreaded, because my exposed bum would freeze every time I sat down to do my business, only to discover that I was bleeding.

Infrequent spotting wasn't uncommon for me, so I wasn't entirely surprised, but I was annoyed at the inconvenience nonetheless. After an unwelcome series of chores—washing my hands, retrieving my menstrual cup, going back to the privy, again exposing my bum to the elements, inserting the cup, washing my hands again—I was back in business.

Over the years I'd used a menstrual cup to make it through the long days on my feet working wholesale gem shows, but my confidence with inserting and removing it wasn't that of a frequent user. Typically, spotting is not an ideal circumstance for using a cup. When flow isn't heavy, it can be sticky and painful to insert and remove. This is where my ADHD sometimes feels like a superpower. Crouched over the pit privy, I was so hyperfocused on willing dexterity into my numb fingers and preventing the escape of what little heat I had into the single-digit night that I barely noticed any cup-related discomfort and had an issue-free insertion.

The next evening I caught up with my tramily—trail family— right around golden hour at a spacious clearing between towering trees that were becoming darker by the minute. After tackling my camp chores, making conversation, and cramming calories down the hatch, I heeded nature's call and wandered away with my trowel and toilet paper to do my business. While I prefer a privy, catholes are sometimes an inevitable responsibility. It's proper Leave No Trace procedure to discard menstrual cup blood into a cathole. It may not sound ideal, but when the alternative is packing out bloody tampons, the cup proved more convenient in my eyes (and uterus).

With the sun went down, the hand sanitizer felt bitingly cold on my fingers. I impatiently blew hot breaths into my cupped hands for five long minutes to prepare for the task ahead.

Based on past patterns of spotting and my consistently frozen fingers, I hadn't emptied the cup in the twenty-four hours since first inserting it the night before. With the cathole dug, my hands sanitized, and my brain hyped up, I pulled down my cold-weather tights and underwear and squatted. Once again the biting cold chilled my bum, but there was moisture where I wasn't expecting it and the cold intensified. Blood was smeared on the insides of my thighs where my underwear had failed to absorb the spill.

Menstrual cups are designed to hold two ounces of liquid before needing to be emptied, which is plenty of capacity for eight to twelve hours. If a cup overflows or is inserted slightly ajar, blood will leak out. Even if your menstrual cup confidence is airtight when you're in the comfort of your own bathroom, try your technique while crouched over a cathole with the sun going down and no familiar sanitation in sight and you'll see how quickly things can go awry. I was no stranger to the imperfect insertion, so I figured that was the cause.

Blotting my underwear with toilet paper, I pulled away square after bright red square in an attempt to clean up, while using as little of the finite resource as was necessary. My spare pair of underwear was back at my tent, surrounded by my all-male tramily. I accepted my fate of eventually having to pull my damp, bloody underwear back up over my now-numb bum. But first, I had a job to finish.

I removed the cup and realized with horror that the leakage wasn't due to an imperfect insertion. I'd underestimated my flow by a long shot. Blood dripped from the cup, coating my stiff, throbbing fingers. Frustration overflowed in the warm tears streaming down my frozen cheeks. If I had ever had a bail-out button to use once on a thru-hike, that would've been my moment. But once more, my ADHD hyper-focus superpower kicked in and there was little on my mind beyond the task at hand and the inescapable aching pain from the cold on my exposed skin.

Several minutes of crying, bleeding, and freezing later, I succeeded in my endeavor—if you could call achieving my task at the expense of a brief, half-naked breakdown in the woods a "success."

Half an hour later, I was snoozing peacefully, snuggled up in my sleeping bag, just happy to be there. My period remained highly irregular the rest of the trail, eventually disappearing around the same time I began developing constant urinary tract infections. I counted my blessings that I never had to face both at the same time. I could handle frozen period blood, and I could handle peeing fire every quarter mile. But both would've been a doozy.

Whenever I get particularly stressed about a situation I find myself in on trail, I repeat a simple mantra: *I've made all the decisions to put myself in this position, and I'll have to deal with it, and make all the decisions to get myself out. There are no other options.*

On the AT, I started to see the simplicity of such situations— hiking ten to twelve hours a day, sleeping outside, taking care of my body as issues arose, and existing in the moments of beautiful solitude. In the 3,000 miles I have hiked since then, hiking has become as much a meditative practice as a physical exercise—a way to untangle my thoughts, my anxieties, my ADHD brain.

———

KATIE "OATS" Houston (she/her)

Asheville, North Carolina—ancestral land of the Miccosukee, Tsalaguwetiyi (Cherokee, East), S'atsoyaha, and Mànu peoples

Oats thru-hiked the Appalachian Trail shortly after graduating with a BS in environmental science in 2019. She realized she needed to make the trail community the center of her life, so she pivoted to freelancing in the outdoor industry. Now, when she's not hitting the trail with her husky, Thru, she helps long-distance-backpacking gear and media companies engage with their audience in online spaces. Through this work, she fosters good trail ethics and an outdoor community where everyone feels like they belong.

She can be found on Instagram @oatshikes and at oatshikes.com.

soar

It is day thirty-five of forty. A bone-dry summer season in mid-August deep in the pandemic of 2020. In this amount of time I have hiked, often painstakingly, 387 miles away from my home in Denver. I have entered the double-digit-mileage and single-digit-day countdown, ninety-nine miles from finishing the entire Colorado Trail, and I'm bleeding. From my uterus via my vagina, that is. The monthly shedding of uterine lining signifying there is still no baby growing inside me.

My hard-earned trail legs tenaciously hustle to ascend above 13,000 feet in elevation. My toned calves and thighs scream out as I clamber up and over boulders and stumps, carrying my weight in water because it's so dang hot. Turns out this will be one of the hottest and driest Colorado summers on record. I traipse nerve-rackingly through precarious scree, navigate the dense deadfall of avalanche fields with oodles of branch scratches and almost-poked-out eyes, and doggedly labor along with a paradoxically aspirational *Sound of Music*–like attitude across high-altitude mesas. I'm audibly cursing. "Fuck! Fuckity fuck, fuck, faaaawwwwwkkkk." This four-letter word has never, in my entire adult life, so comfortably traversed my vocal cords and slipped from my lips as it does now while on trail. Climbing, cursing, sopping in sweat, breathing heavy, and high-stepping, trekking poles serving as my third and fourth legs. All whilst pumping out blood from my body's southernmost orifice.

Womb, for reals?! What are you trying to tell me?

Obviously, my sacred uterus wants to remind me of my femininity despite how badass manly strong I feel, after hiking close to 400 miles in every imaginable condition. *Wait, I guess I'm even more of a badass for doing it while bleeding from my fucking vagina!* Because I'm still not pregnant.

And there, echoing in my feminine badass ears, is my mom's voice the moment I told her about my plans for this trek. "Forty days?! That's two menstrual cycles!"

Yup, in all her glory as the mother who birthed and raised me. At that moment, she could not convey any sense of pride toward my aspirations, or what I'd already been through and triumphed over in the last five years. Her first thought and first words were in reference to the grandchild I hadn't yet given her. To her chagrin, I would not become pregnant in these weeks while on trail. It was the tone of immediate disappointment, that I may be missing out on conceiving for two whole cycles this summer. The summer after my first failed IVF (in vitro fertilization). The summer after six years of failed fertility treatments. The summer of a global pandemic. The summer she wouldn't get to become a grandmother—again. Yet another summer I wasn't going to become a mom.

> *Heart drops.*
> *Another devastating failure.*
> *Nonfulfillment.*
> *Breathing stops for a quick moment.*
> *Big sigh.*
> *Broken. I'm broken.*

Every time I bleed, the possibility of a new life departs. It screams: *Well, there's nothing growing in here after all!* Life not formed. Death exits through my vagina every twenty-eight to thirty-two days. The grim reaper that is this infertility journey. I have bled not once, but twice in these forty days on the Colorado Trail. *Womb, again, you've got to be kidding me!* I'm hiking my feelings—hiking to heal. One foot in front of the other in an attempt to prove my body's non-brokenness, my body's strength, my body's fertility. Confirmed! I am indeed so fertile that I bleed like clockwork—twice in five and a half weeks.

The first cycle occurred over days nine through twelve. One hundred miles away from home. Somewhere around segments 6 and 7 in a sweltering mid-July. My period. Every month for the last twenty-five years. An indication that things are working as they should be. Or at least showing up just as middle school health class taught me. Happening just as our female elders have informed us it would. Heavy flow, gentle throbbing, and a constantly blood-encrusted pointer finger courtesy of the natural, applicator-free wad of cotton that I forcefully shoved into my birth canal every three to four hours. Unfazed am I. Animalistic and raw. A perfect match to the on-trail environment.

Segment 6 broke me. This pass is most oft traveled by ski lift. Everyone forgot to tell me that it is typical to "slack-pack" this one-day section. Instead of allowing my pack to be shuttled to the next trail-head, I carried my full weight, plus an eight-pound burrito from my cousin's restaurant in Breckenridge and my standard three liters of water. I added to my pack several blood-soaked tampons over the course of the day. I painfully rolled my ankle on a bridge crossing. I kept that torment a secret for quite a few more miles before earning myself an ankle wrap by trail magic in segment 9. Numerous false summits broke my spirit but prepared me for the perseverance and aspiration required to continue again and again in the face of devastating disappointment. One of so many lessons on the Colorado Trail.

My second period showed itself twenty-six days later, on August 12. Why? Why was my body still bleeding? She could barely hold herself up when not in constant motion, but she could still climb up, scale over, and flow with joy, accomplishment, and menstrual blood. My last four days of hiking were to be spent bleeding. Depleting my body further of iron and nutrients. I was exhausted. Any gumption I had left poured out of me via my sweat, my tears, my blood.

There weren't enough natural, applicator-free resources to absorb this fucking flow. Wilderness living preaches caution around food smells and scented toiletries. As a lady thru-hiker with two cycles in forty days, my blood smells and bodily scent, from DNA excretion, were unavoidable. The four men I was hiking with—my brother and husband being two of them—honored the rock star–ness that my body is because she could hike swollen, steadfast, bloated, sore, and throbbing. She could carry upward of nine liters of water during a twenty-five-mile day. She wore bloody boy shorts underneath her hiking skirt and the weight of the world on her back. She smelled rank —not of sweat, really, since the body begins to no longer smell when sweating at this point. Something called "stench equilibrium," coined in *Backpacker* magazine. Where a thru-hiker won't smell any worse after nine weeks in the wild than one would after three weeks. I'd certainly reached this threshold, since to save weight, I wasn't carrying or using deodorant. I wore the same hiking shirt and bra daily. Both items were crunchy at this point. Stained beyond repair. It was my boy shorts that were the worst smelling. I was getting sloppy with my "pull back one leg to pee" while standing up technique. Most of my urine was ending up on my leg and drip-drying on the material. Add that to the menstrual blood that was caked in my crotch at this point and "rank" might seem like an understatement.

My body began to enter the beginning stages of toxic shock syndrome during the final six miles of the Colorado Trail. I couldn't change my tampon because I didn't have any more to replace it. For almost three full days, I wore the same wad of cotton within me. I felt sick—nauseous and sweating. Was that the smidgen of giardia I picked up two weeks back? Was that my womb getting mad at the old blood remaining imprisoned inside me? Was it my body breaking down after forty days of sleeping on the ground, setting up and taking down my tent each day, eating those favored instant mashed potatoes with powdered bone broth deliciousness? Was it because all I wanted was sugar right now? Maybe it's the sickness that comes when one realizes that the end is near. Little did I realize at the time, my mom's premonition was correct. I did experience two menstrual cycles after all! I may not have conceived a baby while on trail for forty days, but I conceived a better version of myself.

Breathe. Keep breathing. Breathe deep and often.
Lighten that load you're carrying.
The climbs are temporary. The pain is temporary. What's trying you is
temporary.
Relief comes in the decline, the down. When we descend.
Slow down.
Rest.
Wait. The wait game is real.
Not broken, not one bit.

I've been getting periods since one fateful day in eighth grade. My family had just moved houses and I had switched from being one of the old students at a K–8 to being one of the lowest at a new junior high school. It was the year 1993. In one of the last class periods of the day, I felt some wet thick stuff in my underwear. With a trip to the girls' bathroom, I discovered the deep crimson stain and chose to ignore it. Later that afternoon, my piano teacher noticed the bloodstain on my stonewashed jean shorts. She had me play a few pieces without her as, I realized later, she called my mom to inform her of my entrance into this new season. The fertility season. The season of womanhood. Once home, I sensed a fog of hush-hush within the family. My father kept mentioning that I was a "woman" now. The term and his tone of voice when he said it made me cringe, blush, sweat in places I didn't know I could sweat. I wanted to hide myself for the rest of adulthood. Truly, I didn't even want to grow older back then.

I was deep in doom and gloom. Nothing would be the same anymore. I would now endure monthly discomfort, monthly pain, monthly grossness of body fluid, the kind that stains, the kind that no one seemingly talks out loud about, a sort of shame-induced weirdness silently experienced.

I'd known that this was coming, since my mom told me about "the birds and the bees" two years earlier. She had broached the subject while picking lice out of my hair and chopping it into a short bob, during an infestation that had taken out my entire sixth-grade class. It was then that I had started secretly dreading the entrance into womanhood. I didn't want it to change me, let alone become a bother every month. I don't remember the talk being focused on the gift or honor of creating life, the beauty or power of fertility. I only saw the future of my womanly body as something I wanted to avoid. Could I have sabotaged my future Self right there and then? Could "the talk" have been reframed to be received and perceived in a more positive light? I only ask these questions now as I write this story at forty-four years old. I only now recall and reflect on this moment on the back porch, with my mother's hands in my hair and her words in my ears, as I enter into my ninth year of invasive infertility treatments. In this ninth year, my mom has indeed changed her tune. She has evolved from her quip about two menstrual cycles. Where she was once against anything that might prevent us from making a baby, she is now pro–anything that will help us create a family.

Fear into Fearless.
Worried into Warrior.
Multiple chapters. New beginnings. Head trip. Heart opening.
Soul validating. Spirit healing.
Reframe.

I had no idea that come day thirty-five on the trail, I'd have dropped twenty pounds from my frame. My hip straps needed to be pulled tighter to keep my pack in the best ergonomic spot, yet the straps wouldn't cinch any more. I first noticed the difference when I turned sideways with the rising, already boiling sun behind me. The stick figure of a shadow that I saw on the high-altitude marshy meadow took me by surprise when she nearly disappeared. In fact, for a split second I thought someone else was standing behind me and this was their shadow. *Whoa.* My twenty-year-old self would have been pleased with this discovery. I aspired differently back then. The aspiration was thin. Skeletal. Straight. Narrow. No curves or soft edges. The feminine form of a perfect pencil. My forty-year-old self did a much healthier job of recognizing that my body had worked hard—SO HARD—these last thirty-five days.

I knew I needed to stay strong and keep myself fueled to make it to the end. Food was fuel. I sensed I would feel so much stronger if I ate every one of those allocated-for-five-days cheese packets rather than just one. *Yes, if I eat the tuna packet that I've been saving for tomorrow today, I'll be satiated and charged to do the miles I need to do. Heck, if I have two tuna packets, a handful of cheeses, and as many of the gas station salty junk food snack-y things that I have, I'll really feel superhuman. Give me the salt, the crunch, and the fast-burning "cheap" calories!* A fellow hiker shared some Crystal Light packets with me that completely rocked my world. I didn't know why I hadn't been drinking those the whole time! They were fake-color, fake-flavor deliciousness that my body drunkenly devoured. Gummy bears were passed around, and even when the entire bag accidentally emptied onto some sticky pine needles, I gleefully scooped them up and popped them into my mouth, Lysol effervescence, crunch, and all. Self-judgment dissipated. My newly acquired thru-hiker body LOVED herself some junk food, something my younger self never would have allowed herself to consume or would have quickly purged right up. Junk food denial was replaced with a salty, crunchy junk food love affair. Food as fuel and body celebration. That night for dinner? The two-person rehydrated bag meal didn't have a chance against my hunger or my stomach capacity. Ravenous! Consumed! Fed. Fueled. What a phenomenal reframe in how I felt toward my body—an unintended consequence of my thru-hike.

The more I consumed, the more confident my footholds were, and the stronger my thighs became to lift me up and over markedly tall rock steps or hold me steady on the extreme slopes that descended into the valleys (only to climb back up again). The more I fed myself, the better hiker I became. I liked myself. The more I fueled up, the more I loved my body. The more I loved my body, the more miles I made. While thru-hiking, I relearned to respect food. Food as fuel. While thru-hiking for the last forty days of my fortieth year on this planet, I fed my body lovingly, with respect and utmost care, and I reveled in how she responded. Almost three months post-trail, I found that I could barely eat full meals of any kind. I could only nibble, snack sporadically. When I tried to clean my plate during a late-August barbecue, my body physically couldn't handle it. I grew exhausted, fatigued. The only consumption it seemed my body wanted was gas station junk food snacks. In acceptance of this newfound awareness of food capacity for my post-trail body, I didn't force it. I listened to what my body needed, how she needed it, and when to fuel her in the optimal amount. My body, a beautifully fed badass. She needed me to respect her. She had earned that. I could only do her justice by abiding by her needs, offering anything that helped her continue to thrive post-trail. Another trail lesson: love my body.

We can do hard things.
Third 11,000-foot climb today.
Turn around and look from where you've come.
So hard.
The desire in your heart to be a mom is there because it was meant for you.

For the duration of my husband's and my two-year engagement and, at the time of this writing, nine years of marriage, I got my periods regularly, despite partaking in very conscious, often strategically planned acts of baby-making, more often with a sense of urgency and obsession on timing—the right timing. I bled no matter what. No matter the position, the time of the month, the amount of love, the supplements, the substance moderation or abstinence. No matter the amount or frequency of using ovulation synthetic stimulants (ten monthly cycles in total). No matter how many IUIs (intrauterine insemination—basically the turkey-baster method; five in total). My body was broken. My period, which should have been a sign of fertility, became a sign of confirmed *in*fertility. My body wasn't doing what I was told it would do. Those health class teachers had lied. The whole "first comes love, then comes marriage, then comes a baby in the baby carriage" singsong we'd bully each other with when in elementary school was a complete lie! *Why am I different? Why is it not happening to me? For me? Am I doing something wrong? Is something wrong with my body? Is something wrong with me? Is my body broken?* I had been told I would be able to do this; I expected to be able to do this.

I believed I was broken.

That's why I needed to thru-hike the Colorado Trail. It was both an outward expression of an awesome feat accomplished, as well as a massive internal transformation of how I felt toward myself. Toward the very existence of my being. Infertility teaches us to question our purpose on this planet. Receiving relentless negative results, negative outcomes despite consistent positive action—it takes a toll on the soul. My spirit was in need of deep healing.

I hiked to discover the version of myself that would exist at the end of an extreme physical effort. The only way out was to become someone entirely new.

Unanswerable. Unknown. Undetermined.
Infertile versus Fertile.
Shots to the vulnerable parts.
Pain on the surface, deep down full and achy.
Hope divorced.
We aspire instead.

The day of my fortieth birthday, one year before my hike, we had facilitated quite the party: it was equipped with a silent auction, a live band, two food trucks, and an enormous amount of joy, anticipation, and hope. The silent auction was to fuel our bank accounts with the funds needed to put ourselves through IVF. You see, nothing we had done in the last four years of marriage had worked thus far in our family-making journey. All those monthly menstrual cycles, all those tampons, all that blood and we weren't successfully conceiving. What a waste of a life force! We had spent thousands of dollars on lotions, potions, spells, medications, supplements, treatments, more treatments, and even more treatments. This IVF was our gift to ourselves, with the generous support and loving embrace of friends and family near and far.

The shots and appointments started in late September that year. This expensive and intensive process begins with day one of a menstrual cycle.

Blood kicks off the IVF process (any infertility treatment, actually, is calculated from the start of a menstrual cycle, day one of blood).

My bleeding commenced phase one: in short, excess egg creation stimulated by hormone-filled syringes painfully delivered as a shot to my belly twice a day, every morning and every evening for two weeks or more. Then, when the size of the hormone-pumped eggs looked ideal, when the moment scientifically seemed correct, said plethora of eggs was extracted from my body (we got ten), then was combined with my husband's sperm outside of my body in a beaker filled with room temperature saline (only seven of them were fertilized).

Exciting, right? Maybe not.

Science had stepped in. Science is pretty remarkable. We celebrate a shared belief in science.

A waiting season.

We waited five full days. Five painstakingly long days. What were once frequent visits and practically daily phone calls from the clinic turned into hauntingly silent, loooooonnnnngggggg days. I cautiously anticipated their phone number showing up on my cell phone screen as my phone mirrored my caution with its dainty vibration while ironically in silent mode. It's excruciating, really, this waiting time. Those of us who go through waiting seasons: we are left with our own thoughts and Dr. Google either validating or denying symptom-spotting. We are left to sit in the unknown. This is not a feat for the weak. Like on trail, just because the map shows a climb, curve, or change in elevation ahead doesn't necessarily mean it'll feel bad or be hard or even all that noticeable. If we don't anticipate what's ahead, we can enjoy the present. In the case of those of us navigating infertility, we learn to call this the Pregnant Present.

The phone rang on that fifth day. We had only one surviving embryo, one champion. This was a miracle. A combination of me and my husband. An already very loved, living mini-almost-baby, lying frozen in a petri dish until my next monthly bleed (well, not really monthly anymore, my days had been all out of whack since science intervened).

Freeze.

Day one of the next bleed would tell us when to transfer our frozen mini-us back into my body to thrive. More blood. Bleeding started phase two—transfer and implantation. Another excruciating waiting season. This time a full nerve-racking eleven days. The hauntingly silent cell phone returned. Dr. Google. Grasping peace, clinging to clarity, asking for signs. Cautionary dainty vibration in an ironic silent setting.

All the shots, all the money, all the time spent at appointments, all the invasiveness, all the energy, all the hope, all the belief that this was it, this was going to be our time. One miracle, champion embryo.

So much love from near and far. *It's just gotta work, right? It just has to.* No. Nope, it didn't. All of the possibility, gone. On December 25—Christmas Day of 2019—we learned that *she* didn't stick. We were not pregnant.

When undergoing infertility treatments, your entire care staff and even office staff know information about you prior to you knowing it. In this case, they knew the sex of our embryo. It was written in our notes. During one of my phone call updates with a nurse, this information was accidentally revealed to me. I told them we didn't want to know the sex. This nurse realized it after the fact. We shared a long few seconds of silence as this information left her mouth, entered my ears, and went straight to my heart.

All the blood, for nothing.

We had nothing to show for it other than our broken hearts and debilitated spirits. We wailed in devastation. Animalistic and raw. Defeated. Tears would well up at all times of day, in all situations, like in a coffee shop, during a work meeting, or in the middle of a treasured time with best gal friends. Grief is a gnarly creature to tame, let alone navigate well. It sometimes comes out of nowhere and sometimes leaves for a long stint. Then reappears to knock our socks off, in deep, empty, broken sorrow.

Loss.

We made it to day one of January 2020. Shook off a lot of that sorrow (really because we worked through it, sat in it, stared at it, and let it go only when it was ready). We intentionally took time "off" from fertility-focused things. We nourished our beaten-up bodies with healthy shakes, we moderated our grieving souls from alcohol, we got back to us, got back to joy without being so tied to the act of baby-making. We were prepping, bodies readied, spirits emboldened. If I wasn't to become a mom in my fortieth year, then I would surely prove to myself that I was not broken. I would thru-hike the Colorado Trail. My husband would start and end it with me and be my resupply every sevenish days. His journey of healing would equate to at least 150 miles of trail and over 400 miles of driving while going back and forth from home to meet me. The last forty days of my fortieth year would be BIG. I would complete the journey on my forty-first birthday. This was the plan.

Then, in March, the world shut down.

There is no lack and scarcity. No sense of urgency either.
Return to you, the basics, the base. Return to what really matters.
Persevere.
Fucking Fertile. There's nothing wrong with you.
You are not broken, not one bit.

I hiked to heal. I hiked to prove I wasn't broken. I hiked to relearn that food is fuel, food is a nourishing friend. I hiked toward motherhood. Hiked toward a future full of dreams and aspirations. I hiked to let go, release the old, untether what no longer served me. I became

Yardsale: the giving away of what is no longer needed. The releasing of items that are taking up space. The removal of the old to make space for the new. That is me: Yardsale (also not exempt from the other definition of *yardsaling*, when all of my belongings are splayed out in a hot mess at camp for anyone to view). Yardsale. Untether what no longer serves me. Be okay with a mess. Let it go. Put it on display. Release and welcome the "new."

I yardsaled the devastation, defeat, debilitating sadness, sorrow, and grief. I dropped twenty pounds off my body and carried twenty pounds of my better, stronger self. I hiked myself into my forty-first year. Renewed, refreshed, recharged. I hiked to know *I got this*. To remember that *we've got this*. Bleeding with two cycles in forty days, it was like a giant FUCK YOU from my uterus to my heart. But my heart knew that I could do hard things, I could be a warrior. I could be a Trying-to-Conceive-Lady-Thru-Hiker-Infertility-Warrior who bleeds. *We'll be pregnant real soon after this*, I told myself as I neared the bend in the trail where I thought camp would be after a seventeen-mile day (and it wasn't, of course, no campsite around that bend). *Keep going! Our family is coming. Our family is just around the next metaphorical bend.* Another trail lesson: There's always something different, possibly something better, up ahead.

Trust.
Trust yourself, trust your body, trust the process, the path, trust the trail.
The trail provides.
What's up ahead doesn't need to live in your head.
Stay curious.
News is just more information. The map showing the trail ahead is:
Just. More. Information.
You have no real idea until you actually get there.

Three years after I completed the Colorado Trail and nine months into my forty-third year of life, we gave IVF another go. I felt abundantly nourished, fearlessly confident, and bountiful in my belief in myself. This time, my forty-three-year-old body performed exuberantly. So many eggs, two beautiful embryos, a nourished, clean, strong bleeding body who was more ready than ever to receive life. She rocked it so much better than three years earlier at age forty.

The embryo transfer worked!

I was pregnant on Mother's Day 2023.

The fertility clinic staff was WOWed! I had beat the odds. All the foreboding statistics, I had paid no heed.

All that bleeding, my body cleansed each month in all my seasons, readying me to receive this month. My thick-blood-lined uterus was growing a mini-us, an almost-baby.

What I've learned over the last nine years of being on this infertility/trying-to-conceive journey is that there are sometimes no true reasons why. Although I am not a trained doctor, and in my case, my diagnosis is "Unexplained," my body wasn't ever the problem. Through extensive mindset training coaching investments, I've learned that infertility is not something that has happened *to* me. It is not something that is happening because of *me*. Most importantly, when navigating infertility one will benefit from not ever blaming, shaming, or judging oneself. No amount of diets, lotions, potions, science, or treatments can backfill my mind, or reteach my heart that I was never broken in the first place. There was never anything wrong with me. Our bodies are indeed designed to do what they know how to do. Far better than our own brains. Our bodies, they know. It's best if we trust them. My infertility journey retaught me to trust my body. It may strike us as odd, but I now believe that infertility happened *for* me. For me to be exactly the mother I was meant to become.

The Colorado Trail taught me to trust. My favorite lesson from the trail is: Trust the trail. The trail always provides. In life, my body is the trail. She will provide.

We got to see the heartbeat. Quick, slow, quick, slow, quick. We were told that this little "bean" was a few days behind in development. "It's okay," we told ourselves. "We aren't going to give up on you."

My body made it to the eight-week mark. Our mini-us was too mini and had not continued to thrive. Our once-seen heartbeat dwindled, faded, and finally stopped for good.

Then on a Sunday morning, with extended family gathered around the brunch table, I felt that familiar warm feeling of fluid draining from my body.

Thick, rich blood, clotty with slight variations of human tissue colored pink in relation to my own skin tone, passed through my vagina. My legs and arms shook with emotion and grief as if I were lying supine and naked in the Arctic. The following day, my birth canal was triggered by the synthetic stimulants of the abortion pill regimen. A medicated miscarriage. My uterus convulsed. My body was undergoing activated labor. My womb emptied the life it had begun to feed after all those cycles of menstruation across all those seasons, throughout all those years. Throughout the miles, despite the smiles. My body let go of the life she desperately wanted to keep. It was simultaneously excruciating and terrifying. Now if that's not some fucked-up shit, I don't know what is. We women, we female-identifying folx, we are brave, we do hard things, we are warriors.

Bad News equals just more information.
Meandering. Flow. Surrender. Let go.
Anticipation isn't necessary.
Each moment is the present, an actual present, a fucking gift.
The motto of those in the Trying to Conceive Club.

A little over a month later, I ventured out at golden hour to complete the Collegiate West portion of the Colorado Trail—a promise I had made to myself when I completed the trail in 2020. Back then I was a southbounder and I took the Collegiate East option—the original trail that flows and rolls up and around the Collegiate Peaks without the requirement of summiting. Three years later, I would return to experience "the West"—a seventy-five-mile stretch of mountain passes, ridgelines, and deep valleys through the Collegiate Peaks Wilderness of Colorado. This time, I was a north-bounder, heading from Monarch Mountain to Twin Lakes. I was still healing. I didn't feel strong. I didn't have "trail legs." I "off-the-couched it" this time. I was solo. Truth be told, I wasn't 100 percent internally motivated either. Yes, being on the Colorado Trail specifically is spiritual for me no matter what or when. I was rather more externally called to complete this goal, as if it was a to-do I'd set for myself to check off. Something to once again remind me that I wasn't broken. That there wasn't something wrong with me. That our family was still a possibility.

During this route, I was content in my smiles, not miles. I was reflective of my great smallness against giants. I hiked as a mother—even for the short amount of time I got to call myself one. I hiked as an infertility success story. I hiked as a badass lady thru-hiker who had grown three years older (I was almost forty-four) and realized there was no longer a need in my heart or spirit to be on top of mountains anymore. My mountains were at home. Already conquered. Loved, thriving, and celebrated. Bleeding monthly brought me here. Life force pulsing through my veins, fueling my muscles, firing my synapses, pushing me forward. Bringing me over, on top of, through, and back down again.

This time on trail I did not bleed.

I mothered the next chapter, a new class of Colorado Trail thru-hikers, as each one passed me on my trek north when theirs was south. I was mothering with my care for embracing each of their journeys. I was mothering myself as my body worked SO VERY hard to hike me to my final destination. I even mothered my decision to end a bit early, saving my body from the last two summits. I was content where I was, looking up at them from a distance. True honor. Mad respect. Tremendous gratitude. During the quiet solo moments when I had the trail to myself, either grooving with my growing-stronger, return-of-my trail-legs pace or running from looming, deadly-looking late-afternoon storms, I spoke with my future babies. I shared with them the ideas for our future family adventures. Painted them a picture of what it would feel like to be a part of the family their dad and I had co-created for them, with them. Spoke enthusiastically about the possibilities they'd have in the great outdoors and of course the adventures we'd partake in on trail. I felt like they heard me. They knew how much they were already loved.

Feet grounded. Feet aching. Feet destroyed. Feet enable us to soar.
When your feet are sore on trail, I say soak them in the closest cold creek
until your uterus freezes.
Keep brave in your footing.
Stay planted in your belief that:
This. Can. Fucking. Happen. For. You.

Post-trail, I ushered in my forty-fourth year of life with radiance, joy, receiving, believing, and another attempt at conceiving. Cheers to our bleeding moments, to our blood-filled scars, to the memories blood stains onto our spirits. Cheers to the bloody, rich life force in each of us. We began again with my blood. Two mini, meatball-shaped miracle embryos we made. Another waiting season. This time a ridiculous thirteen days. *No problem now, I know exactly how to do this.* Sort of. I didn't feel the twangs, twinges, pangs, or pulls. I didn't feel like I was pregnant. Our doctor's phone call confirmed it.

She also said, "Let's try a different route so we don't have to have sad phone conversations like this one anymore. Get back to me on your decision."

A month later, another bleeding cycle later, we did. We got back to her.

This journey is an invitation for growth. It is here for you. Take it. Hold
tight.
Grasp so tightly that blood rises to the surface.
You see it pumping:
Heartbeat.
You got this, mama.
You are brave. You matter. You are a warrior.
Soar.

Our fertility journey towers ahead like the metaphorical mountains I've summited the last nine years and the actual ones on and around the Colorado Trail. I honor my inner Yardsale as I release whatever doesn't serve me and enter another waiting season. A new chapter of my journey has begun. The epilogue forthcoming. It begins with blood all over again. Bleeding kicks off the next chapter. Our trust in us, in my body, in our future family is unyielding. Nine years when blood prompted us to begin again. There won't be any bleeding from this one for another nine months. This we believe in our hearts. Forever grateful for the forty days on the Colorado Trail. Feeling empowered and fearlessly fertile four years past forty. Our aim now is to make it to forty weeks. This is still an aspiring journey. I'm ready to mother my thru-hiking infertility warrior self. I'm ready to be a mother. A mom-to-be. We are ready to soar.

LAUREN "YARDSALE" Jones (Austin) (she/her)

Englewood, Colorado—ancestral grounds and sacred land of Ute and Cheyenne territories

Lauren grew up camping with her family, which turned into backpacking in high school and thru-hiking the Colorado Trail in adulthood. She holds several degrees and certificates, including an MA in counseling psychology and counselor education and a permaculture design certificate; she is also a Nationally Certified Counselor (NCC), a Licensed Professional Counselor Candidate (LPCC), a Certified School Career Development Advisor (CSCDA), an Ordained Clergy Person (OCP), a horticultural therapist certification candidate, and a certified postpartum doula (CAPPA). Alongside her husband, Matt, she is a 'mama' to her dog, Journey, and three pesky chickens. She has been previously published by Hyperlite Mountain Gear, with her piece "Putting It All Out There and Getting It Back Together on the Colorado Trail."

She can be found on Instagram @sol_y_luna_soilpluslove and @stillaspiringjourney.

SWEAT

how to become a rugged outdoorswoman

I'm FALLING BEHIND AS JONAH SCRAMBLES ACROSS ANGLED slickrock. He seems to know where he is going, though I see no obvious indicators of a trail. I'm out of breath. I'm always out of breath. The pressure to keep up is intensified by the sun hanging low in the sky, and the knowledge that we haven't brought headlamps, or even water bottles. Sweat prickles under my arms, though the night is comfortably cool.

"Wait for me!" I call.

My hand reaches out and I make what I hope is a cute-girl pouty face. Jonah rolls his eyes but allows me to hold on while we navigate a steeper section of rock. Logically, I know the treads of my trailrunners are more than sufficient to grip the gritty sandstone of Sedona's famous red rocks. But it's my feet that I mistrust, not my shoes.

"Didn't you hike the Appalachian Trail?" he asks.

"Well... not all of it."

The qualification still stings only a couple years after my unsuccessful attempt at a thru-hike.

"You're kind of a princess, though, even after that."

"No I'm not!" My indignance is a front. I *am* kind of a princess. I'm not the hardcore hiker that I thought I'd be by now. My body is still slow, sweaty, struggling, something to be ashamed of. "I'm a rugged outdoorswoman!"

He laughs. I laugh. We share in the joke at my expense.

But the words stick in my head. I've never named the woman I want to become. I know that she is braver than me, stronger than me, more adventurous than I am. She doesn't gasp for air when nobody else is, or wonder if her heart is going to explode on an "easy" hike. I don't know how or when the words rugged outdoorswoman came to be in my subconscious. Rugged is a word reserved for mountains and men. But I like the sound of it—even if only as a joke.

I spend the rest of the evening chasing a shadow. The desert is blanketed in stars on a new moon night, which seems enough light for Jonah to see by. He leaps down from boulders, skipping along as smoothly as walking. I stop at the precipice but cannot understand the depth of the fall below me. I lower to my butt and dangle my legs over, before scooting to the edge and dropping a couple feet. He's a quarter mile away by now. Gone.

A moment of panic washes over me. The night air pulses in rhythm with my pounding heart. My eyes swim. The trail is as much a mystery to me as ever, and now I'm on my own.

What would a rugged outdoorswoman do in this situation?

Probably not stand here spiraling into tears and nothingness because she couldn't keep up. She wouldn't even be in this mess in the first place, because she *would* keep up.

I start walking again, focusing my eyes in the darkness, searching for some sign of a trail, some feature that feels familiar, and heading in what I hope is the general direction of where we parked.

———

Since that day, I've moved into a van and started living full-time on the road. I've backpacked another 1000 miles or so. I've trained for a 50k trail race that never happened.

I continued to call myself a rugged outdoorswoman. For years it felt like a joke, until it slowly began to feel like an aspiration, until it slowly began to feel just a little bit true.

Things never really got easier. I'm stronger than I was, but I still struggle in this body. In late 2020, at 30 years old, I was diagnosed with POTS, a form of dysautonomia. Suddenly my racing heart, bright red face, ragged breathing, and profuse sweating were explained by something other than my own lack of effort.

After diagnosis, I grieved the vision of my future self that had been driving me for so long. I realized I would never become her, because she doesn't have this broken body, and I do. And then I began the work of forgiving the version of myself I'd been trying for so long to run away from. The real one. I had never given her credit for everything she'd done. I could never see her as the best version of myself, always the before photo. I had been trying so desperately to put miles between us, but she always managed to make it just as far as I did. Perhaps she is stronger than I realized. Perhaps someday she can forgive me.

In 2021, I hiked the Colorado Trail. Before I left Durango, I told myself that these 500 miles were not about pushing my limits or fixing my brokenness. I wasn't going to be able to hike to the body I wanted, I would have to hike with the body I had. I planned to apply everything I'd learned about living with dysautonomia in the previous year. I carried enough food (unlike what I had done on the Wonderland Trail—purposefully underpacking in an attempt to lose weight). I'd been practicing with my hydration and carried little baggies full of salt tablets in my waist belt. I strategized about taking breaks throughout the day, elevating my feet, paying attention to the heart rate data on my watch. I intended to tune in—to really listen—to the signals of what felt good and what didn't. I hoped to leave the trail at peace with my body.

Forty days later, I walked down Waterton Canyon, with sweat salt crusted at my hairline in a dry September heat. Back at home, I peeled off the clothes I'd been wearing for over a month, and threw them away. There was no saving them. I admired the intensity of my sock tan line—the physical evidence of 500 miles that had gone off without a hitch. The deep soreness in my glutes and quads and the bottoms of my feet would take a few weeks to truly disappear, and I would miss it once it was gone.

I tried to sum up my experience on the Colorado Trail. I wanted to tell a story of overcoming. I wanted to believe my work was done, and that I was now okay with the body I was in. I had learned a lot. I was pleased with my body's performance—but only because my body had performed well.

It was a good season. Harder ones would follow. When you are chronically ill, some days are better than others. And sometimes the bad ones fall one after the next. Sometimes six months of sickness will leave you a shadow of your former self. Sometimes the darkness seeps into the recesses of the mind and you wonder if you will ever be your former self again. And then you realize you won't. Because time only moves in one direction. And even if your muscles become as strong as they once were, you are changed by the experience of the low. Maybe you won't take those muscles for granted this time around. Maybe you will delight in the movement of your own feet over the earth. Maybe you will carry a subtle sense of dread, knowing that another low is inevitable and so you will try to squeeze every last drop of joy out of the pushing and pulling of your body through the universe. Maybe you will be angry at the unfairness of your broken body. Maybe you will become tired of always overcoming. Maybe it would be nice if peace with your body didn't feel like an endless and all consuming task. Maybe forgiveness isn't as easy as forty days on trail.

WHEN WE SPEAK of the ruggedness of mountains, it is their wildness that we venerate. We admire exposed rocky faces and inhospitable reaches. We find beauty in the sharp edges and the brokenness. The harsher the environs, the more we burn to know them.

When we speak of the ruggedness of men, we think of callused hands and bulging muscles—the evidence of strength and hard work. We know that they are capable because of their five o'clock shadows. We understand that rough edges come with the territory.

Rugged men conquer rugged mountains. Somewhere along the way, I realized the mountains were never my conquest. I do not think that ruggedness is just for mountains and men.

My body is as broken and unforgiving as the deepest reaches of the Rocky Mountains.

I am as strong and callused as any man I've ever met.

I am a rugged outdoorswoman.

———

CHRISTINE REED (SHE/HER)

Full-time on the road, but most often in Denver, Colorado—traditional territory of the Ute, Cheyenne, and Arapaho peoples

Christine is the founder of Rugged Outdoorswoman Publishing, whose first publication, *Blood Sweat Tears*, is a perfect example of the mission to promote the adventure stories of women and gender-expansive folks. Her award-winning debut memoir, *Alone in Wonderland*, shares the story of her personal transformation via thru-hiking. She has been forged by nature and movement, and she firmly believes in the power of story and representation to invite every body into the outdoors where we can see ourselves more clearly.

She can be found on Instagram and TikTok @ruggedoutdoorswoman and at ruggedoutdoorswoman.com.

if you give a girl a chainsaw

THERE IS A LITTLE GIRL INSIDE OF ME, AND SHE LOVES TO play in the dirt. She is tomboyish and lanky, red hair chopped blunt at her shoulders and freckles on her forehead. She wears Eddie Bauer pants and does not know how to make friends with the other girls in her grade; something is lost in translation between Aéropostale and the L.L.Bean Outlet that makes her rubber boots feel like lead. At recess, she follows the half-trail along the creek, just out of sight of the playground monitors, and sits in a patch of sun until the bell rings and the rest of the kids run for the door of the middle-school wing.

After school she sits directly behind the bus driver in the seats that are usually meant for troublemakers, avoiding the back of the bus in favor of a book and a seat near the kindergartners. Once off the bus, she walks up the wandering driveway and drops her backpack in the hall before going out the door again, off the front porch and down the hill, across her cousin's driveway, and behind the woodlot to where the forest drops down to the marsh. There, spilled across the side of the hill, are bottles and cans and shards of pottery and ladles and spoons with the bottoms rusted out and blue enameled pots and pans that have been rotting under the New England duff for fifty years or more. In a cluster of trees above the old dump is a fort, and back across the driveway and up another hill is a brushy shelter built around some deadfall. Down the hill the other way, almost to the water, is a beech tree with her name carved into the bark on the side facing north. She climbs this tree and sits for hours, blending into the murmuring canopy in the quiet spot where the lakeshore meets the pines and waits and watches for something further on.

In a year or two she'll be at her grandparents' house exploring their woods and she will find an axe-head. It will be short and heavy, sharp but rusted. The eye will be filled with dirt. She'll ask her grandfather to put a handle on it for her, and when he does, she will carry it everywhere. She'll put hockey tape around the handle for better grip and spend hours wandering the forests and bogs with it by her side. She will smack at downed trees like she can shatter them with will alone; all force and no finesse. Eventually, the axe will get leaned up against the cement wall of the garage, where it will be found by a spider, and then three. The girl will go to high school, grow her hair long, and trade Eddie Bauer for Lilly Pulitzer. The beech tree will stretch beyond the initials she carved, and rust will creep over the axe once more.

––––––

AFTER GRADUATING FROM COLLEGE, I took a job on a trail crew in Montana. With piles of dorm room boxes still packed in the corner of my parents' house, I stuffed my tent and some work pants into a backpack and headed west with my sister. We passed through the familiar Green Mountains and Adirondacks, drove along Lake Erie and out into the midwestern landscape which, as die-hard mountain girls, we had spent most of our lives avoiding. We spent a night outside the Badlands and another in Wind Cave National Park, grabbing the last spot under a stand of pines that rolled out and out across the prairie. We stopped again at Devils Tower and walked the winding mile around it.

As the Black Hills fell back in the rearview mirror, we realized that we had made it out West. From Wyoming we drove into Montana, wondering at the open prairies and skyline that seemed so impossibly vast. We were used to the improbable claustrophobia of the East, the way the mountains and towns and wildernesses and cities crashed into each other in improbable claustrophobia—where capital *W* wilderness areas were only two hours north from the Amway, bears and people mingled quietly, and water seeped from every crack in the bedrock. In Montana, lodgepole pines clung to windblown hillsides, and mile after mile of wire fence stretched across sagebrush range. I-90 roared by in both directions, and even in May the sun seared the pavement under the wheels of my old car.

For the first three weeks in Montana, I lived out of the trunk of that car in the back corner of a KOA campground, directly under the flight path of the Missoula International Airport. After a cursory attempt to get to know the dozen other crew members, I adopted my usual spot on the outskirts of the group and spent most afternoons exploring the surrounding hills alone. During one of those weeks, I picked up an axe again. This one was sharp and well-balanced, and my shoulders burned from the weight when I swung it. Back in town, airplanes roared overhead, and Reserve Street thundered by just on the other side of a TJ Maxx. As the preseason weeks went by, I worried and I wondered about the season ahead and whether I would be strong enough to meet it when it came.

———

THE ANCIENT WORK-ISSUED Suburban lurched over potholes and washboards on the way up to the campground where we were staying during one of those training weeks. I glanced over my shoulder from the passenger seat to make sure that the water jugs my crew leader and I had just filled at the ranger station hadn't spilled.

"My parents . . . yeah, they're not . . . I don't think they're that comfortable with ambiguity," I explained. "I came out as a lesbian when I was sixteen or seventeen. It's not true anymore, but I haven't really bothered to say anything. I'm not sure they'd get it, and it just feels easier this way."

"Do you want them to know?" he asked, quietly.

"I don't . . . maybe. I don't know. I just figured I'd cross that bridge if I ever brought a guy home or something."

He laughed. "That's one way to do it, I guess."

That ambiguity pointed at something else I had been grappling with for a while. A year before, I had sat on the banks of the Grasse River in the St. Lawrence River valley and cried to my friend on the phone because I hated the feeling of my chest, hated my hips and the rest of my body, and hated the way I felt a step out of time with an identity that was supposed to be innate, but was feeling less and less so with every month that passed. Half a woman, half a girl, half something else I did not know what to call.

The fall after that conversation,

I had slept with a man for the first time. He was my best friend and someone whom I adored. For the first time, I felt my body in contrast—so different from girlfriends and stolen party kisses. He was gentle and kind and I loved him, but in spite of his kindness, I spiraled. His hands on my chest and my hips made me want to run. I shoved that feeling down as hard as I possibly could. *You're always like this, stop being an anxious fuck for once in your life and just calm down.* As maybe could have been expected, he and I didn't last.

Now, in Montana, the same creeping anxiety persisted. I was the only "girl" on my crew. The only not-man, anyway. Although we were all finding our stride, all clean boots and soft hands, I wondered. Wondered what my place was in this group, or ever could be. At least now I knew how to use a shovel and pack a backpack. The rest, I figured, would come later.

And it did. I cut off my hair a few weeks in and I fell in love with the crosscut saw: the way it bowed and slipped and sang, the dance it led between the bodies at either end. I loved, too, the quiet pace of the days as the sun dried out the rainy spring and hauled in the scorching summer. Through hundred-degree days we worked, clearing trees and brushing trails while the world slipped by outside our Wilderness. In early July, my crew leader gave me a two-pound axe-head on a child-sized handle, and as the weeks passed, it rarely left my hand. I learned to swing it how I'd been shown in training, adjusting the angle so the head bit deep into the wood. I remembered the hatchet leaning against the wall in my parents' garage, rusted over and claimed by the spiders since I'd seen it last.

———

WHEN I WOKE up each morning in the pale green dawn, I felt the previous day's work in my back and arms. I felt the places on my hips where my pack rubbed, and on my palms where blisters cracked and pulled. As I ran my hands over my chest and shoulders, feeling for bruises and massaging the sore spots, I felt muscle connecting to bone, tendons pulling tight, sinew and power intertwined. This body that I had stopped recognizing was becoming mine again. I didn't hate myself as much, not anymore.

Halfway through the season, our crew merged with another, and for the first time, I had company. Jessa was cheerful and strong, a fierce advocate for herself, and a quick learner when it came to complicated tree work. She asked lots of questions, poking right back when the guys teased her. Our spike camp was on a lake, high in the mountains that separate Idaho from Montana. There, rocky crags slashed the sky and subalpine fir prickled the ridgelines, nestling into the lee side of cliffs and scattering across the cols. Firmly declaring ourselves fed up with the dude energy in our group of nine, Jessa and I set up our tents on a small island in the middle of the lake. There was a rock to dive off and a screen of trees to hide us from shore. After work every day we would strip, spread our sweaty shirts out on a rock to dry, and run to dive off the rocks. We'd slip, naked, through the water and swim over to the other side. There was another rock, tucked behind the point from camp, and we'd sit there and talk, our same bodies perched on the rocks that rose and then spilled and fell and tumbled, all the world spread out before us.

———

WHEN THAT SEASON ENDED, I took a job back in New Hampshire in the White Mountain National Forest as a backcountry caretaker. All alone that winter, I split wood, carried water, managed the solar panels, and spent those months in a frozen, easy quiet. I wrote, drew, and thought. I switched posts around New Year's, moving to a small stone building set deep in one of the northern notches. As the snow wrapped around the hut, I remembered the way the wind rippled the waters on that mountain lake, the last heat of the red sun slipping through the smoke over the divide. Sometime in mid-January, I caught a glimpse of myself in the tarnished mirror that hung over the radio desk. My hair was greasy and matted, my skin blotchy. I ran a cold hand over a patch of dry skin that ran from my cheek down to my chin and there was snow- and wind-sung clarity in my eyes. *She* had melted away. The girl. I did not see her in my face anymore, not in my too-short hair, not in the way my shoulders hunched from months of packing. Someone different lived there. I liked them.

In February of that year, before I left for another season in Montana, I found that old hatchet again. I ran my fingernail over the chip in the blade from when I'd nicked it on a rock, and I felt a sudden, intense compassion for the little girl who'd carried it. She was fierce and shy and she had known who she was and she had not known what was coming. I wondered what she would think of me now. Would she think I was cool? Brave?

I felt an unexpected sense of responsibility to her and to the person we were becoming.

———

AT THE BEGINNING of that second trail season in Montana, I was offered the leadership of a women's chainsaw crew.

"I'm not a woman, though, at least not. . . like that, I don't know," I remember telling my new boss on the phone. "I'm not. . . I mean, is that okay?" It was one of the first times I had owned that uncertainty out loud. In private I had accepted it, I had turned the feeling over and over during those long months alone, but speaking it aloud to a stranger, somebody who held my work in their hands, gave it new weight.

"I don't see why not," she had said. "It's a space for non-men, more than anything. But it's up to you, whatever is comfortable for you."

I wasn't a woman. I wasn't a man. I was something in between that didn't belong to either group. In that simmering discomfort, though, I remembered Jessa. I remembered our camp on the island and the warmth I had found in her company. We were not the same, but there was sameness there. Maybe I could help someone else find the same peace I had found in this work. A few days later, I said yes.

I met my crew in May, and from the very beginning their joy and humor filled our camp to bursting. Their curiosity and earnestness were a buoy in the rainy spring. The months slipped by as we learned and grew together under the fir trees.

The start of our season, though, was not without growing pains. When we stepped out of the truck, when someone came upon us while we were working, when we stepped into a district office for the first time, there was always a sizing up. I could always see them doing the math—one, two, three, five, all . . . women? And then there was my response in posture, the straightening of my back to be as tall as five feet, two inches could be, and the way my voice fell to meet theirs. There was always that nagging, insecure voice: *Don't ask too many questions, but make sure you ask the right questions to prove you know what you're doing. Eye contact, firm handshake, absolutely no giggling.*

When we met a rafting group on the Middle Fork of the Salmon River, they asked where the men were. The intern in Plains called us "girls": "Thanks for the work, girls!" they had said before we parted ways for the week. A ranger asked if our periods had synced up yet. My grandmother asked me if our crew could get as much work done "without all those men around." A parent of a friend said they could never be on an "all-girls crew." "All that drama," they had said. "How would you ever get anything done?"

Here's the kicker: if nobody had brought it up, we would not have thought much about the lack of men, except to acknowledge that it felt safer, that it let us be ourselves more quickly, and that without the confines of masculinity, we were free to work hard, be kind, be gross, and have it mean nothing more than that this group was ours. We never once questioned our own capabilities—that was other people's problem. The posturing that happened in town was forgotten as soon as we were in the woods and on our own. Out there in the mountains, in the river valleys and under the sun, we had freedom from all of that. We had a job to do and nothing more.

In July, we were dispatched to a drainage south of the Selway River in Idaho. Outside the bunkhouses in Elk City, we loaded up our boss's UTV and followed him up the winding roads. Where the road turned to trail, we parked the rig and continued on foot, stopping here and there to pick the first huckleberries of the year. Higher up, we saw the places where the UTV had run into the last of the snowdrifts that were still clinging to the mountain. As we hit the ridgeline and walked out into the clearing, the old Anderson Butte lookout towered fifty feet above and views stretched for sixty miles in every direction. Directly to the north we could see the Selway River drainage, and to the northwest the jagged landscape of the Crags slashed the skyline. Rolling mountains plunged into river valleys and it was blue and blue and blue forever.

We camped up there for two nights, watching thunderstorms and sunsets clash and roll, great oranges and yellows meeting purple and towering thunderheads slouching off to the east. We fired up the chainsaws, broke one or two, and practiced dropping hung-up deadfall that blocked the trail in many places. On the third day we packed up our tents and bumped camp down into one of the drainages below the butte.

Sawing while hiking goes like this: You move along, picking your way around rocks and roots, not able to lift your head fully because of the brim of your hard hat. You're wearing Kevlar chaps over your duck cotton work pants, plus a long-sleeved shirt and heavy leather boots, and in midsummer in the mountains it's almost never less than eighty degrees. Your backpack weighs seventy-five pounds, so there's that to contend with too. You have to carry your chainsaw, your gas, your repair kit, two pounds of food per day, four or five liters of water, and whatever else you need to be able to sleep and stay warm and dry. Your shoulders, knees, hips, and feet feel bruised from trying to manage the weight, and when you want nothing more than to lay your entire body down in the creek and float away, you come across a tree. You might kick it, see if you can pick it up or roll it off, but usually you have to cut it. So you pull the saw off your shoulder and undo the scabbard before putting your right hand on the wrap and slipping the pull cord between two leather-gloved fingers. With the weight on your back, pulling the cord all the way out is hard. The engine might turn over, or it might not, and if it doesn't you throw your pack down and mess with the choke, full to half to idle (maybe?), and yank the pull cord over and over until the saw starts or your shoulder gives out. Sweating and cursing, you get the saw to start eventually, finicky carburetor be damned. All before you've actually cut a single thing.

We repeated this process a hundred times as the miles and trees stacked up behind us and we continued to descend, subalpine fir blending into Douglas fir and Engelmann spruce and eventually into cedars. Late in the afternoon, we came alongside running water, and a quarter mile later, the cedars cleared to reveal a pack shed, a bunkhouse, a cookhouse, and an old barn. Exhausted and clumsy, we dumped our chainsaws, gas, saw bags, chaps, and other tools on the porch of the pack shed before stumbling, off-kilter now, to the yard by the cookhouse door.

Meadow Creek had been a working guard station for decades. Now, several of the outbuildings dripped with rat shit, and many of the old mattresses and bags of feed had been shredded by packrats in the years since the station had shut down. The cookhouse, though, was clean. Big windows let in the distant sun. The dusty chairs seemed sleepy in their light. Outside, a field of deep grasses meandered down to the creek and the porches butted up against thousand-year-old cedar trees, their branches like fingers tracing the cabin roof while we sat, stiff and salty and grimacing, in the grass by the cabin door.

We worked out of Meadow Creek for the next few days. Our

assignment was to clear the trail to the top of the ridgeline a bit east of us. Every day we pushed a little farther, repeating the steps to sawing while hiking over and over. We walked until a tree blocked the path, then dropped packs, started saws, cleared trees, killed and sheathed saws, picked up our packs, and continued on. We worked in pairs sometimes, one person sawing and one person moving branches. The earplugs we wore kept conversation to a minimum. It got hotter as we moved up, the trees thinner and shorter, the hillside sandy and exposed. Under my chaps, my pants were soaked, and the sweat sliding down my face mixed with sawdust and dirt, itching and dripping and pooling in my bra and around my waist.

On the third day we started early. The four of us ate breakfast and made it to the last day's stopping point on the ridge before the sun had even crested the ridge. The higher we pushed, the denser the trees got. The burn we had cut into was twenty years old, maybe more, and the understory was dense with huckleberries and bear grass in full bloom. The fluffy white stalks waved in the wind, sending pollen everywhere, making our eyes and noses drip as the stalks smacked us in the face with every step. The wood we cut was dense—fire hardened and dry, branches gnarled and twisted, snaring every bite of the saws. Many of the trees had sunk into the ground, five or six piled on top of each other in a jackstraw. It was hard to make heads or tails until you started cutting into it. A bruise formed on the back of my right hand from every time I slammed the chain brake on. Even with the saw off, my hands hummed with phantom vibrations. At morning break, I blew a snot rocket into the grass. I'm pretty sure it was half sawdust.

Around noon, we collapsed in a cluster of bear grass. We dug into our packs for lunch and ate in silence, curled up in what little shade we could find. I pulled out my phone and checked the map.

"Guys, I think we're, like, less than half a mile from the top. I think we can get this done today." We were backed up against a three o'clock end time, but we looked at each other and nodded. It felt doable.

Four hours later I looked at the tree in front of me and then down at my hand clenching the saw. There were woodchips in my gloves poking into my fingers, and sweat dripped down the back of my neck. I turned back down the trail to watch Kate pulling branches away from where Perry was sawing at a furious pace. The pull of the end-of-day heat dragged me down, the still air creeping but not cooling. My arms shook, my legs were jelly. Half a plan ran through my brain and petered out. Right after lunch we had hit the densest cutting yet, trees piled on top of each other, limbs caught and bound and twisted, brush so crowded there wasn't even room to move. I hadn't put the chainsaw down in hours. Faced with yet another tree, I cut the engine. I looked at Brooke. When I stopped moving, I could feel my heartbeat in my swollen feet. I could hear every *thud* behind my earplugs and every pulse in my hands and arms and neck. My skin felt too hot; my mouth was dry, and my lips were cracked and salty.

"I can't fucking do another one, I just can't."

They looked back at me. "Fair. Be done." We sheathed the saws and started the long hike down the ridge. We didn't get back to camp until after seven.

I think about that day a lot when people ask me about trail work. I think about the things it can do for you, about my favorite days and my hardest days, and the ones that have meant the most to me. We pushed harder than any of us had thought possible, tackling sections of trail that would have been beyond us even a few weeks before. When we got back, we found out that that week had been one of the hottest so far of the summer. In spite of all that, the faulty saws and the heat and the flies, it was done.

———

BACK AT CAMP THAT NIGHT, after the saws were cleaned and sharpened for the next day, we wandered down to Meadow Creek. In the fading light, we took off our dusty boots and tossed our crusty socks and pants onto the rocks before taking off our shirts and wading into the water. Even in August, the creek was freezing. We wandered out to where the last of the sun flickered over the water's surface and savored the heat on our bare, gritty skin. My body—and it *was* my body—pushed back against the current before I slipped under the water, the cold rushing over me. I came up gasping. I looked around to see everyone else doing the same, all bare bodies and hard muscles in the summer dusk.

The little girl hiding in the beech tree stirs. *I've gotcha*, I told her, *we're here, now.* She hugs that old tree tighter. *We've found a place to belong, and it's golden.*

———

LIESL MAGNUS (THEY/THEM)

Missoula, Montana—traditional territory of the Salish people

Liesl grew up hiking, backpacking, running, and working in the White Mountains of New Hampshire and later in the Adirondacks. They hold a BA in government and environmental studies and have been previously published in *Appalachia* and the *Northern New England Review*. They've completed three seasons on trail crews across western Montana and northern Idaho and two seasons as backcountry hut crew for the Appalachian Mountain Club. Trails and outdoor work are Liesl's life, passion, and drive, and how they've met some of the most important people in their life. They believe in the power of authenticity, the expression of genuine experiences, and the importance of creating deliberate space for non-men in the outdoors.

uncovering strength

I WAS SIX YEARS OLD WHEN I FOUND OUT MY BODY WAS something to be ashamed of.

In the honey-thick humidity of a Michigan summer, my dad stripped off his shirt while working in the yard. I followed suit. It was much cooler. A few minutes later my mom called me into the house. "You need to put your shirt back on."

"But Dad isn't wearing a shirt. It's hot," I countered.

"Yes, but you're a girl," she explained. "You need to wear a shirt."

I put my shirt on, embarrassed that I had done something wrong. That there was something about me that was wrong. Something I could not control. My gender itself was wrong and must be hidden away. I never went shirtless again, and even well into adulthood the idea of running in just a sports bra seemed unfathomably indecent.

My parents were not ones to force gender stereotypes on me. I had Barbies and GI Joes, Matchbox cars and Care Bears. They never had a son and in many ways I filled in as one, strong enough to carry fifty-pound bags of grain and throw hay bales by the time I was ten. But I always knew my body was something to be kept hidden. Something I was reminded of daily as I made my way from childhood into my preteen years.

"Moooo." It was quiet but meant to be heard.

I walked by, head up, pretending I didn't hear it. Or at least that I didn't care. I knew I was fat. Every kid in school had reminded me of that fact every day for five years—since second grade. I pulled on the hem of my oversized black T-shirt, wishing it could do more than cover my D cups and tummy. I wished it could make my body vanish altogether. Unlike that overheated little girl, now I wanted nothing more than to hide under a shirt.

After another decade of draping my body in baggy clothes, I found hiking at the age of twenty during a summer job working at the Grand Canyon. I'd arrived there by accident after finding a brochure in the college career center to clean hotel rooms. Hiking was a revelation—something clicked inside me. This act of moving through a landscape was the missing piece in my life. It made me feel whole in a way I'd never felt before. Never had I experienced a form of exercise that made me forget how much I hated to sweat. I decided that I wanted to thru-hike the Appalachian Trail when I graduated from college.

Two years later, I started north from Springer Mountain with no clue what it would be like to backpack—to live in the woods for months on end. Yet, I made it to Maine in four months, madly in love with the experience. Along the way, I discovered new aspects of my body—its strength and durability in the mountains. For the first time I felt proud of what was under my baggy clothes.

On the summer solstice, hikers on the AT gleefully strip to their birthday suits and amble through the woods, celebrating the longest daylight hours of the year with an unofficial holiday: Hike Naked Day. The night before, as we all sat in our sleeping bags in the shelter talking over bowls of ramen, the others discussed their plans for doffing apparel while still keeping certain areas covered in case they encountered non-thru-hikers. The various applications of bandannas and socks were discussed while I listened wide-eyed. *Was I really expected to march through the woods with no clothes on to be a "real" thru-hiker?*

In the morning, I left the shelter before everyone else was awake and was soon treading down the chilly trail alone. My days were always spent this way, my legs enthusiastically carrying me northward faster than everyone else. I enjoyed chatting at overlooks and shelters or whenever I encountered other people, yet the solitude of the walking was what I loved. Shortly after passing a side trail to a shelter, I saw two backpacks wobbling along ahead of me. Protruding below them were tanned, strong legs—and pale white buttocks. *People really are hiking naked!*

"Hello!" I called out as I approached. The man closest to me half-turned and made a squawking noise as I saw him fumbling with—and dropping—a bandanna.

"Hello!" the other man said, deftly swiping his ball cap from his head to cover his crotch.

"Have a good day," I said, rushing past them, my face turning crimson.

Hours later the heat and humidity of the mid-Atlantic summer had settled thick on the forest. I'd seen no one since the two men and —with shaking fingers—I pulled off my shirt. The air on my bare stomach was foreign, but cooling. I felt exposed and awkward. Yet I also felt something else as I charged up muddy peaks: free.

The Appalachian Mountains were sweltering in late June. Sweat trickled down my cleavage and soaked the band of my cotton-blend sports bra. The fresh sweat rejuvenated the stench of six weeks of dried funk in my clothing and my pack. I didn't care. At an overlook I stood on a rock outcropping, gazing at the rolling farmland of Virginia. A slight breeze chilled my damp skin. Goosebumps sprang up along my arms and neck. Voices approached and I dove for my pack, yanking my tank top out of it just as a family emerged from the tree cover.

"Hello!" they cheerfully greeted me.

I mumbled a reply, my face flaming red, as I sought refuge inside the safety of the bedraggled burgundy shirt.

I DIDN'T REALIZE it at the time, but my life would be dedicated to hiking. I'd noticed there were very few solo female hikers, and none who seemed to hike as fast as I did, but it hardly seemed important. I felt alive in a new way, fully devoted to this lifestyle. I switched from poor-fitting cotton-blend clothing from Walmart's activewear section to beach-style sarong skirts. I loved the pop of bright color as I put on the same clothes every day. It was interesting how, in the simple lifestyle of backpacking, little things like colorful clothes could boost my mood, even when everything else was bad. The comfort of a skirt was unparalleled for me, and I delighted in not experiencing the chafe of soggy shorts bunching up between my thighs as I walked.

As time went on, I switched to thrift store sundresses and logged thousands of mountainous miles as well as thru-hike after thru-hike—finishing the Triple Crown at age twenty-five. In 2013, I donned a lightweight, zebra-print sundress I'd purchased for a quarter and bested the long-standing men's fastest known time (FKT) on the Pacific Crest Trail—hiking the entire 2,600 miles in sixty days.

In the weeks that followed, I struggled to understand how my chubby, embarrassingly female body had accomplished such a task. *Was it an accident?* The media also began to pay attention to my gender. In interviews, I was asked leading questions: *Do you think women are better than men at long-distance hiking? Why do you hike in a dress? What's it like being a woman on trail? What made you think you could break a man's record? Why did you break Scott's record, rather than go after the [much slower] women's time?*

For the first time since I was a child, I was reminded that my body was wrong. Women don't do these things. Women aren't this fast. Women shouldn't go alone into the mountains. *Put that proverbial shirt back on.*

But I couldn't.

Even as I struggled with having my womanness overshadow my experiences, I became aware of my body's abilities. Abilities that perhaps stemmed from the fact that I was a female. In the realm of hiking, I wasn't just "good for a girl." I was shattering overall records and outhiking men and women both. Not because I wanted to prove feminine superiority—something that had never crossed my mind, but that the media liked to posit—but because I was doing something that I was truly, deeply devoted to. Something that fulfilled me in the deepest sense. Something my female body was well equipped to do.

I will never have children, but I know my biology came preprogrammed to do so. As a woman I am hardwired to tolerate intense pain, to function without sleep, to hold many logistics in my mind at once, and to carry on even in the face of famine and starvation. Men may be intrinsically stronger and faster in many arenas, but these profoundly feminine tools serve me well in the extreme conditions of long-distance hiking—effectively leveling the playing field.

I came home from the PCT nearly skeletal. My body fat percentage had plummeted from a healthy 18 percent to 10 percent. I felt weak and exhausted—every bodily system was dysregulated. While I struggled to cope with a new identity as an athlete and the scrutiny of the media, I also felt shattered by the constant "compliments" from my friends and acquaintances. *You look great!*

In other words, I looked like I was supposed to. Like an athlete should. Like a woman should. Like every ad and movie told me I should look—size zero. It didn't matter that I felt less healthy than I ever had in my life and my blood work backed that up.

For most of my life I had hated my body. It was a rectangle rather than an hourglass, with a propensity for weight gain. It was larger than most women's, with big, dense bones inherited from my Norwegian great-grandmother. My feet were bigger than my dad's and I could never seem to be coordinated enough to walk in heels. My body would never match the images the media had fed to me throughout my lifetime. Now I knew without a doubt that my body-shame had been true. My body in its healthy form *was* something to be ashamed of. If it was going to be strong, it had to meet the prerequisites of stick-thin femininity too. If I had been self-conscious before, I was doubly so now. *You're a woman, cover up. You're a woman, you can't be better than men. You're a woman, if you're strong you better look pretty.*

I layered my too-big clothes onto my FKT-thin body and tried to hide.

In 2015, only a few days shy of smashing my second multi-thousand-mile self-supported FKT—this time on the Appalachian Trail—I was walking across the aptly named Beauty Spot on the Tennessee–North Carolina border by the light of the full moon. As I looked at my shadow striding across the mountain at the end of yet another nearly fifty-mile day, I was overcome with a sudden sense of gratitude. This body that I had always wanted to hide was more powerful than I had ever given it credit for. It didn't matter that my legs were unshaven, that it had been hundreds of miles since my last shower, or that I stank to high heaven. I was thin now, but I would regain weight once I stopped—weight that kept my endocrine system regulated and my bone density healthy. I didn't care whether I met a single standard of attractiveness or femininity. I dropped my trekking poles and hugged myself tightly. For the first time, I whispered "I love you" to myself. I finally saw the beauty that exists in strength rather than minimization.

This trail—and all my journeys in the wilderness—had taught me to love and appreciate my body. To hold tight to the certitude that my strength out there did not run counter to femininity. It was a product of it. That when I am dirty, stinky, and wild, I am strong. I am beautiful. I am a woman.

HEATHER ANDERSON (SHE/HER)

Washington—traditional territory of the Lummi, Nooksack, Samish, and Semiahmoo

Heather has hiked over 47,000 miles since her first thru-hike in 2003. She was the first woman to complete the Appalachian, Pacific Crest, and Continental Divide National Scenic Trails three times each. This includes her historic Calendar Year Triple Crown hike in 2018 when she hiked all three of those trails in one March–November season, making her the first woman to do so. She holds female self-supported FKTs on the PCT (2013) and the AT (2015). She was named National Geographic Adventurer of the Year in 2019. She is the author of *Thirst: 2600 Miles to Home* and *Mud, Rocks, Blazes: Letting Go on the Appalachian Trail* and co-author of *Adventure Ready: A Hiker's Guide to Planning, Training, and Resiliency.*

She can be found on Facebook and Instagram @_wordsfromthewild_ and at wordsfromthewild.net.

obscured by light

AT DUSK ON THE FIRST NIGHT OF MY SPEED RECORD attempt on the 485-mile Colorado Trail, I chugged a bottle of caffeinated peach-mango Crystal Light. It was the first caffeine I'd consumed in weeks; I'd been abstaining to prepare for the effort. Dirty energy coursed through me as the light paled. I'd been moving for thirteen hours and had covered the first forty miles. My body now wouldn't be able to sleep for another four or five hours. I turned on a disco playlist and watched through the trees above as a bank of clouds oozed down the ridge I intended to climb. The mist was slow; the music was fast. I didn't want to ascend into the fog, and I didn't want to keep walking into the night, but now I had no choice.

The current record stood at fifteen days. I'd announced on the internet that I planned to complete the trail in fourteen days, and secretly I hoped for twelve. But I couldn't do the mileage necessary for that goal during daylight hours. If I wanted the record, I had to get over my fear of the dark.

By the time I turned on my headlamp, thick fistfuls of cold air had gathered between the trees. The world outside the beam became a watery void punctuated by hazy talons of fog. I popped out my head-phones and night sounds rushed at me: rustling leaves, crunching sand, my breath. Beyond, an eerie, damp silence.

A few miles later, I reached for my phone in the pocket on the front of my shoulder strap. The next moment, I found myself on the ground in the trail. My wrists stung. A cool bead of blood slid down my shin from a raw knee. My headlamp had twisted around to my ear and was pointed uselessly skyward. I checked my pockets in panicked pats: phone, GPS tracker, mace, trowel, water bottles—all present and accounted for. What if something had fallen? Would I be able to find it in the dark? The night seemed enormous.

I picked myself up, testing my full weight first on one leg, then the other. My body could still walk, so I kept walking.

If you'd asked me then why I was attempting a Fastest Known Time (FKT) on the Colorado Trail (CT), I would have told you about the four preceding years. I had hiked the Pacific Crest, Continental Divide, and Appalachian Trails—nearly 8,000 miles in total. With that kind of background, a record-setting attempt might have seemed perfectly logical. But another past trailed me, too, one I thought I'd left behind.

Six years before the CT, halfway through my freshman year of college, I spent a few days locked in my dorm room watching every documentary I could find about the Jonestown Massacre. After about a week, I began to suspect my fascination had something to do with taking my own life. I called to make an appointment with campus counseling.

The triage call came the next day. I was walking home from class. People were studying on blankets in the sun. In the distance, a volleyball game was in full swing. Pomegranates and rosemary grew in mulched beds.

"Are you thinking of harming yourself?" a disembodied voice asked.

The truth of it—how often the Swiss Army Knife in the plastic tote under my bed had bubbled into my thoughts—washed over me. "Yes," I said. A Frisbee whizzed past my head.

I saw a therapist shortly after. When she asked how I was, I started crying and tried to pretend I wasn't. I couldn't tell her about the Swiss Army Knife or the Jonestown people; the whole affair seemed sort of derivative. I said: "I'm having trouble adjusting." I said: "These people in my dorm don't even know how to do their own laundry." What I meant was: *I don't know who I am, and I'm beginning to worry I will never know who I am again. I don't feel seen by the people around me, and I don't know how to reveal myself, or if I have a self to reveal.*

She told me that she, too, had struggled making friends in college. She had felt lonely her entire undergrad career, but in grad school she had moved in with an acquaintance and they formed a little community. Things got better.

I was nineteen. I had three and a half years of college left. That was one-fifth of my life so far—an unfathomably long time to wait for things to get better.

"Are you exercising?" the therapist asked.

"I backpack on the weekend sometimes."

"Why don't you try exercising regularly? If that doesn't work after a few weeks, you can come back for another appointment."

Shame coursed through me. I had given her no reason to think something was wrong, but I was still desperate that she believe it. I didn't want exercise to be the solution; I didn't want there to be a solution within my power. Everything felt out of my control. I couldn't stop thinking about my future, about the path ahead: I would get a degree and a job, obsess over arbitrary metrics of success like salaries and promotions, maybe bury myself in marriage or motherhood. It seemed inevitable that I would grow old regretting my lost youth. I couldn't bear it. I wasn't sure there was a point in staying alive.

After the appointment, I walked straight to the campus bookstore, where I bought a sheaf of X-Acto knife blades.

AFTER MY FIRST night on the Colorado Trail, I was too tired to be afraid of the dark. I fell into a rhythm: two hours of sleep just after nightfall, walk through the coldest part of the night, two more hours of sleep before dawn. Shortly before the trail, I had listened to an audiobook about long-distance speed records. It called sleep an emotional need, stating that our bodies don't need sleep, only stationary time to recover. But our brains do need sleep—more time than our bodies need to be stationary. There's apparently science behind this idea, though I haven't double-checked. My plan to optimize the record attempt was to spend only as much time sleeping as my body needed to be stationary, and then I'd white-knuckle through my brain's complaints.

I was finding out quickly, though, that when you don't meet your emotional needs, you run into emotional problems. I fixated on lost minutes: the morning I snoozed my alarm for an hour, the night I stopped walking and just stood for ten or fifteen minutes, staring at the canopy, scratching my butt, mesmerized by shadowy branches. I counted miles, divided by hours, got confused, and redid the calculations. I constantly felt I should have been going faster.

I called my partner, Troy, on the fourth afternoon. I'd skipped my morning sleep, so I'd been hiking for eighteen or twenty hours straight. I blubbered, "This is so, so hard."

"What did you expect?" he laughed.

I didn't laugh, but I should have. Really, did I expect it to be easy?

Of course not. I had wanted it to be hard. I had wanted the difficulty to be legible in my body, and it was. My eyeballs were perpetually itchy. My nose wouldn't stop bleeding. My tongue broke into white pimples that stung when I ate sweet or salty food. All my food was sweet or salty. One day, the sight of a family cutting into a loaf of French bread—blessed, bland bread—brought me to tears.

Crying on the phone became a daily ritual. After years of hiding my tears in front of friends, family, therapists—now I wailed.

Cry as I might, I met each challenge with a new solution. I held my bleeding nostril shut until a green-bean-sized clot formed. I broke my food into little pieces and swallowed them like pills to bypass the tongue bumps. When my toes swelled into translucent grapes and blood blisters formed on my heels, I burrowed the tip of my Swiss Army Knife through each callus until pink liquid frothed out. It was all business. It didn't even occur to me that I'd once imagined the same tool embedded in my elbows or shins.

I NEVER WENT BACK to that therapist. I don't think I ever used those X-Acto blades either, though there are some other memories from the following years of sharp objects and hot objects pressed against my skin. A few fading teardrop-shaped scars persist on one of my forearms from the hot back of a spoon. I don't like to ascribe rationality to these actions, but if I had to, I'd say I was telling myself a story about suffering, about the great ineffable sorrow I felt swirling around me. It didn't feel real enough, good enough, until I made it physically manifest.

I left school at the end of my sophomore year. A year after that, I arrived at the southern terminus of the Pacific Crest Trail, intending to walk from Mexico to Canada. I wasn't there to exercise; it hardly even registered that I would be walking all day. Mostly, the trail was a desperate thing. I had spent the two previous summers working at a camp near Desolation Wilderness; I considered it a magical place. I had made a deal with myself that if I reached Desolation, mile 1,500, and still didn't want to be alive, I could jump from the cliffs of Mount Tallac.

When I started the PCT, I expected to struggle to walk ten or fifteen miles per day. I had never considered myself an athlete. In nine years of playing ice hockey as a kid, I'd scored about half a dozen goals for my team, and about as many against. I once finished a one-mile track race a full lap behind everybody else. But fate had other plans for me on the PCT. The first person I met on trail was a man eager to explain everything to me: stove fuels and weather patterns and why he'd never let his wife do the trail alone and why Cheryl Strayed was irresponsible for encouraging all these unprepared women to try thru-hiking. I spent all week trying to outpace him; I was far too proud to slow down and let him go ahead. I did twenty, twenty-one, twenty-two miles per day. My fifth day, another hiker told me I'd need to do thirty miles to reach my resupply box before the post office closed on day six. I hesitated for only a moment, then started walking.

All day, I expected to collapse. I expected one of my bones to break. I expected my organs to fail, or my uterus to fall out. I expected to vomit and pass out and need to be saved by a helicopter. But instead, I walked, and I walked, and I walked. My trekking poles rubbed raw patches into my palms, my toes and heels grew ugly blisters, and pain shot up my shins with every step. I kept walking.

I reached my campsite around dusk and collapsed against a cottonwood, totally beat. My feet buzzed. A breeze fluttered against my neck. My shoulders, free from my pack, floated. I, too, was buoyant. For twelve hours, I'd unlatched myself from past and future. I had been present with my body, observing its discomforts and struggles, and together we had done something I'd believed impossible. My body—my body was incredible. It turned food and water into movement, nothing more, nothing less. It was exactly what I needed it to be. It was perfect and powerful.

I wondered why I hadn't believed I could walk the distance. And in what other ways I was holding myself back with an inability to fathom my own strength.

I dedicated the following years to chasing the edge between mental and physical limits. I hiked through Achilles tendinitis and shin splints and all kinds of chafing. I hiked through ice and snow and rain and extreme heat. I hiked before the sun rose and after it set. In Washington, on the PCT, I ran out of food and hiked for a day on a bag of trail mix and all the salmonberries I could pick. In Wyoming, on the CDT, a poisonous plant made my legs break out in quarter-sized boils; I kept hiking. In Maine, on the AT, I was caught in a thunderstorm on an exposed ridge and fell waist-deep into a bog while running to safety; I checked that I had both shoes and kept hiking. The next year, I got pulmonary edema during my first ultramarathon. I couldn't take a full breath for the last eight miles, but I walked to the finish. I enjoyed it.

Through these trials, I learned to love my body for its ability to carry me. I thought that loving my body would teach me to love myself. I made gestures at an off-trail life in between hikes—I went back to college and then to graduate school, signed leases, got jobs—but I was always scheming about the next trail, the next race. How far, how fast could I go? How strong was I, really?

By day six on the CT, I was three days ahead of record pace. I felt strong with every step. I hauled myself over blowdowns; I was sure-footed on rocky descents; my lungs filled painlessly with air even as I topped out on high-elevation passes. My blisters had stopped looking so infected now that I was washing and changing my socks daily, and I'd started rubbing Aquaphor in my nostrils to keep them from bleeding.

My body was adjusting to the effort, but I was still crying a lot. Troy suggested I get a hotel in town for the night.

"No," I sobbed. "I want to keep going. It's just hard."

What I was too tired to articulate was that my body could keep going, and I wanted to keep going until my body failed. To never again be limited by my mind felt like a promise I'd made to myself years earlier, at the end of that first thirty-mile day.

Most of all, I didn't want to stop because I was happy. It might not have seemed like fun, but I felt confident I was exactly where I was supposed to be. Each day, I learned new ways to be grateful to my body and to the trail. Troy was right that I could've taken a night off and still gotten the record, but I wasn't out there to break the record. I had come with the intention of doing the trail as fast as *I* possibly could, and it felt good to follow that intention completely. In each moment, I knew I was being true to my goal—to myself. The evidence was in my body. It was in the pain burrowing into my hips at night, in the band of hunger cinched across my belly, in my eyelids and cheeks going puffy from lack of sleep.

On the tenth afternoon, with seventy miles to go, I napped at Molas Lake Campground for an hour while my phone charged. I planned to hike from there to the end without sleeping. I plowed up the hills and jogged down. The trail stayed above tree line for miles. Stone ridges collided with meadows; shrubs splashed across golden hillsides. Mutters of thunder punctuated the afternoon and smudges of rain hovered over the horizon, but where I was, the weather held. By dark, I had only fifty miles of trail to go.

I was approaching a saddle when the moon rose. The mountain became metal and shadow. Time attenuated. Twenty-minute podcasts seemed infinitely long. I counted miles and calculated my pace, but the numbers didn't make sense. I didn't want to keep hiking. I wanted pizza and veggie sushi and seltzer water. I wanted sleep. My knees throbbed. The soles of my feet pulsed. My temples were crusty and brittle.

The pattern recognition part of my brain began to malfunction. The world at the edge of my headlamp became liquid and ominous. Stumps looked like badgers. Sleeping pads hung from trees. A lot of things looked like IUDs.

At two or three in the morning, I discovered I was out of water with seven miles until the next source. I felt incompetent. I couldn't bear another moment of walking. My plan to not sleep felt pointless. I put on all my layers, including my plastic emergency poncho, and curled up in the middle of the trail with my body against my pack for a forty-five-minute nap.

Near dawn I made the mistake of checking my GPS app. I'd barely moved two miles per hour all night; I'd been hoping for twice that. I still had a long, long way to go, though I couldn't figure out how long. Maybe *thirty* more miles? At least *ten* more hours, *fifteen* or *twenty* at this pace. Numbers ran through my head, but they meant nothing. I still hadn't reached water. I understood vaguely that the present would become the past, that I would one day reach the pizza and sushi and bubbly water, but first I had to walk to the end. The only way to get there was to walk, and I didn't want to.

I tried hiking with one eye shut, then the other, imagining I could turn half my brain off at a time like a shark. I tripped and awoke splayed across the trail, an oblong bruise already forming where my forearm had collided with a rock. I'd fallen asleep as soon as I hit the ground.

A few minutes later I slapped myself. I remember thinking it might wake me up, but I also remember a hot plume of rage. I knew my body could still move; my mind was holding me back. I felt I was getting in my own way. Worse: I wasn't happy anymore. I no longer felt like the walking was a complete thing, meaningful unto itself; I couldn't access the gratitude. Every memory of every long day I'd ever hiked taunted me. I remembered how expansive and powerful they'd made me feel. Now, I felt lazy and weak.

For a minute or two, the pain helped my vision focus. But soon I slipped back into the wobbly beam of my headlamp. The queasy thirst and the anger with myself returned. *I should be moving faster*, I thought. *I should've trained harder. I shouldn't have wasted time in the mornings tallying my aches. I should've packed a loaf of French bread.*

"Are you exercising?" the therapist had asked. I struggle, still, to parse the relationship between exercise and self-harm—is it possible to push the limits of the former without it becoming the latter? They feel so different—one a negation of my life force within, the other a celebration of the bountiful minutes I've been given on this earth— but it's undeniable that they can look similar. Something shifted in those final hours on the trail. The joy I'd felt even in the most challenging times on trail turned to something else, something ugly. I slapped myself again and again and again. I dug my fingernails into my thighs. I gnawed on the insides of my cheeks. Each time, the raw skin or sore flesh cleared my mind briefly, but then the anger and the greed flooded back, bigger than before.

WHEN I HAD VISUALIZED the end of the Colorado Trail, I had pictured myself sprinting from the forest, fists raised, laughing, celebrating. Instead, I stumbled shivering and mumbling into the trailhead parking lot at dusk. Troy was there; he helped me into a chair and wrapped me in a sleeping bag and gave me a bottle of San Pellegrino and twelve roses and put a pizza in my lap. I curled in on myself, clutching the glass bottle and the bouquet, bawling. I was crying too hard to eat the pizza.

I don't really remember all of this, but I know it happened because Troy took videos. They're hard to watch, even now. My face is scrunched, my lips flapping. I can barely catch my breath.

I'd completed the trail in ten and a half days. I'd beaten my most optimistic estimates by a day and a half—I could have been crying tears of joy. But in the first moments I spent in that chair, I mostly remember feeling scared. I kept thinking of how I'd slapped myself, how out of control I'd felt. It had been years since I'd felt that way.

"That was so hard," I kept saying. "That was so, so hard."

I DON'T LIKE TALKING about the time in my life when I thought a lot about harming myself, about taking my own life. I was embarrassed, then; I suppose some of that embarrassment has lingered. For a long time, it felt as though to say it out loud was to invite it back; it had never felt finished enough for me to speak of it in the past tense.

Here's what I can say: when I was really in the thick of it, when I was nineteen, twenty, twenty-one, I thought there would be no end. I had a vague idea I might be okay when I was older, but I couldn't imagine how I'd get there. I wanted another life so badly it hurt.

I am dazzled, these days, by how rarely I feel that way. I have a community; I make art; I do work that I find meaningful. Sometimes I think everything happened the way the therapist said: I got older and things got better and the exercise, the walking, all those thousands of miles, gave me something to do while I waited. But it's no small thing, the walking. I had been afraid of losing time; instead, I filled my days in a way that returned me to myself. I gave myself that gift until I didn't need it anymore.

"That was so hard," I kept saying. I was talking about the trail, but I was talking about all of it, too, all those scary years before I started hiking. I had never really cried for myself, never felt it was finished enough to look right at it and admit how much life I had lost. But the longer I sat in that camp chair in Colorado, the more I trusted it was over. I knew I would go home, and I would sleep, and I wouldn't hurt myself again. All I'd needed was to reach the end of the trail.

———

MIKAELA OSLER (SHE/HER)

Albuquerque, New Mexico—occupied Tiwa land

Mikaela holds the Fastest Known Time (FKT) on the Long Trail in Vermont and once held the FKT for the Colorado Trail. She has an MFA in creative nonfiction, and her work has appeared in *Hippocampus*, *Trail Runner*, *Long Trail News*, and *Archetype*. She was born into an outdoorsy family in the Green Mountains of Vermont and now works as a backpacking guide throughout the Western US. She feels that many of us interpret our outdoor experiences through a canon mostly written by men; she wants to work together to create a new canon that affirms who we are and how we walk through the world. She is currently writing a memoir.

She can be found on Instagram @mikaelaosler.

the way i walk

As I came around the north side of Mount Hood for the first time, a sharp gasp escaped my mouth. I breathed, dry and heavy. I was too dehydrated for any tears to fall but I stood, taking in the most hidden side of my favorite mountain. Its rocky summit pushed through the melting snow, white and still draped over its shoulders even in the July heat.

I was only and already halfway.

Somehow my poor feet had carried me here. I stood still, feet and heels throbbing in the confines of my heavy boots. They were waterproof, and although they seemed like overkill in the baking summer sun, I knew there would be snow farther down the trail. My knee was wrapped in the same black-and-gray elastic knee brace I'd brought on every trip for three years. Hood looked down on me with reverence and I breathed a sigh of exhaustion and disbelief that I'd made it this far. Or that I was out here at all, hiking still.

The Timberline Trail is a forty-two-mile loop around Mount Hood, at and right below tree line. Hikers ascend more than 10,000 vertical feet over the course of the trail. They cross deep rivers, navigate scree fields, and come face-to-face with evidence of past wildfires —blowdowns and exposure and heat.

I had a plan to hike the trail in three fourteen-mile days. After a relatively smooth first day, I woke up this morning in pain, like I do most days. It sits between my shoulders, in my hips, in my knees. Mostly my knees. Despite the pain, I wasn't going to stop heaving myself up and over mountains and passes with a pack on. Over the years, my injuries have come and gone, but my love for the trail has stayed. Doctors have always been largely out of the question due to my nomadic life, but I've spent months sitting, hiking, walking, tuning in to my body and its pain, and learning how to manage it on my own.

I lowered myself onto a round piece of basalt, letting its curves support my pack and lift it off my hips. I straightened my left knee so that the brace didn't fold into it in that weird and often painful way that it does. The flies began to swarm, landing on my exposed arms and legs. I swatted at them, but they insisted that I keep hiking.

My relationship with my body and my relationship with Mount Hood are inextricably connected. Three years earlier, I had attempted to summit Cooper Spur, a smaller peak on the east side of the mountain. I'd never been in the alpine before, nor had I accomplished anything of that scale—twelve miles with 5,000 feet of gain—so I'd originally planned to turn around halfway, at the Tilly Jane A-Frame. My partner, Michael, would continue to the top alone. By the time we got to the A-frame, I'd convinced myself that I could try for the summit too, and so I lugged my body and my dog up and into Mount Hood's wilderness for the first time, trying my best not to slow Michael down. Mount Hood towered over me, calling quietly in the harsh alpine. At a view of the Eliot Glacier, we paused. The ice stretched blue beneath us, and I was in awe. And on we hiked. The wind whipped so hard and fast that it could've knocked me over, but Michael was solid. Loose scree tumbled down the slope beneath my feet. We slipped and slid across snowfields. I pictured us sliding halfway down the mountain with one wrong step. I didn't know anything about snow gear or microspikes—I hadn't grown up with snow the way Michael had. The wind and the scree and the snow got the best of me, and I turned around before I could make it to the top. Michael summited without me.

Feelings of failure nagged at me as I sat in my van that night at the base of the mountain. Failure was still new to me, but I was getting used to it, as I pushed myself into more difficult territory as a hiker. But this time, it was accompanied by yet another new feeling: a soft throbbing in my left knee. This, my first knee injury, started quiet, nestled just below the kneecap, somehow sharp and dull at the same time. It grew louder over the following months with every trail I tried to hike. Eventually, Cooper Spur haunted me across state lines: to Idaho's Sawtooths and Crested Butte, Colorado, the pain constantly announcing its presence.

But I couldn't stay off the trails. My right leg took a beating on behalf of my injured left, and by July, the same injury plagued both knees. Pain when I bent them, pain when I straightened them, pain when I inevitably tripped over rocks because the best I could do was stumble along trying desperately to keep up with Michael. He and I were mountain people—it was part of what brought us together in the first place. The mountains called to me in the same way they did him, but while I had lost my confidence on Cooper Spur, Michael marched on without a single thought. I wanted so badly for the mountains to feel accessible again, so that I could enjoy them too.

But there's something about us mountain women. We always find a way to keep going.

Now, I sat cradled by my basalt rock, staring up at Hood again, this time from its wild backcountry. The first day had been rough in the way that the first day with pack weight always is, but by day two my pace had become slow and painful. My knee brace was buried at the bottom of my pack, in the crevices of my sleep system. I hadn't needed it for over a year. I had summited Mount St. Helens, trekked the Palmer Glacier, and thru-hiked California's Backbone Trail—all pain-free. But I was superstitious, believing if I didn't have it with me, that would be when I needed it most. Maybe I should've put it nicely on top, where I could have grabbed it without unpacking.

I was in pain, but quitting was never an option. I had made it to the end before, so I knew that I was capable. I'd hiked the seventy-mile Backbone Trail across the Santa Monica Mountains in six days. That trail had taught me that I was capable of doing big things, but it had also given me a voice. I'd started the trek with the goal of raising awareness about how the mountains' proximity to the city is affecting them. Through blogging and social media, my voice had been amplified, I'd created connections in the outdoor industry and community, and my backpacker identity had been solidified. Now, it was about more than just showing myself that I could do big things—it was about showing the women who were watching me what was possible, despite any doubt. The reality was, some of them were cheering me on, and some of them were waiting to see me fail.

On the Timberline, I breathed in the subalpine air, my poles still in one hand. I finally rose, wiped my sweaty face with the sleeve of my yellow sun shirt, and escaped the flies as I began to walk again, the view of Hood's wild north side now behind me. Bear grass dotted the landscape as the trees parted into meadows. I used to call bear grass "ghost flowers." Wispy and white, they swirl upward to the sky, barely tethered to the earth with their green stems. As I trekked past them, I thought about the ghost of myself. How she had stood at the base of Cooper Spur surrounded by the same flowers and thought, *I can do this.*

The trail led me down and then up again, and the pain in my knee came and went. It hurt more on the downhills, so I prayed to go up instead, or for a flat meadow full of those white flowers. It hurt more when my ibuprofen started to wear off, so I stopped often to sit, opting to take more breaks rather than more medication. I would sit somewhere long enough for the flies to really start to get to me before being forced to move forward again. I had this idea that the flies lived in the dying logs. I pushed myself up to my feet, again and again, trying desperately not to be mistaken for one, to not become a home for something biting and painful. I trudged on through the dark tree line, my knee now nagging on the uphills too. Blowdowns littered my path and the trees left standing were dead and unreliable. Hood peeked through the silent branches of the Douglas fir forests, nodding. My knee ached, sharp, biting.

I moved more slowly than I ever had, dragging myself and my

heavy pack up and over dozens of fallen trees. A branch scraped deep on the inside of my thigh. Blood dripped thick and quiet down my leg, nearly meeting the top of my knee brace. My Garmin dangled from my pack's left strap, blinking that it was tracking me. I thought about using it to text someone to meet me at Cloud Cap and drive me back to Portland. A fly landed on my knee, near the blood. I swatted it and kept walking.

In the time between my Cooper Spur attempt and my Timberline loop, I'd made the seemingly natural transition from full-time vanlifer and digital nomad to outdoor industry seasonal worker, injecting myself into the world of guiding via the climbing industry. Sitting in the woods of New River Gorge National Park, where I worked my first outdoor industry job as an assistant rock guide, I had daydreamed about the Pacific Crest Trail, but ultimately decided to pursue the easier and shorter, but still fulfilling, OCT—the Oregon Coast Trail. And after a summer of jugging kids up Nuttall sandstone, I decided to pivot and throw myself headfirst into anything and everything back-country—seeking wilderness and hiking jobs out West. I led student expeditions through Henry W. Coe State Park and North Cascades National Park, and day hikes for tourists around western Oregon. I had found myself in a place I felt like I belonged for the first time in years, with my boots on the ground, showing people why our trails and public lands are so special.

I stood now, looking out at the clear view through the burnt forest below me, and thought about the men I worked alongside, and how this trail would've been no big deal to most of them. And I thought about my knee. I thought about how I'd told my friends that I was planning to hike forty-two miles in three days, only to be met with "Why? Don't you ever do anything normal?" And I thought about my knee. I thought about how guests on the trips I guided called me brave and tough and questioned what my parents thought about me heading out into the woods alone so often, all within the same breath. I thought about how those men I worked alongside weren't called brave—crazy maybe, in the eyes of tourists, but never brave. These things weren't incomprehensible when it was a man doing them. I thought about how I was here, on a shakedown for the over 400-mile OCT, and how I needed to prove to myself that I was going to be able to make it out there. And I thought about my knee. And I thought about my knee.

I knew that people doubted me because I am a woman. I looked inward and doubted myself because I was in pain. And despite these two truths not being connected, my pain made me question the confidence that brought me out here in the first place: What if they were right? What if I was too weak?

The blowdowns got worse as the trail went on. I crawled over one, acquiring another cut on the inside of my thigh, walked twenty, thirty, fifty feet— another blowdown, another climb over, and repeat. More than the pain in my knee, I was discouraged by my pace, which only got slower as I took off my pack again and again, throwing it over into the dirt. Before climbing over, I would toss my trekking poles after my pack, only for them to bounce away from each other in the metallic way they always did. Some of the blowdowns were on the edges of cliffs and I was suddenly thankful for the fact that I climbed rocks. I trusted my body not to fall. I crimped hard on the cracks in the tree trunks and hung on, pack weight and all. I knew these might have been precarious moments for some people, but I was unafraid.

Until I stood on top of the steep scree hill overlooking the Eliot Branch, the river fed by the Eliot Glacier. Nearly every hiker I'd passed going the opposite direction had warned me about this crossing. They'd described swift, deep water, and told me to avoid it in the afternoons when the rate of the snowmelt was the highest. It was 2 p.m. It was clear from above that they were right: the Eliot was deep and fast-moving and so silty it was gray. Across the ravine stood Cloud Cap, the backpackers' campground that would be my saving grace. I had to cross this river.

I gripped my trekking poles in my right hand and dug my heels into the hillside to avoid tumbling down toward the water directly below. My left knee shook, unstable on the shifting scree beneath me. I pushed my share of the mountain into the river as the other hikers had before me.

Choking down tears, I took a breath, trying to convince myself of confidence. I took off my pack, then my boots, then my socks, and put on my Tevas to cross the river. This wasn't like climbing a rock, where I could study each move as I went, take it slow, and do it right; this would have to be fast and deliberate. I stepped in, got scared, and stepped out again, pack unbuckled and heavy on my shoulders. The cold was shocking. I stood on the bank, my feet drying, sharp and icy. I gripped the cork handles of my trekking poles tight, but I couldn't get one down to the river's bottom without it being washed away. Doubt rang as loud as the rushing river. I had made it twenty-seven miles, but I didn't trust my body to make it ten feet through the freezing, turbulent water.

Another solo hiker descended the scree hill behind me, swapped his shoes, and crossed, dropping his pack on the other side. For a second, I refused to believe he was doing what he appeared to be doing, but then he was back in the water, halfway across, in the current of the thing with his hand extended toward mine.

For so long, it had been just me and my injured body. I hadn't been prepared to ask for help, and I didn't want to now. But underneath my stubbornness, I knew that my own two feet couldn't get me safely across the Eliot, despite all the miles they'd hiked. The word *failure* briefly entered my mind, and I considered the outstretched hand. I considered how asking for help made me feel less capable, and what did that mean for all of the people who encouraged me to keep going? What did that mean for the people who expected me to fail?

I braced for the cold of the river and walked toward him. Halfway across, my feet were mostly numb. All I could feel were the foam soles of my Tevas being pulled by the water. The other hiker grabbed my hand as soon as he could reach it and pulled me across. I dropped my heavy pack from my shoulders at the edge of the river and collapsed onto a rock. I looked at the man who had just potentially saved my life. My knee brace was soaked but the cold felt good on my sore leg.

"Thank you," I said.

"Glad I could help," he said, changing from sandals to trail runners while the river rushed quickly by.

We chatted for a bit. His name was John, and he was from here—Oregon. He had just section-hiked the OCT: the trail that I was getting ready to attempt myself. His knee had been bothering him too, after an eighteen-mile day one. I felt bad for a second about the fourteen-miler I'd struggled on the day before, but I realized I'd hiked more than he had today, only for us to end up in the same spot. We trudged uphill toward Cloud Cap together until I fell behind due to the heat. I'd catch up soon enough.

I'd made it this far.

I stared down at the Eliot Branch, shrinking below me. While I felt slow, it had grown so small already. I stopped often, the late-afternoon sun beating down on my bare legs, my head, my arms. I would have a knee brace tan line to remember this trip by.

My eyes scanned the trail behind me, past the river and the scree hill and up into the trees. I had walked nearly twenty-eight miles in two days. My feet were tired. My knee hurt. But I smiled. I knew that I belonged out here.

Maybe I had nothing left to prove.

John waited for me at Cloud Cap, and we camped together, chatting until hiker midnight while watching the alpenglow caress Hood's rocky summit.

The wind kept me up most of the night and I woke at 4:45 a.m. I was determined to get as far ahead as I could before John got on trail. I knew this would be the hardest of the three days because of the elevation profile: the most gain and loss of the whole trip.

The trail started with a three-mile ascent into the bright alpine at sunrise. The trail was sandy ash, and the wind blew hard, nearly taking my hat with it. I pulled my hood up over my head to secure it. Cooper Spur loomed above me. I was steady. I was moving. Something about being above tree line—the timberline—motivated me to push on. I remembered the winds that had forced me to bail on Cooper Spur three years ago, how Michael had summited, and how I felt I'd been left behind. I thought about all the times I'd stayed back in the van feeling sorry for myself. Not anymore.

If I finished this trail, I could finally let what happened on Cooper

Spur go.

The ground crunched beneath my feet. As I moved and warmed up from hiking, I kept thinking about taking off my fleece, only for the wind to pick up again each time. I wasn't quite out of breath, my legs weren't quite burning, so I kept on, walking up toward my high point.

When I finally did stop to take off the fleece and replace it with my sun shirt, John caught up to me. It had only been about an hour since I'd started walking, but I knew his natural pace was faster than mine. He fell in behind me, opting to hike my pace, and I took point for the rest of the ascent. We crossed snow and scree and rivers and hobbled the whole way because of our knees. Part of it—most of it—felt good, having a teammate, having someone to talk to.

"What are you doing next weekend?" he said as we dropped into Meadows, the bear grass making a reappearance.

"Resting. I'm supposed to start the OCT in a few weeks and my knee needs to chill by then."

"I was gonna ask if you'd want to do Salmon River with me."

"I appreciate the invite, but I don't think it's a good idea for me to do another—what is it, twenty-eight miles?—before I'm pain-free again."

"I've had pain all summer, but I'm still going out every weekend."

We hiked on, toward Timberline Lodge, and I thought about my decision to stay home next weekend, and about all of the decisions I'd made in the past three days. I was jealous that John was going back out, even if his knee hurt. I wanted to be able to go too. But in the world of trails and mountains, it is just as important to know when not to keep pushing as it is to reach for greater unknowns. There's power in that, and I thought for a second about how, maybe, that knowledge is worth more than the pride of finishing trail after trail.

The mountain looked down at me, giving me a knowing nod, as I pushed through my final miles toward the White River. I'd chosen this trail for myself and had a wild enough idea that I'd be able to complete it alone. I'd packed for it and put myself on it and had walked all the miles. I had been ready for this, and even if I was in pain now, that didn't make me any less capable. If anything, the presence of my pain showed me just how capable I actually was. I was going to finish with it as my companion.

I would eventually come to treat my body like the places I loved—with care and gentleness and respect for its resilient power.

The last miles weren't easy. My knee was getting worse, and a blister formed on the bottom of my left foot. Other hikers marched past us, descending to the river. I resented them for a second, wishing I had a body that could fly downhill like they did. But we made it, too, and the White River's silty water quickly numbed my feet with strange relief. I was almost home.

Timberline Lodge stood in the distance, on the other side of an ash-filled trail. John had run ahead, suddenly met with a burst of end-of-trail energy that I envied, and I set to finish the trail the way I'd started it: with no other company but my own body and Mount Hood, looming above me. I reveled in what was left of it—in the vast and demanding wild I'd pulled myself through, in the ways I walked, and the places. Hood stood regal and towering. There were no flies and no dead trees, just trail, and so many and so few steps left to hike.

———

HALLE HOMEL (SHE/HER)

Nomadic and living out of a camper. Originally from Los Angeles, California—traditional territory of the Tongva, Tataviam, Serrano, Kizh, and Chumash peoples. Currently based in Portland, Oregon—traditional territory of the Multnomah, Kathlamet, Clackamas, Chinook, Tualatin, Kalapuya, Molalla, and more.

Halle is a backpacker, hiker, climber, and outdoor recreation guide. She holds a BA in creative writing and has been published by *The Trek, Outdoors.com* and *Rootless Living* magazine. Her biggest passion is the mountains and keeping them wild, and she believes in telling the stories of the places she visits, as well as the experience of the female body on trail. She travels full-time with her dog, Lassen.

She can be found on Instagram and other platforms @halletreks.

as nature is

The first time God felt real to me
Was clenching the crown of Christ in my hands
The crucifixion thorn
That rich Sonoran Desert plant
I remember the sand, the quartz, the slate, and river rocks
Sometimes the river rocks were in pieces and you could tell how long it'd
been since the dawn of time that they'd been cleaved, based on the sharp-
ness of their edges
You could break the slate, startle an animal in the brush and not know
if it was a bunny, a bird, a lizard, or a snake—they all look the same
covered in the same sand backlit with the same dry dirt,
Everything painted in the same value
Except the bright sparkles of quartz and fool's gold
I ran for these desert diamonds
Spit-shined them and collected the best
Watched the cacti with their long arms,
Stretching,
Melting into the skyline
I've never felt this tired before,
I thought

Beneath the vivid stars so clear and bright I could see the heavens aglow
above us in the starlight
Even through the tent nets
Even through the tent nets
Coyotes howled much of the night
So I was told, I could never hear them,
Except once, and then I knew
They were close

LIVING AS A PERSON WITH DISABILITIES HAS ALWAYS BEEN difficult. I have been hard of hearing since birth, always living my life on the fringes of society, struggling to get my needs met and to be understood and respected by the hearing people around me. Academic settings were competitive and often didn't provide the necessary accommodations for me to have access to learning material to the same degree as hearing students. Yet I persisted.

There is one place where I've always felt at peace, like I truly belong, and that is in nature. From bushcrafting as a kid in the ponderosa pines of the Apache-Sitgreaves forest, to camping in the Sonoran Desert as an adolescent, to traipsing through the redwoods and Douglas firs of the foggy Pacific Northwest as an adult, I've always found that nature accepts me as I am.

I can be myself, as nature is, with no need to explain or feel shame or judgment. I can simply exist. Nature doesn't question why it is the way it is. It grows, it evolves, it employs ingenious tactics to preserve its genetic material, it displays altruistic traits for reasons unknown to its external observers. And yet, it simply is.

My narcolepsy developed in 2016, after a severe viral infection. It was during my sophomore year of college, and my parents were determined to fix the problem. We saw so many specialists, I had so many scans done of my head, and I tried so many different medications to help my condition. My symptoms still weren't well managed. Not at all. I couldn't stay awake through my own graduation. Imagine working four years for a degree, then falling asleep uncontrollably during your commencement.

After getting my master's degree in applied biological sciences, I learned that my research position at the university had been terminated, and I was told to come back "when my narcolepsy symptoms improved." Unfortunately for me, narcolepsy is a permanent neurological condition. That same year, I started dating my first girlfriend, to the surprise of my parents, who later would not allow her in our home. All of this change turned out to be too much for them to handle. My parents sent me away to live with relatives in the mountains of Arizona. When my time there was up, my parents told me I couldn't come back to live with them again. Luckily, I was able to get a room in a group home near the Apache-Sitgreaves forest. I wasn't invited to family holiday celebrations. I felt discarded. Forgotten.

It was there, exploring the forests and rivers of Pinetop-Lakeside, Arizona, with my service dog, that I found a new purpose. My purpose was to enjoy the nature that surrounded me, and to find my place in it. My favorite hike was just up the road from the group home, a short trail that took me to the edge of the Mogollon Rim. I watched the ponderosa pines sway and stretch beyond the horizon, and I cried rivers of tears and wrote depressing poetry. I mourned the broken parts of my life that I will never get back—the medical and research career I was studying for before my diagnosis, and the friends and family members who pushed me away. The birds chirping and fluttering among the dry grasses and skinny branches helped me to feel safe enough to let out my own songs of the heart. These words were sometimes the only words I'd hear for days at a time. But the trees and clouds and grasses soothed my pain. The trails became a shoulder to cry on. The desert trees and flowers were thankful for the watering. And every time I left the trail, I felt renewed again.

As I learned to cope with my narcolepsy symptoms and become a new version of myself that lives with this illness, I was grateful for access to nature so close to home. Driving long distances had become difficult, if not impossible. Once I started getting sleepy, I was in danger of getting lost. I became disoriented. It was scary to be exploring wild trails deep in unfamiliar territory, unable to come out of a groggy stupor. On these trails that became mine, I could stop to nap if I needed to. And perhaps recognize my surroundings upon waking.

In that little mountain town, I took my dog camping on a whim. I found a campground close enough that I felt safe driving to. Camping meant that I could explore the trails and lake, but then sleep before driving home.

The hiking trails near the campground stretched for miles, following the lakeside waterfront. We watched herons skim the rippling surface of the lake in search of their breakfast. The only sounds I could hear were the crunching of gravel beneath my feet and the chirping of birds above my head. The sky was an impossible blue, with fluffy ivory-white clouds.

As the day passed, clouds continued to roll in, bruising to dark purples and greys. I realized the hard way that I hadn't checked the weather before planning this last-minute excursion. A thunderstorm hit us that night at the campground, and even though I had water-proofed my new tent before the trip, it leaked quite a bit. In the cold and wet, bundled in all my clothes, I shivered with my dog in a pile of blankets. I felt like a silly little idiot with no one and nothing. I was overcome by the tears. The emptiness. The shame. The fear. I questioned my sanity, I asked myself why I had even tried.

But morning came. And when the groundskeeper checked on us, she exclaimed, "I'm glad y'all survived the long night!"

And we had. We really had.

I'm not Religious anymore, but I am Spiritual.
The trees are my new Gods
I was reborn at the base of their trunks,
In the sleepy mountain town of Pinetop, Arizona—
Nature was beautiful there
So close to town you could taste the forest in its veins
Here, I hike a rugged trail
To a viewpoint of the Mogollon Rim
My only companion, a furry four-legged friend,
A sleek and bright German shepherd

Ponderosa pines whisper around us
The dirt and rock are gritty beneath us
We sit at the end of the trail
Where we watch the bandstands sway with the wind
Overlooking a vast valley of stately trees
I smile at passersby
I feel safe as rain with my dog lying at my side
So I write bad poetry
And soak in the sunshine, the breeze, the ease
With which my lungs breathe
But narcolepsy, she is always there
To weight my lids, heavily
Before long, my eyes begin to blink in the sun,
It shutters like a camera,
From bright to dark, over and over
Until darkness overcomes
When I wake, the world is still there
Both loud and quiet
The birdsong chirps brightly
I hold on, tightly

My new home is Portland, Oregon. The nature here is so different from what I grew up with. I visit Marquam Nature Park and walk among the tall stands of Douglas fir. The trees are so often knotted, twisted, pulled by the degrees of the slopes they sit upon and the weight of gravity inflicted upon them, garnished with messy lichen, leaking resin droplets, their barks painted with natural sunscreen based upon the level of sunlight each side receives. Yet each tree serves its role. It is connected to the earth, using microbial fungal networks to communicate with the community surrounding it. Communities use these networks to redirect nutrients to other trees that may be struggling to survive. Appearances and differences are not mourned or celebrated among the trees. They simply are. No matter their species, they all sway with the same breeze and feed from the same sun.

TATIANA MARIA CORBITT (THEY/THEM)

Portland, Oregon—traditional territory of the Cayuse, Umatilla, and Walla Walla peoples

Tatiana is a Hispanic artist and writer living in the Pacific Northwest. They love hunting for mushrooms and a nice cup of coffee. They graduated *summa cum laude* from Barrett, the Honors College at Arizona State University, with their MS and BS in applied biological sciences. Tatiana is a volunteer facilitator for Wake Up Narcolepsy's LGBTQIA+ Narcolepsy Support Group, and their writing is regularly published by Narcolepsy.Sleep-Disorders.net, RareDisease.net, and SocialHealthNetwork.com. They are looking forward to their first book, a poetry collection entitled *Wild Brujeria*, being published by Curious Corvid Publishing in August 2024. They are currently writing a semi-autobiographical fantasy novel starring a queer and narcoleptic ex-scientist who hikes into a new world.

They can be found on Instagram @authortatianamaria.

coming home

I WAS BORN AT THE UNIVERSITY OF MINNESOTA IN A hospital room overlooking the Mississippi River. As quickly and surely as I learned that my birthplace was the origination point of North America's largest waterway, I came to believe the state I lived in was inadequate. The list of complaints I internalized included but was never limited to: the mercurial weather, oppressively hot in the summer or dangerously cold in the winter, a landscape devoid of mountains and oceans, sing-song "Don't ya knows" and "You betchas," and now the notorious home of George Floyd's murder.

Over the years, I came to see the same inadequacy in myself. I swallowed whole the religious doctrine that I was born utterly and totally depraved and because of my sinful nature deserved little more than pity from God. As often as this message was repeated, at church and at home, it was followed with the "good news" that God loved me in spite of my unworthiness. It was as confusing to me as a kid as it is as an adult, and now a mother.

In 2016, my husband found me sitting in the driver's seat of my car with the windows open and the garage door closed. My right foot hovered over the brake and my index finger rested on the ignition. I wanted to escape myself as badly as I wanted out of Minnesota. He took the keys and my hand, leading me back into the house. In those first fragile moments, he begged me to understand. *I love you. The girls love you.* I refused each plea. *No.*

The following morning, I stood in the pothole-ridden parking lot of the food shelf where I worked and left a message with a therapist. Through tears, I sputtered, "I need help."

TWO DIFFICULT YEARS LATER, I heard about the 197-mile Minnesota State Parks Hiking Club from a chatty hygienist while my dentist applied composite resin to the gaps between my teeth and gums. "Alicia," he had warned after my last examination, "you need to ease up on your toothbrushing. You're close to exposing the root." Unbeknownst to me, toothbrushing had become one of my many self-improvement projects; gum recession just the latest iteration of my never-ending quest to rid myself of all I thought was wrong with me. Reclined under the fluorescent spotlight, I squeezed my eyes shut, trying to stall the torrent of memories, all the ways I'd scoured myself to the bone.

The hygienist, undeterred by the mounting pressure on my gumline and unfazed by the sound of saliva vacuuming through the plastic wand, explained: "There's a designated trail at each state park. There's a small fee to join. You just look for the blue hiking club sign and go!" Mistaking my raised eyebrow to mean *Tell me more!* rather than *How much longer is this going to take?* she prattled on. "My husband and I usually go once a month. We make the day of it. It's fun."

I tried to remember the last time hiking had been fun.

Hiking had once been a respite for me. On the trail, the self-blame and internal judgments—the flood of accusatory *I should have*s and *I shouldn't have*s, the braided currents of *Why am I like this?* and *What is wrong with me?*—dried up like a vernal creek. When I hiked, I was attuned to the accumulation of heat after a steep climb; I could feel the pinprick of a sweat droplet forming, the moment it would sit poised in the dimple of my sternum before falling and soaking the elastic band of my sports bra. Hiking was like a spring-fed creek that percolated out of bedrock. It provided access to the glimmer of goodness that had been obscured by the religious messages and experiences of my youth.

My husband, Chris, and I had met twenty years prior and bonded over our shared love of the outdoors. We said "I love you" for the first time under the sagging eaves of Paradise Inn on Mount Rainier after a hike through the alpine meadows on the Skyline Trail. On subsequent trips—honeymooning in the Rocky Mountains and backpacking in the High Sierra and Denali National Park—we dreamed of sharing the trail with our children. But as dreams go, the reality of children growing into their own personalities, desires, and schedules had rewritten the vision of our family spending weekends in the great outdoors. The hiking club was an opportunity. The idea of getting back on the trail grew into the physical restlessness of possibility. I adjusted my legs on the beige vinyl as my dentist applied the last of the sealant.

A MONTH AFTER THAT APPOINTMENT, I handed over my spruce-green, tree-embossed REI credit card to a Minnesota Department of Natural Resources employee at Lake Maria State Park. In the first three months of membership, I hiked the seven state parks within an hour's drive of where I live in the Twin Cities. The trails guided me up and then down upland prairie knolls, through sandy river flats of floodplain forests, on traverses down and then back up steep river terraces, in and around basalt potholes (some as deep as sixty feet), and under arched tree boughs of oak and maple woodlands. My internal landscape responded to the swells and sways, soft soil, and protection of the forest. My shoulders dropped from their perch near my ears, the tension in my lower back relaxed. I walked with my head up and heart-center open. For once, I wasn't in a race to chase down approval or outrun mistakes.

As the range of my hikes expanded in concentric circles from home, so too did my awareness of the state. In the spring of the following year, I discovered that beginning in April and throughout the month of May, overnight thermal images of Minnesota scream radar red from the birds flocking to the state to mate and nest. My dismissive, nothing-to-see-here attitude about Minnesota as "flyover country" was challenged. On another hike, a heavy and hot July day, I was as startled by the number of snakes on the trail and their sudden, slithering movements as I was to learn that pre-settlement Minnesota was home to seventeen species, including a rattlesnake.

After a rushed hike through wet woodlands besieged by swarms of hungry mosquitos, my opinion changed about these bloodthirsty "state birds" when I found out that only females bite. They sup on our blood protein to nurture and sustain their young. As a mother, I resonated with their ferocity. And who knew that Minnesota was home to a cactus? I didn't. A latitudinal anomaly, the prickly pear is found in the state only on the hundred-foot rise of pink-and-purple Sioux Quartzite at Blue Mounds State Park in southwestern Minnesota.

This was also the year I realized that hiking all 197 miles was *my* goal. I'd tried, with varying levels of frustration and resentment, to include my family in this journey. The frequent "I hate this!" and "Why are we doing this?!" lobbed from behind flew in the face of my hopes that this could be a bonding experience for us. The hiking club was something I wanted. Something *I* needed.

One Easter Sunday, I hiked the three-mile trail at Banning State Park. Like most spring days in Minnesota, the weather was impertinent. The trail was an obstacle course of snowmelt puddles and muck from the day's drizzle. I was soaked from head to foot and back again but was more comfortable than I would have been in a church pew. The trail led me to Hell's Gate Rapids, a place beloved by experienced kayakers across the region. Flush with snowmelt, the red-faced waterway spewed the spittle and brimstone of a resurrection sermon. Instead of drowning in shame, I was buoyed by the eddies' homily.

On another spring day, I cantilevered myself over the edge of a four-foot-wide boardwalk through delicate sphagnum moss to get as close as possible to a pink lady slipper at Lake Bemidji State Park. Other hikers had to take high-kneed steps over my prostrated body to pass. I took one picture and then another picture of the fuchsia orchid. My face flushed to match the bloom—the first I'd ever seen. I flipped the camera to selfie mode to capture my own bright smile and wide eyes.

The more time I spent hiking the more I learned to appreciate the diversity of the state. Some trails were dirt-packed and narrow like those along the cliffs of the North Shore. Others grassy and wide like the prairie itself that runs the southern edge and western spine of the state. I began to differentiate the sound of each footfall on the weathered wood planks of peatland boardwalks from the impact of each step on exposed igneous rock. I developed an affinity for the tenacity of the tallgrass prairies and the intrepid ecosystem of tangled root systems and adaptations that survive the extremes of exposure.

My fledgling appreciation and affection for the state I call home midwifed the same within myself. I began to recognize my own strength, my beauty, my inherent worthiness. Like my home, I am complex. I am tenacious and intrepid and can adapt to survive.

MINNESOTA'S REPUTATION, boiled down to one descriptor, is *cold*. The state's latitude and its vulnerability to polar vortexes make it an easy place to lament and despise. The hiking club invited me out and into the freezing cold to tromp through hardwood forests in a foot of fresh snow and kick-glide alongside a downcut river terrace. I found that the most beautiful winter days, when the sun was shining and the sky was a translucent cerulean, were also the coldest.

The description in the hiking club guidebook assured me that the two-and-a-half-mile trail at Split Rock Creek State Park was hilly but not steep. But on a frigid February day, the knee-high snow made mountains out of molehills. The push and pull of the aluminum frame and synthetic rubber of my snowshoes generated more than enough heat to warm my body against the firm hand of polar air. At an overlook, the heat of my body reached a boiling point. The vault of blue sky and the basin of glacial blue Lake Superior collided with the milky white of ice-covered cliffs and snow. Coils and thick ribbons of giddiness rose up from within. Like Minnesota's "too cold," I had always believed my mercurial temperament, my "too much" and "too big," to be evidence of my unlovability. I had found something to love in Minnesota's harsh winter. A bond was forged as strong as the iron ore in the bedrock.

In August 2023, five years and two months after joining the club, I hiked my last mile at Scenic State Park in northern Minnesota. The wide fronds of red and white pines held their whorled branches like open arms as I walked over the threshold. Since finishing, I have often been asked, "What was your favorite park?" or "What was your favorite hike?" I've never thought of the hiking club in those terms. Each park, each footfall, was a step toward transformation. There is, however, one experience that stands out as a conversion of sorts.

In September of 2021, I was set to hike the two-mile trail at Forestville/Mystery Cave State Park and decided to register for a tour of the cave as well. Our small group followed the DNR guide, clad in tan shirt and brown pants, over a footbridge and through a set of thick metal flood doors. When the last of us filed in, the doors swung closed. Intended to guard the cave system from spring-melt flooding, the doors also sealed us off to daylight and the need for meaningless chatter. A metallic echo moved its way down the chalky bedrock passage. In return, the *plink* of a single drop of water off flowstone came back to us.

The tour guide led us through a labyrinth of stalactites and stalagmites. Features and formations I would have previously expected to see in *National Geographic* or as a backdrop in a sci-fi movie. This part of the state escaped the snowplow of ice and the dump-truck loads of till during the last glaciation. The so-called Driftless region has deep-cut ravines through sandstone, hidden valleys of limestone, and rock outcrops of dolomite. Water that isn't swept toward the Mississippi River in one of the region's numerous tributaries seeps into the ground, bringing carbon dioxide with it, creating sinkholes and cave systems that meander underground for miles.

In one of the narrow, forty-eight-degree corridors, our guide stopped. Using his flashlight, he drew an outline around the six-foot-long fossil of a cephalopod over our heads. Under the remains of the 450-million-year-old shell, a woman pressed against me in the dark. She exhaled her hot, ninety-eight-degree disbelief into my ear. "I can't believe this is Minnesota."

By then, I could.

At the end of the cave, our guide corralled us in a semicircle of darkness. He held us captive with silence. Feet shuffled in anticipation. Finally, he spoke with the intonation of a much-anticipated surprise: "This is Turquoise Lake!" He flipped a light switch and a pool of phosphorescent water appeared before us.

The millions of atoms that make me *Me* vibrated and pulsed as I waited to get a closer look at the luminescent water cradled in the palm of limestone. When it was my turn, I placed my hands on the cool carbonate rock and leaned over the lip of the pool. I inhaled, drinking in as much of the goodness as I could. I held my breath as the image of the turquoise water settled in the well of my solar plexus. After a moment, I exhaled what remained of my disfigured sense of self. It joined the barely perceptible ripple of water as it moved over the bedrock and disappeared into the limestone.

ALICIA GATTO PETERSEN (SHE/HER)

Mahtomedi, Minnesota—traditional territory of the Wahpekute people

Alicia geeks out on identifying plants, fungi, and animals where she lives. Among other outdoorsy ventures, she has backpacked in the High Sierra and Denali National Park, and she worked and hiked in Mount Rainier National Park. She has previously published poems in *Mothers Always Write*, as well as flash/short stories in *Feminine Collective* and the *Stillwater Gazette*.

She can be found on Instagram @agattopetersen and @phenologyofhomemn.

improvise : bike-the-hike

no tears fell. one or two *did* brim up but were quickly batted back by the fierce flick of lids and one quick swipe of the back of the palm. *this is just an unexpected chapter. an unexpected chapter writing itself on the trail . . .*

> *how boring of a story would it be*
> *if you just said "ya I hiked the gdt*
> *no problem . . . oh you've never heard*
> *of the GDT?! The GREAT DIVIDE?*
>
> *Ya I hiked that . . . and got evacuated . . .*
> *stayed in a nowhere town . . .*
> *and then hit the trail again!*[1]

i had pushed the SOS button.

> *Hi Bronwyn, it's 911 dispatch . . .*
>
> *we have numerous emergency services*
> *coordinating to get to you. . . .*[2]

we have your location and are
coordinating a response—

the ambulance was dispatched....

[we] have a helicopter on the
way.

there are paramedics coming
on foot[3]

i am barely able to walk.

only ten kilometres into today and i had to make the call. ten agoniz-
ingly long kilometres, metred in pain, and lengthened by limping...

this had never happened before.

debilitating, throbbing, shooting pangs and swelling in both ankles.
anti-inflammatories unable to ease the stress: *i was keeling over, desper-*
ately trying to push on. i was in agony.

you're one fucking mighty woman!

by the time the long line of the helicopter was dropping down, exactly
three hours later, and i was harnessed into the "screamer suit" by a
member of the *mountain rescue team,*

i was only able to crawl.

———

i *was* trying to thru-hike the great divide...
a rugged and remote trail up and down the spine of the canadian

rockies . . . the northern continuation of the continental divide trail, starting where it ends, at the international border:

> *The Great Divide Trail traverses the continental divide between Alberta and British Columbia, wandering through the vast wilderness of the Canadian Rocky Mountains for more than 1100 kilometres. It is one of the most spectacular and challenging long-distance trails on the planet.*

> *The Great Divide Trail is wild and not always even an actual trail, sometimes merely a wilderness route, inspiring modern-day adventurers to walk the same paths of the original Indigenous people and explorers to the area.*[4]

the great divide travels through the Traditional Territories of the Niitsitapi (Blackfoot Confederacy), Ktunaxa, Tsuut'ina, Îyârhe Nakoda (Stoney), Cree, Lheidli T'enneh, Secwepemc, Métis, and Sinixt.

i had humbly, as a visitor to these Ancestral Lands, begun my trip, backpack on, two weeks previous, where i had found myself standing at the trailhead, on the lakeside border. next to me was *my daughter.* waving from an offshore boat: *my mother.* it was my late grandmother's birthday.

three generations together.
four in spirit.
four generations of strong, independent, supportive women . .

sending me off on my solo,
nine-week hike-and-write journey . . .

there i had stood, some fourteen days ago, at a concrete monument. a historical—*and divisive*—marker. *[un]paralleled.*
treaties and dates embossed upon it.

———

there were many divides i was contending with in that moment—
standing at, and on, the border—*and would be throughout this whole
trip* . . .
beyond where the continental waters longitudinally part ways, *choose
sides:*

but, where

Lands and Peoples are caught between notions of preservation
and purgation; extraction, eviction, exaltation, and appreciation; perpetuity and precarity; where vulnerability, value, and
values collide, coincide, and divide—

often hidden from popular view

by the very views themselves:

the spectacular snowcapped peaks, shimmering turquoise
lakes, creeping glaciers, rushing rivers, lush valleys, alpine
meadows, and an abundance of wildlife . . .

those which have attracted and housed people for millennia.

and here i was, *there i was,*
trying to walk this line . . .

to trace these footsteps through footfalls, *northward.*

and *now*, here,
with search and rescue's helicopter hovering above me,

i am suddenly contending with another, and unforeseen, divide—

the split from what i had hoped to do, had spent endless months planning for, coordinating the logistics of, and training for . . .
and a sudden new reality . . . *unknown* . . .

———

i am an avid multiday backpacker. i am, equally, a site-sensitive poet, who chronicles as she hikes, writes as she walks: translating traversed landscapes into language, trail experiences into engaged narratives, synthesizing into words my ever-deepening understandings of self, Peoples, and place, as a person of predominantly settler descent visiting unceded Ancestral Lands. i have a practice of documenting, from the backcountry, these unfurling relationships, overlaps, challenges, hopes, and their inextricable reveals in situ. my writing aims to capture snippets, sound bites, moments, geology, geography, ornithological-envy, botanical reverie, history, and gaps. my trail documentation travels through many territories and ethical terrains, remaining at once personal and poignantly political . . .

neither the book-to-be, nor the hike, were quite what i'd ever anticipated either would be . . . now both had a crux . . . a climax a mere 250-something kilometres in ...

———

my thoughts drift back to my daughter gifting me a mountain necklace, on the eve before i left, scribed with *"the best view comes after the hardest climb"* . . .

it had been nearly a year and a half since my full knee replacement, as well as the insertion of a full metal rod down the length of my tibia. i had, previously, been living with an acutely crooked, valgus knee, post a leg-shattering sports injury which had happened almost two years before the eventual replacement. i kept hiking during all this—*albeit, extremely slowly, labouriously*. i engaged a determined and focussed multifaceted, dynamic rehabilitation regimen: *positivity and persever-ance. perseverance and positivity. and an exorbitant amount of physio-therapy* for the better part of three-plus years.

you are so ready for this Bronwyn, my physio had texted, on the eve of departure.

i was.
or, as best as i could be.
but, ankles? never had i ever had issues with my ankles.

but strapping on a pack with eight-day food hauls, carrying water over long dry stretches . . . and the weight, despite the ultralight gear, bearing down over repeated long days—in dehydrating terrain, and over all manner of steep footing, with more than 1,000 metres of ascent and descent on average per day—seriously aggravated my feet. *even as an experienced backpacker.*

diagnosis: *ACUTE* tendinitis.
unable to walk, i am wheelchair dependent and hotel-housed for days.
i move in with my parents, where i can just kick up my feet . . .

the preparations for this expedition had been all-consuming for the better part of half a year—

from permits to planning, from passes to packing, from researching histories to the logistics of resupplying.

The GDT passes through:
- 5 National Parks: Waterton Lakes, Banff, Kootenay, Yoho and Jasper.

- 8 Provincial Parks: Akamina-Kishinena, Castle, Elk Lakes, Peter Lougheed, Height of the Rockies, Mount Assiniboine, Mount Robson and Kakwa.
- 3 Wildland Provincial Parks: Castle, High Rock and Don Getty.
- 2 wilderness areas: Beehive Natural Area and White Goat Wilderness.
- 2 special management areas: Kananaskis Country and Willmore Wilderness Park.[5]

each with different rules and regulations.
there is no one pass for hiking the great divide, the GDT. rather, more than thirty individual permits had to be obtained—*aligned and timed*—ranging from random camping to public land use ones, to backcountry reservations and resupply location accommodations in between. *this process was, and continues to be, anything but easy.*

given my desire to write on the trail—being "the backcountry poet"—along with my semi-bionic status, i was not attempting to crush the same miles as the twentysomething crew. i am no longer in that age bracket. i had sixty planned trail days, seventy days in total ... many of which would require route-finding and way-making skills through trailless terrain ...

the healing prognosis for this one: *time.*

time, on trail, becomes elastic.
time, in recovery, can become static.
the task becomes how not to make time stagnant.

tears would not—did not—blotch my ink. i was, after all, @poetichiker.

i stay focused, proactive . . . determined to return, intercepting the trail farther north, as soon as possible.

this is, *sadly*, all too familiar territory. i had been in rehabilitation mode for more than three solid years—i knew how and what to do . . . how to stay positive, zen . . . *but, honestly, i thought i was through that. i was going to hike the great divide and was mentally and physically prepared. i had done my time.* and now the world is suddenly demanding more of it from me. *and not the type of time i readily wanted to partake in . . .*

    i want to be engaged in two-foot, bipedal propelled-time.

it's tough when an active person is forcibly made sedentary.

i will not to fight it. if i do, i will be the only loser.
i will not feel sorry for myself, nor wallow in sadness . . .

however, the increments of improvement are slower than i could have ever imagined.
i mean, *ever.* and along with that comes the harder and harder realization that my anticipated projections of great divide reentry points will need to be pushed further and further ahead. *from a week, to two, to more.* reservations are being cancelled, refunds reimbursed, and resupply boxes chased up for return-to-sender mailings. in between, i slowly attempt to hobble less than a quarter kilometre's worth of distance. struggling hard with 250-metre stints . . . all of my meticulous planning and my big dream: dissolving, or more accurately: *morphing . . .*

––––––

i have now been staying with my parents for more than a couple of weeks—their banisters and furniture still strewn with my gear—left out, as if to colourfully flag that it will necessarily soon be packed up;

to stuff my tent, sleeping pad, and quilt away would be to acquiesce to a different possibility. a possibility that has yet to be known or determined . . .

with feeble feet, i find that the ability to make a plan is still elusive . . . *this i do know:* i will not yet return to my own home. to do so would somehow signal defeat. the desire to salvage not only a hiking project but also a creative one is still fuelling me with inspiration, rather than desperation.

i come up with an idea: i will stay put, but "bike" the divide. *on stationary wheels.*

a lover of rituals, on the three-week anniversary of being plucked off the trail, i set out again on a new way of approaching the GDT: cycling in place. next to me: *my mother,* holding a photograph of my grandmother. FaceTiming in from work: *my daughter.*

> two generations physically together.
> three, technologically.
> *four in spirit.*
> four generations of strong, independent, supportive women . .
> together, *again,*

> sending me off anew on my (anything but)-solo journey . . .

> i will pick up where i left off,
> biking in stationary klicks, my daily planned itinerary.

> i will further research the places i will be passing
> vicariously through, and the people who shaped themselves
> with and within the folds of the hills i have in part stepped
> into, with and alongside...

> here, i am

going nowhere, but going places,

truly, bi-pedaling time.

and then something shifts . . . i both feel and hear, "the" adjustment, "the" crack, "the" realignment . . . *what the hell just happened?* . . . i can suddenly move with a new range of motion, an ability to flex. an instantaneous 180 degrees . . .

i get *really excited.*
i do my first, flat three-kilometre walk. then, several hours later, i "charge" out again—for another one-kilometre flat jaunt—arms swinging, smile beaming . . .

suddenly hope turns into a tangible trail-returning possibility . .

and the unsolicited comments from others that tendinitis can take over a year to heal, if at all, evaporate.

i am soaring . . .

well,
up until the next day.

i had pushed it. in my exuberance, i had lost sight of the idea of incremental improvement . . .

three kilometres + another one = feet rebelling in angry defiance.

back to the physio i head, who asks, "*what on earth have you done?!*"

i had set myself way back.

it had been my talus bone that had adjusted itself and, in turn, relieved some of the pressure it had been causing on the tibialis anterior and other top-of-the-foot tendons. and that foot continues to feel better. however, due to the shift, new pains and strains are developing else-where with it. the right foot screams in peroneal pain and swelling to match its vocalizations. my happy strides had been longer, faster . . . just too much, too soon.

> reality check: *how did i think i could head off into some of the wildest and most rugged sections of this trail—and attempt elevation, multiple sketchy water fords, the strong possibility of inclement weather, snow, and a first day that called for over thirty kilometres—in the time i have?!*

reality can sometimes hurt more than anything.

i have to call it.

tendinitis has developed as a result of repetitive stress, and returning to the trail *so soon* would be asking too much of my still-healing tendons. *there is too much to risk and at risk.*
it would be unfair to do just that again: to repeatedly stress my tendons through the repetitive movement of backpacking.

i will attempt to hike the great divide trail again next year, picking up where i left off.

in the meantime, *how will i salvage some form of something?*

rehab is not quite as simple as "just riding a bike" . . .

———

i suddenly live in a world of axioms, aphorisms, and maxims: *four wheels move your body, two wheels move your soul* . . .

i buy a car.

i return to the rockies, *"solo."*

with me, i bring the stationary bike.

> *if the plan doesn't work, change the plan,*
> *but never the goal . . .*

my hike-to-bike rehab suddenly becomes an inspired, *and inspiring,* piece of public performance art.

i bring my backpack along too. but i will wait to don it until one significant date on the calendar: september 19.

three years ago, on september 19, 2020, i marked the sixteen-week anniversary of my initial leg-shattering injury by donning my backpack and crookedly setting out—at a similarly slow pace as i am presently pacing—with the goal to eventually reach the world-famous berg lake at the foot of mount robson, the tallest mountain in the canadian rockies and originally a part of the great divide trail. my first night's stay was seven flat kilometres away with little more than 150-plus metres of elevation gain. it took me over four hours to get there. *but i did.* it took me six days in total to reach berg lake and back. *but i did.* the cumulative distance of a marathon: a full day for an "average" thru-hiker or, at the time, a marathon-of-meaning for your not-so-average, rehabilitating long-distance walker. *this* is when exhausted, overwhelmed, triumphant tears did fall.

and then, on september 19, 2023—nine weeks after being plucked off the great divide—i, *again,* ceremoniously sling my backpack onto shoulders that have tattooed between them the word *improvise . . .*

and, again, *smiling,* i set off, *slowly,* invoking edward abbey's blessing:

> *May your trails be crooked, winding, lonesome, dangerous,*

*leading to the most amazing view. May your mountains rise
into and above the clouds.*

❤

BRONWYN PREECE (SHE/HER)

Whistler, British Columbia, Canada—traditional territory of the Lil'wat and Squamish Nations

Bronwyn is an avid solo backpacker, a "backcountry poet," and a community-based arts practitioner. She holds a PhD in performance and an MA and BFA in applied theatre. Previous publications include *knee deep in high water : riding the Muskwa-Kechika, expedition poems* (Caitlin Press, 2023); *Sea to Sky Alphabet* (Simply Read Books, 2023); *Gulf Islands Alphabet* (Simply Read Books, 2012). Forthcoming books include *hiking beyond...* (Caitlin Press, TBC) and this story will appear in part in Hiking Thru Divides: Solo Along the Spine of the Rockies (Caitlin Press, TBC). She loves sending handwritten letters and is eager to see more female-authored narratives entering the outdoor literature canon.

She can be found on Instagram @poetichiker.

---

1. inReach message received from my daughter.
2. inReach message excerpts from 911 Alberta Health dispatch.
3. inReach message excerpts from EMS dispatch.
4. "Canada's Great Divide Trail," The Great Divide Trail Association, https://great dividetrail.com/page/7/.
5. "Discover the GDT," The Great Divide Trail Association, https://greatdividetrail. com/discover-the-gdt/.

pace of resilience

I was as ready to fail as I was ready to succeed.

At 10:03 p.m. I stood on the sidewalk outside the Appalachian Trail-er, my toes kissing an AT symbol, and started my watch. I headed down the quiet main street of Hot Springs, North Carolina, under the light of streetlamps. I was soon climbing out of the summer humidity and into the mountains.

I moved at a strong pace across the first ridgeline and over Big Butt Mountain, trying to ignore the familiar tension in my low back. I slipped and fell twice that first night in the darkness. As the initial pain of slamming against the rocks decreased, I checked myself for blood and injuries, my whole body shaking from the trauma. I needed to be more careful, smarter, calmer. I had a long way to go.

Before I began my record-setting attempt on the recently established, 340-mile Appalachian High Route (AHR), I considered my goals clear. My intention was to test myself and explore my limits. I wanted it to be a great adventure. I wanted to complete the route. I hoped I could put down a serious time (under six days) that might hold up, at least for a bit. I balanced both a tangible fear and a realistic acceptance that I may not actually be able to meet my goals. I was open to the possibility of failure. As long as I did my best, I would be okay with it.

It had been seven months since I had a total hysterectomy. I finally had relief after ten years of chronic pain, misdiagnoses, unexplained symptoms, and self-doubt. I had run through all of it, finding that my body withstood longer distances at slower paces best. The challenges of running ultra distances had never outweighed the challenges of getting answers about my own body.

After surgery, I took my doctor's advice and eased back into running cautiously. Fifteen weeks post-op, I stood on the podium at my third 50K in as many months. Another few months and I was crossing the finish line in first place at a dream race, the Old Dominion 100-miler.

Since being open on the operating table, having my most problematic parts fully excised, I had performed well. I was becoming more confident, but still carried the fear of my body failing me again.

The AHR loop connects the Appalachian Trail, the Mountains-to-Sea Trail (MST), and the Black Mountain Crest Trail (BMCT) using the Burnsville Connector. The route also provides access to most of the 6,000-foot peaks in the Appalachian Mountains.

The sun rose and I continued on through midafternoon, completing the initial fifty-eight-mile segment of the AT and beginning the Burnsville Connector, a newly mapped linkup of single-track trail, Forest Service roads, and secondary roads. I trod through the mess of poorly maintained trail segments. Unstable rocks on a steep grade threatened to twist my ankles as I navigated through many downed trees. Fear, anger, and frustration bubbled up. I tried not to slide off the trail into the unknown below.

Once I reached the other side of the connector, I took a one-hour nap before pounding the pavement for twenty-odd miles through Burnsville, North Carolina. As I neared the end of day one with eighty-seven miles in twenty-six hours, the ache in my feet deepened to a burning throb. I lay down to rest at midnight.

Three hours later, I began the BMCT and climbed through daybreak, though I remained in thick cloud cover on Mount Mitchell. The vibrant greens of grass and treetops contrasted with the sea of white that boxed me in.

My muscles quivered on the steep, rocky ascent. My determination battled the part of me that begged to stop. It was far too early for that kind of thinking, though. I knew I could handle this climb and so much more. I wasn't even close to my limit. I'd dealt with far greater discomfort and fatigue in the past. Before the hysterectomy, I ran with chronic pain—and I always managed to push through. When my paces had grown slower and my symptoms progressively harder to manage, I may have questioned my abilities as an athlete, but I never quit. I adjusted my goals.

After crossing the parking lot at the top of Mount Mitchell, I began the descent, now on the MST. The exhaustion was heavy. The sun had broken through that gray cloud cover, creating a glitter all around me. A calm breeze blew across my body, cooling my sweat. Tall grass along the trail invited me to lie down and fall into a deep sleep.

Soon dark clouds covered the sun, releasing an afternoon thunderstorm. The massage of raindrops on my exposed skin energized my dragging body. I began to run again, moving fluidly over the rocks and roots. Hours later, I completed my goal for the day—51.2 miles—and was treated to three hours of rest in the back of my crew leader's van, Pegasus.

I should have been sleeping, but instead I writhed in discomfort. My stomach ached and burned, my elevated feet throbbed, and my thoughts looped on the detriment of lying awake during the short window allotted for rest. Before I knew it, it was time to hike on. I forced myself to eat some chocolate cake with peanut butter and drink the rest of a milkshake. Although not great choices for my stomach, it was easy fuel—rich with calories and fat. And as a bonus, it required very little chewing.

I struggled through the third day. My stomach burned despite my attempts to manage it through nutrition, hydration, Pepto-Bismol, and ginger chews. By lunchtime, I was dry heaving between eating, anytime my stomach felt empty. I was determined to stick to the "A" goal mileage plan and snap out of this low. I pushed as hard as I could, but I was beginning to break emotionally. Cruel thoughts stole my confidence. My body reflected my mind and I moved with hunched shoulders. My whining increased tenfold, broken up by heavy breaths. I couldn't let myself give in to the discomfort.

I started running and pushing harder; I had something to prove. I needed to pull myself together—that's what a real athlete would do. The ever-twisting, ever-turning, ever-climbing trail had other ideas. I couldn't go any faster than I already was. I lost the trail at the top of the mountain. During the tedious and demoralizing process of searching for the last marker I'd seen, my drive fizzled.

I cried out loud to the trail: "What is wrong with me? Who do I think I am?"

There was no record to beat—the trail was new—so I'd be establishing the first mark. My goal was just a list of numbers I had dreamed up and typed on a page. Right as I should have been finding my groove, I was lost and backtracking to find the route. I saw my "A" plan slipping out of my grasp.

Before my surgery, I'd found long multiday runs to be the best for managing my symptoms. In the first hours of a run, pain and muscle spasms would wrap through my lower back and pelvis and not let go. Over many multiday adventures, I learned that the spasms always lessened by the third day. That's when I would hit my stride. Now, without the pain and spasms, I felt that I should be better, that I should be more capable. I had no excuse to quit.

I completed the third day's miles by digging deep into the night. I hadn't broken yet, not my body nor my mind. My spirit had taken the shakedown, though. My friends welcomed me into Haywood Gap at the end of the day. There I could sleep for a few hours, enough time to erase the fear and imposter syndrome from my mind, at least until tomorrow.

At three o'clock, I packed up with lots of food and put my headphones on. I started my day listening to "Higher Love" by Whitney Houston. I was intent on having a *really* good day. My legs felt strong. I danced and sang up the trail into the sunshine like a fool. I was in a full-blown runner's high. I paused long enough to snap photos of the flowers, the views, and even some goofy selfies.

The rest of that day I would be on gravel and paved roads up to

Waterrock Knob and then down into Cherokee, Tennessee. I kept on dancing despite the increasing pain in my feet and waves of severe fatigue. It took effort to hold on to the joy, to focus on the beauty and not to dwell on the discomforts, but I wasn't going to let my good-day energy escape.

Just as darkness fell, the rain rolled in, beginning as a light sprinkle that progressively built into a cold downpour. My feet screamed in pain from the twenty miles of paved and gravel roads behind them. The rain soaking into my shoes was almost a relief against my hot, swollen soles. I felt a single blister on the ball of my left foot open up. Now the dull aching and throbbing was accompanied by a sharp stinging. I searched for comfort and instead stumbled through a mental catalog of pain. A year ago, I was one month away from completing a several-year-long endeavor to run the entire AT in segments. I had been fighting a fairly serious dental infection, and then my mother was diagnosed with breast cancer. The combined stressors led to one of my worst "acute on chronic" flares of pelvic pain. I finally waved my white flag and accepted the referral to see a pelvic pain specialist. After years of medical appointments, I had mostly given up on finding relief. This specialist was different from the handful I'd seen prior. He reviewed my case thoroughly and recommended a total hysterectomy. Surgery was a big deal, and a radical suggestion compared to the solutions—or lack thereof—I had been offered in the past. After some consideration of the long-term risks and side effects, I allowed myself to indulge the promise of a less painful existence. And his promises had come true. On my Fastest Known Time (FKT) attempt, I was grateful that the pain I was choosing to exert on myself was the only one I faced.

There I was sobbing in the dark, shuffling down the road in torrential rain. At my first opportunity, I stopped to fix my foot. I removed the tape from the open blister, examining the pale, wrinkled skin and the newly exposed raw, pink flesh. I dried the area and applied fresh moleskin before pulling on a dry sock and then my wet shoe. I drew from harder experiences, and I continued on to finish out the day, stopping only 1.3 miles short of my "A" goal.

The next morning, three hours later, I began the twenty-one-mile section that would end on top of Clingmans Dome after nearly 5,000 feet of climbing. It was all "downhill" from there, and I would be on a familiar trail for the homestretch back to Hot Springs. The rain started again in the early morning and proceeded to pour down. The lightning flashed around me like a crowd of paparazzi—my moment of fame. I walked through flowing water, placing my feet purposefully on or between the rocks and roots so as to keep my ragged feet from experiencing any more damage from slipping or sliding in the water and mud.

When the rain ceased, I emerged, soaked through and dripping, at the edge of a surging, swollen creek. The trail led directly into the tumultuous water. I scanned the other side and could not see where the trail picked back up. I had to trust it was there. Just as each next step for my body in this journey is unknown, so was the trail in that moment. I climbed up onto a slippery downed tree and walked slowly and carefully across. Not until I'd made it to the other side did I find the trail.

I crossed the creek twice more, but never as treacherously as that first time. Mostly the trail ran alongside the creek through deep mud and across slippery rocks. It was challenging but thrilling. I was enjoying myself. Eventually, though, I began to climb, to really ascend. I was nearly finished with the MST. During this final long ascent, I felt my body shift. I was depleted on almost every level: deficient in calories, electrolytes, sleep, and drive. I wasn't afraid, though. I was too tired for fear.

After four miles of climbing, I marched around Clingmans Dome and then rejoined the AT. With only seventy-five miles left, I was beginning to truly suffer. Either I'd lost the mental control to stave it off or the pain had grown to a level that couldn't be quieted by grit alone. I didn't know. I was sleepy, I was in pain, and I felt weak. I felt so out of it that I lagged behind my friends, letting them pull me through this section. I was delirious with fatigue, existing in a whole other dimension.

I took to the pavement and slept for sixty minutes in the parking lot at Newfound Gap. When I awoke, I stared up at the sky and noticed specks in my vision, like seeing stars. Beyond those specks, the clouds were shapeshifting into glorious works of art. A dancer twirled and a lioness and her cub played together. It was strange and miraculous, the only visual hallucinations I'd ever experienced.

Only a few minutes later I realized my feet needed significantly more work if I was going to do these last sixty-seven miles. I carefully removed the tape, most of which was placed to prevent blisters. The piece around the ball of my left foot where the open silver-dollar-sized blister was required extreme caution. The macerated skin was at risk of peeling right off with the tape. I let my feet air-dry as I ate, packed, and massaged and prepared my body. Finally, I applied fresh tape to the hot spots, with added cushions of moleskin to the blister, before pulling my socks up and then my wet shoes back on. I was still gunning to come in just under six days. The closer I got, the higher the internal pressures and fear mounted.

I don't think I made it a half mile into the next segment before I was crying. This thirty-one-mile section had no access to aid. The rocky trail was cold and hard. My brain reeled. I couldn't find anything positive to latch onto with the pain and fatigue I was feeling. I couldn't dig any deeper. For the next twelve hours I bartered with myself and my friend, and pacer, for every step.

I had been in some level of constant pain for nearly a decade, and in the same way that pain had torn at me, so did this foot pain. It made me feel hopeless and incapable. The fatigue gripped me, choking my drive to walk forward. My brain longed to shut off and slip into a state of unconsciousness. I was momentarily blacking out mid-stride and losing precious time. I took a series of naps, each three minutes in length. I slipped off the trail once and fell over a few times as my brain grappled with why it was still being dragged through this. The long descent to Davenport Gap scared me.

By the time I arrived at the gap, I was swimming in disappointment at my performance during the thirty-one-mile section. I started to feel that finishing under six days had become impossible. If I could move well going forward, I could still do it, but the idea of moving at all caused hot, heavy tears to roll down my cheeks. I needed to pull myself together.

I thought that after the struggle to stay awake, I would fall asleep instantly when I lay down. After a few minutes of horizontal sobbing, I decided that I was just wasting time. When I climbed back out of the van, my knees and hips cried out, each louder than the other. I let out a sharp, guttural cry like a suffering animal. I was miserable, but standing. It was only two miles of easy trail to the next waypoint. I grimaced and groaned, and my conscious mind flickered in and out. I couldn't go on like this.

This time, I fell asleep hard and fast. Luckily, I woke after only an hour. The stabbing forefront of my pain had settled somewhere deep in my bones. The fifteen miles passed slowly, but the hours flew by. It was getting toward sunset when we reached one of my favorite places on the AT, Max Patch. I crested the top of the wildflower-coated overlook where I could see forever into the distance, the trail winding across the grassy bald and back into the forest like a painting, but better. Reaching this point felt significant. I had traveled this path before and knew the way.

As we began to descend from Max Patch, I broke into a run and continued to press forward as hard as I could. My focus returned to the goal of completion. I was so close. I hustled the last fifteen miles, fueled by much too much caffeine, mini croissants, and cinnamon butter until I crossed the pink-ribbon finish line that my crew held up for me across the sidewalk exactly where I'd started six days, one hour, and forty minutes earlier.

I finished, falling slightly short of my sub-six-day goal, but it was far from a failure. It was an outstanding adventure where I learned about accepting and trusting myself. My body didn't fail me, not even close. In fact, I am extremely capable. I am strong, gritty, and determined. I can do hard things and I know myself. I am hardened by the past, but instead of this preventing me from pushing myself, it fuels my passion to explore my limits.

———

MEG LANDYMORE (SHE/HER)

Pasadena, Maryland—traditional territory of the Susquehannock and Piscataway peoples

Meg is an ultrarunner, a wife, a mom of two, a military veteran, a small business owner, a physician assistant, and an ultrarunning coach. She holds an MS in physician assistant studies. She has set course records and podiumed at a number of races from 50K up, and she has set fastest known times (FKTs) on the 144-mile Double SCAR and the 345-mile Appalachian High Route. While she has seen tremendous success with ultrarunning, she has also experienced failure, injury, medical complications, and chronic pain. She believes we should live in a world where women can share stories and resources to be able to find answers, as well as connection.

She can be found on Instagram @mostXtremegirl_adventures and at www.mxgadventures.com.

TEARS

let's be gray

I KNEW THE TREES AT BURNT MILLS WEST PARK HAD heard people crying before, but I don't think they had ever heard the guttural, primal sounds coming from my mouth. I couldn't breathe, I couldn't control my thoughts, I couldn't move. Tears spilled like a kettle boiling over. If someone heard me, they probably thought I had broken my leg. But it was only my heart.

He kept texting me, asking if I hated him. He hoped I didn't. *How's your state?* A playful text we used to share. He lived in Virginia, and I in Maryland—separated only by the Potomac River and forty-five minutes on the Beltway. No, I was wrong; there was more than that separating us.

He had broken up with me two days prior to this hike. I thought he was wrong to break up with me. Not because I thought I was hot shit or anything, but we both knew this relationship was something to hold on to. He was moving to Colorado and said that breaking up would make things easier—he would be a bad long-distance boyfriend. I knew that was fear talking.

The bare trees at Burnt Mills consoled me while I ignored his pleas. I didn't understand why he refused to cut things clean when he was the one who had ended things.

Later that night, we talked for two hours. He called again the next night and the next. We talked about everything: how I was doing, how much I missed his dogs, something AOC had recently said.

Eventually, I mustered enough courage to talk about us.

I said to him, "Let's be gray. No titles. Just gray."

As those words left my mouth, I wanted to reel them right back in.

I didn't want to be gray. I am a black-and-white girl. I wanted to be someone's partner, and I wanted someone to be my partner. Yet, I didn't want to lose him—the first person who made me feel safe and seen. I wanted us to work. I knew I needed to fight for us. I needed to compromise for us. But I hated that I had downgraded myself.

"Yes," he said.

We were together, apart—in a relationship without the pressure of calling it one.

———

WE HAD ALWAYS SHARED a love of hiking. The bluebells had peaked around us earlier that spring in Virginia. The greenery poked through—like our new love finding room to grow—around the Potomac after a cold and dreary winter. I had loved following him through the trees, jumping over mud, exploring new trails. He had dragged me away from the hustle and bustle of Washington, DC, and out into the real world. He had reminded me to turn off my phone and play.

In our newfound grayness, I flew from DC to Steamboat Springs to visit him. I was giddy and fucking nervous. Not only was this the first time I had traveled for a guy, but I didn't know the rules of being gray. Is flying halfway across the country to be with someone gray? Is meeting someone's family for the first time gray?

I'd always been a solo traveler, seeking wild adventures and epic stories. This time a man was the adventure I wanted to be on. A first for me.

Less than forty-eight hours after I landed, we were hiking Hahns Peak with his mom. I kept one eye on the 10,839-foot summit and one eye on her throughout the hike. I had never felt such pressure not to make an ass of myself.

Near the summit, my head began to feel like a pressure cooker slowly building up. My already slow pace grew slower. I stared blankly ahead, forgetting to watch his mom for signs of approval or disapproval. They stopped so I could catch up. We all stood there while he fed me food, water, and Gatorade, to the point I told him if he gave me one more thing, I would throw up from that instead of the altitude.

They both asked if I wanted to turn back. I looked up to the summit; we were so close. As much as I felt like shit, I would feel even worse if we didn't finish. They had done this hike a million times, so it wasn't a big deal to them, but it mattered to me.

I gathered myself, took a deep breath, and pressed on.

When we finally reached the summit, I only wanted to jump on him and kiss him. Instead, his mom took pictures of us and then disappeared around the fire lookout, leaving us to explore this side of the mountain. White puffy clouds looked like icing on top of the mountains, surrounded by shocking blues and greens. There was a lake sparkling up from below.

On the way back down the mountain, I suggested we slide down a lingering patch of snow like we'd seen other hikers doing. He went first, laughing the whole way down, reminding me of all the joyful moments we had shared back before we were gray.

I followed after, losing control and sliding sideways down the snow until I landed at his feet. We laughed so hard that I thought I might pee my pants. *This* was the feeling I had longed for. For a moment, I felt at peace with what we had.

———

THE NEXT DAY, we got a late start to camp in Mount Zirkel Wilderness. After his mom went to her tent, we sat in cozy closeness by the crackling fire. He'd never been much of a talker, but tonight, he was getting going. I could hear the passion behind his words, see the wheels turning in his head. That little smirk he always gave when he had a point to make was driving me crazy.

As I watched his eyes light up, the words became muffled, and my ears became fuzzy.

Love.

Under a bright moon in the wilderness of Colorado, I realized I'd fallen completely in love. One voice screamed for me to climb into his lap beside that campfire and tell him how I felt. The other, saner voice calmly replied, *Do not, under any circumstances, do that.* If he knew I was in love, this would be over before we could walk the five miles back to his car. I kept those words in my head where they belonged.

In the tent that night, I shivered inside my sleeping bag. I was bundled up in yoga pants, a tank top, his fleece hoody, and a jacket. He kept telling me to lose layers—that the sleeping bag would warm me up faster if I wore less. I thought he was fucking nuts and told him so.

Between his sleeping bag and his tender body spooning me in his sleeping bag, I finally warmed up enough to remove his jacket. Slowly but surely, the layers came off. He was right; I was warming up. I turned to face him. His dark brown eyes took me in, putting me at ease as tender warm kisses started. Things progressed quickly and quietly, as we tried to be mindful of the others camping nearby. Everything about that night felt pretty black-and-white to me.

What is gray, if not a mixture of black and white?

The next day at my first alpine lake, he pulled me in to take a selfie, wrapping his hand tightly around my waist. I rested my head on his chest. We'd done this before, but now it felt different because I had a secret. I was in love with him.

———

A FEW DAYS LATER, I returned to the reality of DC—a terrible commute to and from a job that needed to be more fulfilling. I longed to return to the wilderness and escape the drama. Instead, I walked on eggshells every time we spoke. I was watchful of my words because I didn't want him to know about my secret.

A few months later, he asked, "Would you still speak to me if we broke up again?"

I told him, "I would need space to figure out how to fall out of ..."

On an October night, we were no longer gray. He was black, and I was white. I had thought I was heartbroken in May, but this was a new level. I regretted ever asking to be gray. I was pissed at myself as much as at him. I should have let us go before.

He returned to the DC area a few weeks later to visit his family. With some hesitation on both sides, we agreed to see each other. After three minutes of hurt and hate, it was like we were back together that whole weekend. But it was temporary, like our entire relationship.

He had told me before that he had to end things because he was falling in love. After all, this was temporary. I had asked if *I* was just temporary. He had said no, just the relationship. It would never work once he moved away. I'd always taken issue with that. How can you decide to end a relationship with someone you love because it is only temporary? Who gets to decide something is temporary anyway?

Things got worse after that visit. Once again, I found myself in the woods as he texted me that he had started seeing someone new. It had been less than two weeks, and he was with another woman. My only solace when reading that text was the fallen tree I collapsed onto, as well as those still standing who witnessed my tears. In stark contrast to the tumult of our relationship, the log was steady, predictable, and already clearly dead.

———

TIME WENT ON, and a pandemic happened. I was jealous, hurt, mad, and depressed. This was my first heartbreak, and adding the confinement and solitude of a pandemic magnified it. I needed to travel, return to my solo adventures, and remember who I had been before him. Instead, I stayed—locked not just in my apartment but also in my heartache.

All I could do initially was practice yoga, drink, and sleep. I kept myself busy and numb so the days would end and night could come. That was the only time I didn't hurt.

I decided to hit the trails since my options were otherwise limited during the pandemic. I asked anyone I could to hike with me. I didn't want to be alone; I needed a distraction. Occasionally I had someone, but often it was just me. I hiked and hiked. I even ran a few times, which I hadn't done in years. One day, I ran six miles because I couldn't get out of my own head. I couldn't stop the memories of us from flooding in. My body hurt that night from the running, but at least for a moment, I had stopped thinking of him. Then the pain in my body reminded me of the pain in my heart that made me run in the first place. I hated him even more. But I blamed myself.

On social media, I saw him out exploring. Everywhere he went, I decided I would never go. Why would I want to hike to Delicate Arch or Dead Horse Point State Park, knowing my feet were exactly where he had been with another woman? I felt deflated and hurt seeing them do everything I wanted to do with him. He was the adventure I wanted to be on, and she was better at it than I was.

To heal from the heartbreak, I did what any heartbroken girl would do: I upgraded my gear and joined the fifty-two-week hike challenge, committing to hiking once a week for a year.

I wouldn't stop at one hike each week, though. I poured myself onto the trails, hiking four or five days a week. I took short local hikes after work, and then every weekend I traveled the states of Maryland and Virginia in search of new trails. Deep down, I thought that if I hiked enough, I could win him back somehow. Sad, I know, because he had already moved on, forgotten me. But I was so in my head about the woman he was with that I couldn't stop comparing myself to her and trying to keep up. I spent all my time working out, hiking, paddle boarding, anything to get in better shape and get myself out of the rabbit hole I was stuck in. My friends thought I was going to extremes, but I didn't know any other way.

He had once said to me, "Just do your own thing. People will respect you more, and you will be happier, I think. Being a follower is lame." But I'd always been a follower. Trying to be who people wanted me to be was like a second job. I didn't know who I was until a few months before meeting him. I had started to do these little date nights with myself: cooking, reading on a Friday night, and taking myself to new places to figure out who I was when nobody was around. That had started to fade as soon as we met. When we were together, I liked who I was. I thought *this* was the person I was supposed to be—less uptight, more adventurous, lighter, secure.

But he had taken all of that away. Our fights, the harsh things he said, my jealousy—they shaped the way I saw myself. I wasn't trying to do my own thing; it was all a performance. I had slipped back into my old antics, trying to prove my worth to someone else.

See, I can have my own adventures!
I can hike too.
I can be like her too.

I had wanted to hike my problems, feelings, and everything else away. I've always liked to escape when life gets hard. To escape a place, a job, or a person is a way to escape myself. To play at a happier, more playful version of myself—one that is more at ease.

The following October, a year after we broke up, I took a road trip from Denver to Moab. I was ready to stop being a brat and go to places I knew belonged as much to me as to anyone else. On the edge of a cliff at Dead Horse Point State Park, I stood 2,000 feet above the Colorado River. I looked out to the emptiness of the canyon. In the vast opening, I felt seen for the first time in a year. The canyon reflected the emptiness I had felt so deep within myself. I was exposed on this ledge, visible from all directions. I started to tear up. I wanted so badly to be seen. The emptiness of the canyon was layers of sand and rock, purple and red and brown. The emptiness made room for depth, space, mystery, discovery, and the raging river far below. Emptiness was a beautiful thing, and it was every color but gray.

I did things I swore I would never do and saw places I promised to never see during that trip. I didn't follow in their footsteps, hiking twenty miles and backcountry camping. I didn't need to. I made my own way on the trails and treated them better than the ones I'd left back in Maryland. I camped solo for the first time, surviving forty-mile-per-hour winds, and in doing so, I found a little bit of myself again. I don't know that I found the self I'd lost in him; I believe I found a newer version of myself. I started to heal. No longer the sad girl, the girl who was always punishing herself and trying to win him back, I began to have a different relationship with being on the trail. I smiled. I enjoyed myself.

Since then, I have stood at the base of red rocks, among the twinkling leaves of yellow aspens, and beneath endless blue skies. As color reappeared, I started understanding why the universe had broken me down. It was to show me that I could live the life I had been too afraid to pursue before. Now, when I hike my local trails around DC, I see the past version of myself, crying in the trees.

The pain in her eyes turns to a flicker of hope when I tell her: *You aren't fucking gray anymore.*

————

BELINDA ARNDT (SHE/HER)

Washington, DC—traditional territory of the Piscataway and Nacotchtank peoples

Belinda is a solo traveler who is happiest at the ocean, or out West. She holds an MA in public affairs. She feels most at home on the trails, where her wildness is accepted, and she can be her whole self. She has found that the outdoors has taught her that her problems aren't as big as she thinks they are, and that everything will work out, even if not in the ways she expected. She knows that sharing our stories is how we spread knowledge and connection.

She can be found on Instagram and Facebook @Wandering_bel and at www.wanderingbel.com.

my mother's mountain

BECAUSE THERE ARE NO MOUNTAINS, I'D SAY. THIS WAS MY answer whenever my mother asked why I couldn't move back to my childhood home in Lincoln, Massachusetts, where she and my stepdad still live. Yet ever since I can remember, I've dreamed of a mountain emerging beyond the edges of their lawn at night, erupting like a volcano, its jagged crest splitting the hayfields, the wetlands, and the soft forest floors, its summit rising toward the sky until ice crusted over the very top.

There had once been giant peaks in these lowlands, I knew. As a mountain-loving child, I'd paced the surrounding woods, searching for long-lost summits, noting the traces of bygone ice age glaciers: the rounded swells, low ridgelines, and watery hollows left by their retreat, the lines their debris had scratched across the rocks, like the marks of dragons' claws.

Traces of absence and of longing.

I'll build you a mountain, my mother would say, and she always sounded serious. Anything that would tempt at least one of her daughters to stay home.

———

ALL THROUGH MY CHILDHOOD, my mother devised local adventures for my younger sister and me. At night, we'd hike through shadowed woods to skate across the moonlit shimmer of a frozen pond. Or else we'd stumble down steep hills toward the murky edge of wetlands to hear the loud chorus of spring frogs. But it was the long road trips north or west with her or with my father that haunted me: how the seemingly endless sprawls of strip malls and subdivisions dissolved back into open fields and dense forests as we left eastern Massachusetts; how narrow paths entangled with roots and boulders led to the cold, misty air of granite summits; how a summer snowfield flashed against lupine and paintbrush flowers or how a glacial lake turned a strange and incandescent turquoise. Everything hinted at otherworlds infused with something nameless, radiant, essential.

However it happened, my sister and I were both infected with a yearning for heights. I left Massachusetts as soon as I could, near the start of the new millennium, seeking work as a teacher, a journalist, or an editor in places like Mongolia, Wyoming, Montana, and Vermont where an abundance of summits rippled above the valleys and the plains. My sister, in turn, headed to New Hampshire, Washington State, and finally California, where she became a professor and a writer, often spending weekends amid the sunlit granite domes or deep winter snows of the Sierra Nevada. There, she and her husband taught their young children to hike and ski, just as our parents had taught us.

Each time our mother came to visit, she scurried along trails and sprang from rock to rock, her own pace quickened by desire. She loved mountains, too, only she could never stay near them for long. She had her home in the Massachusetts town next to the one where she'd grown up, her childhood friends who lived close by. She had the retirement life that she and my stepdad, Russ, had grown accustomed to: the set of routines, quasi-mysterious to me, that included a vegetable garden, birdfeeders, yard work, book clubs, social events, house projects, responsibilities to local friends and family members— and with all that, a sense of rootedness I'd never felt myself.

So I began to send my mother almost daily photos of the trails I ran, the mountains I skied, the cliffs I climbed: the crimson light of sunset that shone through curtains of suspended ice; the white feathers of rime that sparkled on branches bent like giant wings; the translucent layers of ridgelines that faded to a pale horizon pink. Evidence of reasons to roam.

———

WHEN COVID-19 ARRIVED IN 2020, I found myself sheltering in place in a house that belonged to one of my mother's friends, on the edge of the Bangtail Mountains of Montana, enclosed by fir glades and deep snow. On leave from my editing job in Vermont, I'd traveled there to finish the rough draft of my first book. As the pandemic and the quarantines continued, my planned two-month stay stretched on to six. Unable to venture far from the house, I found my topic—the history of imaginary peaks—increasingly apt.

During the days, I perched in a small, high study, gazing out the window, from time to time, at countless snow-lit peaks above vast plains. I read story after story of the centuries of myths and hoaxes, cartographic errors and persistent fantasies that had once created phantom summits on maps around the world. I wrote about the traces left behind whenever their existence was disproven, of irradicable yearnings for something beyond measurement or sight. During the evenings, I wandered the nearby mountainsides alone, at first on skis across the silent drifts and later on foot along the emptied trails, through meadows bright with glacier lilies. I watched the rays of sunset flicker in and out of the Bridger Mountains to the west, creating a daily magic lantern show. Ever-shifting hues of crimson and violet enchanted the other ranges that rose in all directions. One faraway mountain, higher than its neighbors, became the focal point of my longing. Its summit was shaped like a giant crystal; its facets blazed with alpenglow. It seemed improbable and unearthly, like the peak I'd dreamed of in childhood.

Yet by the time the lockdowns eased, I didn't want to climb it anymore. While reading *A Field Guide to Getting Lost*, I had come across Rebecca Solnit's description of "the blue at the far edge of what can be seen. . . . The color of where you can never go. For the blue is not in the place those miles away at the horizon, but in the atmospheric distance between you and the mountains." The summit that entranced me, I'd realized, was one I could never reach: tinted with the haze and fantasy of distance and desire.

Meanwhile, restless as well, my mother had begun roaming ever more extensively near her house, seeking out each acre of undeveloped forest, wetland, and field along the borders of Lincoln and Concord, looking for neighborhood walks that she'd never done before. Over phone and email, she shared encounters with unfamiliar bogs and forgotten groves. Searching for more than she could find on modern maps, she used the books and journals of the local nineteenth-century philosopher Henry David Thoreau as a guide to patches of wild that lingered beyond the houses and the lawns. These places were already shrinking in his day, yet still full of wonders vaster than their size.

Many people, Thoreau asserted, know even less about their backyards than the European explorers did about the remote islands they claimed to have discovered, though such regions were long inhabited (and well-known) by Indigenous residents.[1] Moments of transfiguration haunt his prose, when the miniature becomes the infinite, the inner world exchanges places with the outer one, reality unveils itself as mythology. He described how White Pond and Walden Pond transformed under bright sun into "great crystals" and "Lakes of Light."[2] His ascent of a white pine, in springtime, opened up views of faraway blue summits to the north and west, mountains that he'd never glimpsed before, "so much more of the earth and the heavens."[3] The tiny red blooms of the pine flowers, glittering from its high branches, awakened as much awe as fallen stars.

Often, he imagined himself wandering along the thresholds of some other land hidden within the borders of the town, until the maps he made as a local surveyor dissolved like dim lines on a pane of glass, revealing an indescribable vision.[4] All it took, apparently, was a more attentive gaze, a more open mind, to find something like enchantment—a practice at which my mother, it seemed, was becoming increasingly adept.

In August 2020, my leave over, I returned to my job in Vermont, but I was haunted by the pandemic deaths of so many of my parents' generation, and after the state quarantines ended in 2021, I drove south more often to visit my mother and stepdad in Massachusetts. There, she guided me to a few of the places she loved: the quiet corridors of trails under the shadows of white pines; a steep hillside where my feet slipped on fallen oak and maple leaves, slick and deep as alpine snowdrifts; kettle ponds that glowed turquoise like the ghosts of lost glacier lakes. There was more to my hometown woods than I'd thought, but I still didn't feel as much wonder as she did: there were still no mountains, only their memory and our imaginations.

That November, at age seventy-five, my mother had a stroke that left part of her face and one thumb without feeling. Within a short time, she learned to compensate for the unusable finger by tying her shoelaces with an elaborate shuffle of her hands. She soon appeared mostly well again. It was as if nothing serious had happened, yet everything had. Our family returned, for the most part, to our usual lives, but with a new, latent dread. We couldn't ignore what this was: *a warning sign.*

————

IN OCTOBER 2022, I moved to Colorado to work on a second book, still pursuing the idea of ice-coated peaks, as alluring as a flash of sunset along the horizon. *Could you do something more practical?* people started to ask me, with genuine curiosity, now that I was in my mid-forties. Yet I'd come to realize that after a certain point, it's harder to settle down than to keep moving. It seemed far too late for me to attempt to go to business or medical school or try to enter some corporate track or steady trade—or whatever might count as practical in our precarious time. Over the years, I'd become too obsessed with writing, teaching, and editing to quit. And I was already on a path of sorts: an unstable literary life. In its increasing uncertainty, I knew I'd continue going wherever the next promising opportunity emerged. Still, I was starting to hope, as I got older, that one of these jobs, eventually, would lead to more security, and to a place I could call home.

I stopped by my mother's home along the way. On our last walk of the visit, we passed by a junction where another trail led to Mount Misery, a mere ripple of earth, just 284 feet high, barely distinguishable from the gently rolling woodlands around it, although it retained the designation of "Mt." on modern maps that other local hills had long since shed. We meandered, instead, toward Walden Pond, and somewhere strayed amid the branching of unmarked paths and dirt roads onto a trail she didn't recognize. Through the trees, an unexpected jumble of gray cliffs appeared above us.

I think we should check that out, my mother said. She began clambering uphill directly toward them. I traversed off to the side, following the base of the rock until I noticed a wide rift with scuff marks of previous scramblers' feet. Halfway up, the steep path passed over bulging stones that had to be climbed. Above the cliffs, I found myself standing on a slab of bare granite, like a mountaintop, gazing out at something rare in this region of dense woods and low hills—a view.

A canopy of green leaves, marked here and there by rust and gold, stretched out to the horizon, concealing all signs of houses and roads. And at the very edge appeared a watercolor wash of hills tinted violet and then blue. Pale clouds rose above the last ridgeline, also bluish, like even higher summits. Dusk drifted across the sky in a haze of pink.

I shouted to my mother, urging her to join me. Slowly, intently, she made her way over the bulge, focused on each movement, until we stood side by side, lost in silence and awe.

We'll have to find another way home, my mother eventually said. *I'm not going down the way we went up.*

I'd forgotten how fragile she had become.

Still, she showed no sign of faltering as we began our twilit stumbling through unfamiliar woods. Relying only on her sense of direction, we squinted through the darkening air.

Shouldn't we call Russ? I asked, and then I clarified, *To let him know we'll be late.*

Later, she said, and I knew she meant: *As soon as we know where we are again.*

We'd always been so alike. Neither of us was going to be good at old age. Neither of us wanted to cause worry. Neither of us could let go of our independence or our pride. Neither of us wanted to be assisted or rescued, even if that help just meant my stepdad picking us up from whatever road we reached.

We kept walking, hoping to glimpse, somewhere beyond us, through the dim, a gap in the trees—where the train tracks would emerge, their lines cutting a swath back toward Old Concord Road or where the shimmer of Walden Pond might appear, still reflecting the fading sky.

Eventually, we saw the train tracks and the pond-shimmer. I don't remember, anymore, how long I'd spent wondering where we'd turn up when we hit a road—or wondering, illogically, as the shadows consumed all memory of houses and pavement, whether roads existed here at all. This was eastern Massachusetts, of course. The wilds are so small that *lost* can only ever be a relative and temporary state, more internal than external, as unexpected as an act of grace.

What remains most in my mind is my mother's figure ahead of me on the tracks. The rhythmic clatter of her trekking poles on crushed stones, the determined cadence of her feet, her body straining forward, the faint light of her headlamp, flickering like a star, moving as if alone, deeper into the cobalt black of the night.

———

I'm NOT sure we could ever find that place again. And perhaps we shouldn't try. Later, thinking of that day, I've remembered tales of doors that opened, only once, into otherworlds.

I've wondered how much of the apparent enchantment of that clifftop was formed by the approach of dusk, by the filtering of recollections and desires. How much a place becomes reshaped by the telling of it. Maybe, under different circumstances, we would have seen it as just another scruffy mound of weeds and rocks.

Thoreau, my mother's guide, had dreamed of climbing a peak in Concord, somewhere near the border with Lincoln, "in the easterly part of our town (where no high hill actually is)," he acknowledged in his journals. He described a vision of clambering up its bare stone crest, past stunted trees, until at last he appeared to cross "an imaginary line which separates a hill, mere earth heaped up, from a mountain."[5]

Our clifftop was not his peak: we didn't climb into the "upper air and clouds," as he did, only among clusters of autumn leaves. But we, too, had crossed some indefinable, unexpected line, if largely in our minds. Like him, we'd had to seek another way down. And we also felt that our miniature peak, as he wrote, could "never become familiar; you are lost the moment you set foot there." From the moment we'd left the trail and had begun bushwhacking toward those cliffs, we'd been *lost*, astray from the maps we hadn't brought, from my mother's extensive memory of local geography, and from my own preconceptions about these lowlands and these woods.[6]

Lost to what we'd call the *real* world as well, perhaps. And *lost* in a story we were creating, briefly, with each other.

———

FINDING the mountain in my mother's backyard didn't stop me from continuing out West. I still had a book to write and contract work to fulfill. I still felt that overwhelming yearning for elusive, greater heights.

In an essay, "Walking," Thoreau had evoked other phantom ranges, including the golden cloud peaks that only appeared right before dusk, "those mountain-ridges in the horizon, though they may be of vapor only," lit into being by the last glow of the evening sun. To him, those illusory summits recalled "a sort of terrestrial paradise . . . enveloped in mystery and poetry," a West that might be perceived only in imagination, like the fabled "island of Atlantis," the source of so many mythic lands: of El Dorados, Perditas, and other realms of seemingly unquenchable desire, but also of the Isles of the Blessed, where the wandering spirits of the dead came, at last, to rest.[7]

I was the one leaving again, and yet I couldn't help sensing that my mother had already set out on a journey that was leading her even farther away. Already, she and my stepdad spoke of topics I couldn't fully understand, as if, in aging, they were becoming residents of a distant country: aching backs, knee and hip ailments, heart monitors, unending medical tests.

It could have been worse, we all said about her stroke. *Take care of yourself*, friends and family kept telling her. I reiterated the usual advice that younger people give older ones like a litany of hope: eat well, exercise, talk with your doctor, stay active. As if the words themselves, spoken often enough, could be a spell to keep her safe. *Keep having adventures*, I added, for I knew, more than ever, she needed them to continue feeling alive.

But the unspoken knowledge lingered in our minds that one day, inevitably, something worse would happen.

———

In late October 2022, when my mother and my stepdad visited me in Colorado, she lunged up the trails above Boulder, scarcely pausing as she balanced with her trekking poles on heaped stones or crusted snow. By now, she'd learned ways of tying her shoelaces so skillfully that the signs of her stroke were no longer noticeable at all. We stopped below one of the Flatirons' sandstone slabs, amid drifts of yellow pine needles, winter in the air. She gripped her poles and grinned up at the vast slant of furrowed rock, pointed toward the sky. *We could just scamper up that one, couldn't we?* she said. High above where we now stood, I'd once seen a pair of climbers moving upward like dark birds. I pictured what it might be like to return here, with her, bringing my rope and climbing gear, how she might grip the edges of the stone with fingers that still had all their feeling left.

On the way back, we encountered a group of gray-haired women and exchanged words of appreciation about the weather and the trail. *People just go into the mountains all the time here*, my mother said to me afterward, *don't they? That's just what they do.*

Her wistful tone sounded promising. I reminded her of other retired people we knew who'd moved out West to join their adult children. She spoke gently and vaguely of considering the idea, yet I was aware that she and my stepdad had too much keeping them in place.

Someday, as their health wanes, I might need to return to Massachusetts to take care of them instead.

Soon, they were headed for the airport, back to their friends and other family members, back to the house they'd prepared so carefully for their old age. I felt the shrinking of the time we'd have together on earth, like the shrinking of a wildwood, still unmapped, but no longer unbounded.

I'm so glad you live in a beautiful place, my mother keeps saying ever since that visit. I imagine that I'm hearing a new, sharp edge of longing in her voice. I don't know how much of it is for the mountains and how much of it is for me.

I need to see more of you, I tell her.

You have your own life, she replies.

And so, of course, I realize, does she.

From time to time, as I hike or run on mountain trails, bouts of weeping overcome me: a sense of helplessness at the inability to slow time, an anticipation of future, inconsolable grief. Whatever remains when the sensory and the physical, when what we call the *real*, is gone —the hollows of vanished glaciers across a forest floor, the shadow of a woman striding deeper into night, the echoes of her shoes on a dim railroad bed—it will never feel like enough.

On that October day after she and Russ left for the airport, the sudden loneliness was as cold as a plunge into a glacial lake. Disoriented, I went back to that giant slab of rock she'd liked. Alone, I made my way over its easiest scrambling route, padding up ripples in the ruddy stone, between the pale green lichen and the black. Below me, the air deepened and the treetops became ever-smaller points. Eastward, the forest ended even more quickly than it did at my mother's home. Beyond its fringes, cities and plains stretched to the vanishing point, golden with late-autumn afternoon sun, blending with the mauve haze of smog that veiled the horizon. Massachusetts lay somewhere beyond sight or imagination.

In the other direction, around the corners of Front Range foothills, I could glimpse the fragments of much taller peaks that continued west in sweeps of ever-paler blue toward more tantalizing, invisible summits. I thought about the kind of love that is longing for what always recedes into the distance. It was that love for mountains, which she'd helped teach me, that had driven me to leave my childhood home. And I knew then: I also feel that kind of love, now, for her.

Scenes of this story take place on traditional lands of Indigenous people, including Massachusett, Abenaki, Arapaho, Cheyenne, Ute, Blackfeet, Apsáalooke, Confederated Salish and Kootenai, Očhéthi Šakówiŋ, and other groups. I have discussed similar themes to some of the ones in this essay in my book Imaginary Peaks: The Riesenstein Hoax and Other Mountain Dreams *(Mountaineers Books, 2021).*
—Author

———

KATIE IVES (SHE/THEY)
Boulder, Colorado—traditional territory of the Arapaho, Ute, and Cheyenne peoples

Katie reads about mountains, writes about mountains, edits stories about mountains, and spends most of her free time in the mountains. She has a BA in literature from Harvard and an MFA from the Iowa Writers' Workshop. She also attended the Mountain and Wilderness Writing Program and a Leighton Artist Studio Residency at the Banff Centre—the latter with a Paul D. Fleck Fellowship. Her work has appeared in many publications, including *The New York Times*; *Outside*; *Atlas Obscura*; *Lit Hub*; *Adventure Journal*; *Mountain*

Gazette; *Panorama: The Journal of Travel, Place, and Nature*; and *The Rumpus*. Her short stories have been included in two anthologies, *Rock, Paper, Fire: The Best of Mountain and Wilderness Writing* and *Waymaking: An Anthology of Women's Adventure Writing, Poetry and Art*. Her articles have made the Notable lists for *The Best American Sports Writing* and *The Best American Essays*. She was an editor at *Alpinist* for nearly eighteen years and was the editor-in-chief of the magazine for more than a decade. In 2016, she received the H. Adams Carter Literary Award from the American Alpine Club, and in 2022, her first book, *Imaginary Peaks: The Riesenstein Hoax and Other Mountain Dreams*, received a Special Jury Mention at the Banff Mountain Film and Book Festival. She loves ice climbing, alpine climbing, rock climbing, backcountry skiing, trail running, skate skiing, hiking, and watching the sunset from mountaintops.

She can be found on Instagram @katie_r_ives and on Facebook.

---

1. See Henry David Thoreau's November 23, 1860 journal entry.
2. Described in Thoreau's classic book *Walden*.
3. From Thoreau's essay "Walking," published in *The Atlantic Monthly* in June 1862 about a month after his death
4. See Thoreau's November 10, 1860 journal entry.
5. From Thoreau's October 29, 1857 journal entry.
6. In *A Field Guide to Getting Lost*, Rebecca Solnit writes: "To lose yourself: a voluptuous surrender, lost in your arms, lost to the world, utterly immersed in what is present so that its surroundings fade away. In [Walter] Benjamin's terms, to be lost is to be fully present, and to be fully present is to be capable of being in uncertainty and mystery. And one does not get lost but loses oneself, with the implication that it is a conscious choice, a chosen surrender, a psychic state achievable through geography." And later, she adds: "Lose the whole world, [Henry David Thoreau] asserts, get lost in it, and find your soul."
7. For more on the connection between myths of the West and imaginary lands, see John Logan Allen's *Passage through the Garden*.

nothing to do but go

DECEMBER 2019

Snow fell listlessly outside the window of my bedroom in Portland, blanketing the once-lush garden shrubs just in time for their winter sleep. Though winter had just begun, I already ached to be outside in the sunshine, hiking familiar trails and lazing days away in the remote wilderness, instead of being confined by these claustrophobic walls. The extremely short, dark, dreary winter days in the Pacific Northwest can feel hellish to a brain that battles depression and anxiety. I considered setting a goal for myself that would hopefully keep my head above water as the darkness encroached. Getting outside had helped me keep myself pulled together during previous years, and I figured it would be beneficial to do more of that.

A lot more of it.

I looked back and realized that in 2019 I'd taken about eighty hikes, purely out of a newfound love of the outdoors. I was a late bloomer to outdoor adventure, only discovering the natural world in my mid-twenties when I was forced to go camping entirely against my will for an undergrad biology course. Since then, nature had become a potent salve for the wounds of young adulthood. I had discovered the unbridled freedom of exploring, the confidence that came from navigating the challenges of the trail with only my pup, Charlie, by my side, and a sense of optimism that had long been overshadowed by grief. The mental fog began to lift—and stay lifted—once the outdoors became a consistent part of my life.

Whatever the new calendar had in store for me, I knew I could get through anything with the promise of a fresh year of hiking ahead. The possibilities seemed endless as I wrote "2020: TAKE 100 HIKES" on a page in my notebook and numbered each line 1–100.

Even though I was an experienced hiker with plenty of evidence of the positive impact the outdoors had made on my mental health, the self-defeating thoughts still crept in. As I reflected on the trail of abandoned projects I'd left in my wake over the years, I was overcome by doubt and shame. The intrusive voice of my inner critic had a point. I needed to set myself up for success by defining hiking in a way that made it accessible and achievable even on days when depression and anxiety had something to say about it.

After some contemplation, I wrote: *Hiking means getting outside for a good long walk wherever and whenever we can. No worries about steps, miles, location, or elevation. Just enjoying being outside, discovering amazing things.*

WINTER

On January 1, 2020, I had water, snacks, and a list of possible places to visit. I grabbed Charlie's leash and slid on my hiking boots.

There was nothing to do but go.

I'd planned to head to the coast, one of my favorite places to hike year-round, but it turned out to be an extra-rainy, extra-soggy day across the region. I still drove toward the ocean but stopped halfway there to hike around a local state park that was familiar to me. There would be plenty more chances to explore the craggy cliffs of the Oregon Coast this year. Today I just needed to make good on my promise to *get outside*.

Low-lying clouds shrouded the woods in shimmering mist, wafting between the deep green pine boughs. Discarded oak leaves piled up in drifts around mounds of freshly opened mushroom caps.

The now-naked tree branches revealed clumps of crusty lichens and bedraggled mosses, glowing neon against the olive drab uniform nature dons midwinter. A recent storm had caused a small landslide, scattering fossil-filled rocks across the trail. As I admired the seashell forms on these stones, I imagined I was hiking through the ancient seabed they once knew, envisioning ghosts of extinct trilobites gliding between the ferns and blackberry brambles lining the trail around me. The morning's mist turned to full-on rain and the cold drops on my face broke my reverie, firmly rooting me back in the firmament of the present-day Pacific Northwest.

I hiked four times in January, recording each on my list with a flourish of satisfaction. February brought with it a bone-chilling freeze, a sudden drop-everything-and-leave move into a new apartment, and no time made for even one short hike. Seasonal depression sauntered back into my life, dulling my thoughts, and warping my perspective. Through the haze, my inner critic's voice called to me like a siren: come back to the pit and rest awhile. You know this place well. The darkness is safe.

Still, a beam of reason shone through, reflecting off the diamond-frosted foliage outside my new apartment's window. There was something to look forward to: ten more months of hiking. I vowed that on the first sunny day—and a sunny day *would* come—I would be out on a trail, thawing my brain and my bones from this all too familiar mental freeze.

SPRING

The first weekend of spring, that sunny day I'd longed for finally appeared. Once I had scavenged through messy closets for our camping gear and loaded up the car, Charlie and I set off east with no clear idea of where we'd end up for the night. We drove away from the city into the promise of a few crumbs of sunlight. I'd put on news podcasts for the drive and half listened to voices whispering about how a new virus sweeping the globe could lead to widespread lockdowns. Brushing off the seriousness of the threat with some upbeat music, I sang along and enjoyed the windshield view of pines towering along either side of the road as I drove deeper into the forest, unaware that this would be the last I saw of the free world as we knew it then.

My arrival in the Cascades saw me hiking with Charlie through a subalpine meadow, soaking up the few dazzling beams of sunlight that peeked through thick storm clouds. I walked off months of stagnancy and depression, feeling lighter with each step, blissfully unaware of the pandemic-induced chaos unfolding at the foot of these mountains.

After checking this hike off my list, I found a clearing along a forest road to pitch my tent and wait out the long, cold night. As the temperature hovered around freezing, Charlie and I squirreled into our sleeping bag, nestled together in a cocoon of down feathers and woolen clothing. I brought out my small palette of watercolors and painted by headlamp, images from memory of a forest understory studded with gemstone wildflowers and sprawling sunny slopes of waving grasses, until sleep overcame me.

Dawn brought with it a light snow. Large flakes accumulated lazily on windswept piles of crisp maple leaves, burying them in an icy tomb. I decided to get down the mountain before the heavy snow made it impossible. It wasn't until I stopped in the first town for a warm drink that I learned of the mandated lockdown that had turned Portland into a ghost town in my absence.

Over the next few weeks, my hiking boots slumped in the corner of the living room while I slumped on the couch, endlessly scrolling through the news, my anxiety escalating with every swipe down the never-ending parade of fear-mongering headlines. The world had come to a standstill. Home was the only place to be, the government said. Stay home, stay safe. Indefinitely. Public lands in and around Portland were shuttered. Then my car broke down and was declared irreparable. Home really was the only place I could be.

My goal of one hundred hikes in 2020 suddenly seemed less like a challenge and more like an impossibility. Though I had been excited for a year of hiking and knew how impactful the experience would be for my health, I almost felt a sense of relief. I didn't *fail* to do one hundred hikes—there were circumstances out of my control that *made it impossible,* you see. If I blamed my car, the weather, the pandemic, then I didn't have to take responsibility.

"Oh well," I practiced saying. "This just wasn't my year."

As enticing as that easy (and familiar) path of noncommitment seemed when it appeared before me, I was already in too deep. Some primal part of me knew how badly I needed this. So with even more limitations to navigate, I sat down to figure out where and how to move forward.

What's stopping me from hiking in the city? I thought. Well, it was almost guaranteed to trigger my anxiety: rushing traffic, aggressive drivers, and the endless parade of people and children and dogs on every sidewalk. A simple walk around the block would invariably deteriorate into full sensory overload among the cacophony of city life.

Despite my initial reservations toward urban hiking, the sense of claustrophobia I felt with each passing day was quickly becoming more intense than my city-induced anxiety. So I brushed off the ol' hiking boots, perhaps overkill for concrete trails, and got out to wander. Charlie and I trudged through trash-littered alleyways, by homeless encampments rising beneath rows of gaudy mansions, between strip clubs, and past craft beer bars and overpriced donut shops. With businesses shuttered, and lockdown orders in place, I was occasionally able to find small pockets of peace, away from crowds and traffic.

Fresh air, albeit tinged with the scent of gasoline and sometimes a nearby neighbor's barbecue, did help ease the spiral I had begun to descend into. Though this new version of hiking was far from what I had envisioned, I slowly cultivated a sense of joy in these excursions. I walked past Frankensteined gardens of native and ornamental plants, stopped to watch ducks at city parks, discovered hidden street art on sunbaked sidewalks, and experienced the apocalyptic silence of a city under quarantine.

My journal reflected the shift from a sense of unease and frustration to one of gratitude for the previously unseen bursts of nature in my neighborhood.

MAY 10, Hike #24: *Found a giant sequoia on the walk tonight! Also found a perfect songbird nest woven with spiderwebs, and watched the giant moon rise over a very empty, peaceful Burnside Street. Urban hiking = achieved. Still going to hit those 100 hikes this year.*

May 18, Hike #26: *Got caught in a sudden, warm rainstorm. Soaked by the time we got home, but saw the moon shining through the smallest opening of the gray rain clouds, Charlie and I chased each other through the soggy grass, and enjoyed a surprise rainbow before night fell and we turned to walk back home.*

June 2, Hike #29: *Sunset and yoga and the park with Charlie after a long 5-mile urban hike through parks and nature trails. Resting our feet, minds, and hearts.*

SUMMER

Despite the sudden narrowing of our homebound lives, the wilderness was still out there. Somewhere beyond the cityscape, alpine wildflowers were starting to bloom, waterfalls were surging with snowmelt, and if I closed my eyes, I could almost feel the sunshine on my skin as I lay on a mossy rock drying off after a cool dip in the river. The initial spark of hope I had found in my neighborhood excursions had begun to lose its shine. Resentment had elbowed its way in.

In June, strict lockdown orders were lifted, allowing us to venture out into the few public lands that had reopened. Understandably, everybody else was tired of being home too, so the trails were now bombarded with throngs of first-time hikers. Rivers, waterfalls, and lakes swarmed with more humans than mosquitos, each as overwhelming as the other.

The few opportunities for typical summer indulgences like wading in cool rivers and lying out in the sun were weighed down by a heavy sense of loss, or perhaps longing. Like I wasn't fully living this summer, merely walking through the hazy memories of summers past. Most of my hikes were frustratingly short, unlike the weeklong expeditions I'd usually embark on, where Charlie and I bummed around the desert for days, utterly alone and perfectly lost. Every moment felt like a desperate attempt to grab the tattered shreds of a summer that was all too quickly unraveling.

As we were offered the small freedom of the outdoors, new limitations materialized. Face masks were now required at all times, both indoors and out, and there was still no definitive answer as to when we could go home to visit family and friends. A series of short, hurried hikes wherever and whenever I could avoid the increasing crowds of rebelliously unmasked people didn't feel like the freedom, adventure, and self-exploration I had planned for 2020. I was lonely and untethered. And this loneliness blew a big wide hole in my life that could no longer be filled with hiking alone.

As much as I needed the outdoors, I needed a reprieve from my indoors. A relationship gone sour left me staring in the face of someone else's struggles with addiction, which all too easily stirred up my own demons. The few short treks I managed to local nature trails felt like a last-ditch effort to get back to myself. When once I had found peace and an unwavering sense of self in nature, I was now bringing my demons with me in a flask tucked into my backpack between my sunscreen and snacks.

I began the search for a new place to live, horrified by rising rent prices, wondering how in the hell I was going to survive the rest of this year on my own. I walked to the liquor store for a handle of bourbon and drank half of it on a filthy park bench overlooking a man-made pond slicked with algae. Sitting in the hazy twilight, the air thick with smoke from a nearby lit joint and the smell of moldering feces, I realized I still felt more at home there than I did in my own apartment. Something needed to change.

Change came swiftly, though it wasn't what I'd had in mind. As a grand finale to this botched season, early September wildfires tore through the region. The ancient forests that had shaped me for the past decade, that had become my home, were gone. Razed. Winds whipped thick clouds of smoke and ash from the charred trunks of old-growth stands into the city, forcing me to breathe the smoldering corpse of the land I had fallen so deeply in love with. The smoke shouldered against my shuttered apartment windows, trapping me even deeper inside.

Watching those forests burn, unavoidably inhaling the charcoal smoke, hearing of the mass exodus of humans and animals from scorched areas, and understanding the weight of all we'd lost hit me hard. Without central air to filter the heavy smoke, I spent two weeks with a sore throat and lost voice, in silent lament. Curled up on the living room floor on a makeshift bed between half-packed boxes of old sketchbooks and dried-up paint tubes, I spent the last night in my old apartment knocking back another few glasses of bourbon, trying to drown the burn of these sudden endings.

With only three months left of the year and forty-six hikes still to go, I accepted that this project was a nice idea, but an idea for a different year. An idea for a different person, even.

Another half-finished project.

Another promise to myself I had failed to keep.

Fall

October swept into the Pacific Northwest as a crisp, cool disintegration. As the leaves fell in a frenzy of gold and crimson, I too was drifting through the days in what felt like a kaleidoscopic spectrum of dizzying change.

Finally in my new apartment, I was free and living on my own for the first time in my adult life. My front door latched behind me, and I was the only person with the key. Charlie was safe when I left for work. I slept more soundly than I ever dreamed of among the revolving chaos of roommates and partners, no longer burdened by the messiness of other lives. The only possessions I brought with me fit in two small carloads. I burned old journals, deleted photos, and pared down my closet to just a few items of ragged thrift store clothing. This bare-bones life may have seemed pathetic from the outside looking in, but I reveled in its honest simplicity. Free from distractions, bad influences, and daily fears, I could begin to process my grief and gain clarity. I made a new rule that liquor was not allowed in my home and replaced my daily drinks with every flavor of bubbly water on the market. I started eating actual meals again. I bought houseplants to care for. I drank tea while reading memoirs and comics to Charlie as we snuggled close on our little bed. I started socializing again. I started laughing again.

And, within a few weeks, I hiked again.

Although I had accepted defeat on my hundred-hike goal, the trail still called to me. Once I felt settled enough to let myself believe the worst was over, I called out of work and ventured through the Forest Service lands east of Mount St. Helens. The pitted dirt roads welcomed me with open arms, their winding paths pulling me into the tender heart of the wilderness. The forest moved tall and proud around me, still dressed in full fall fashion, gliding over a red carpet of alder and vine maple leaves with distinguished grace.

I hiked a trail that was rated moderate, though my desperate gasping for air on the ascent had me questioning that assessment. A quarter of the way up the talus slope, I realized that other hikers were probably right about the moderate difficulty—it was my own body that had atrophied during the months I'd traded walking for whiskey. Though I was weary and out of practice, my mind was grounded and more present than ever. I'd managed to find my way back to the trail and was well on my way back to myself.

With November sun bursting through branches of maple and pine, the forest preached her annual sermon of transience, impermanence, change. Of letting go. In a normal year I'd find myself clinging to autumn's gold-crusted coattails, begging it to stay, reluctant to submit to this ceremony of physical and metaphysical rebirth. This year, though, the season's offering to shed my pandemic-battered self was a welcomed relief. I was reminded that the natural world had always had the power to gently hem my ragged edges. I could find myself anywhere: forest, mountain, desert, wetland, swamp, busy urban city, and even in the middle of personal life crises. Anywhere I was, and any way I was, I could always find my way back.

Once I understood this, the entire world unfurled at my feet.

Through the last few months of the year, I hiked nearly every other day. By hiking close to home and creating a routine of hiking before work and on weekends, I reached ninety hikes by the end of November.

WINTER

The coast is stunning in wintertime, when the land is caught exposed and vulnerable. Gnarled spruces and madrones twisted by spectacular winds give way to jagged rocks being whittled to sand by the impossible power of the seething ocean. Shorebirds slice through crisp, salt-crusted air above spans of wide-open coastline. I visit the headlands and their coves for my last hikes, as one wavelike year recedes and the next prepares to roll in.

After hike number ninety-nine in the small seaside town of Astoria, I turn onto the bridge rising over the yawning mouth of the Columbia River and make my way into Washington State. The saltwater bay rolls beneath me, sunshine gleaming off the waves. Without a destination in mind, I reach the end of the bridge and a massive green road sign that reads: CAPE DISAPPOINTMENT STATE PARK.

"Oh yeah?" I say to no one. "This place can't disappoint me." I cross my arms as if to lock in the finality of my decision.

I know I only have a couple of hours before the sun goes down, so I pull into the first trailhead I see. Cape Disappointment Trail will be my hundredth hike. My heart swells with the culmination of every past version of myself who has ever set off on a trail full of expectation and intention. I marvel at the sunset over the ocean, brush my cheeks against leaves, run my fingers over mossy carpets tacked to tree trunks.

Through fern and fir I wander, navigating roots and mud, watching bald eagles glide above the treetops, all the while whispering thanks for this life and this body. This body that is capable of propelling me along hundreds of miles of undulating trails, breathing sweet air into my lungs, blood coursing through ever-fortified muscles. What a privilege it is to stand at the edge of the land, a speck gazing over the ocean, with a multitude of memories, experiences, anxieties, and fears dissipating into the salty breeze.

At one point I stop to pay respects to the 300-plus-year-old Sitka spruce, dubbed Cathedral Tree for its arch- and buttress-like roots. Jays holler above and juncos flash their striking white tail feathers through the undergrowth. I fall in step with the tune of the woods, shedding the difficulty of the year, allowing myself a moment of peace and awe. Thoughts of the demons who have haunted me and the challenges I have faced are replaced with the pure joy of seeing Charlie bound down the trail ahead of me, always turning back to make sure I'm okay. I breathe in. During the moment of pause I let myself marvel at the glittering woods around me, alive and expansive in the last of the day's sunlight. I exhale, and with my breath flows a year of tears.

While crawling over jumbled roots snaking across my path, I see the jumbled roots of my own life that led me here. A lifetime of anxiety, pain, confusion, stress, and regret pours out of me as I climb higher up the trail. I am physically exhausted when I reach the summit, like all the wind has been knocked out of me.

I sit for a moment overlooking the bay, feeling vulnerable and small. Clouds cover the distant hills in hazy sheets of gray. Cautiously collecting my breath and my thoughts before starting back down the trail, I retrace the same bootprints I left in the mud on the way up, knowing that each step from my past self brings me to the completion of my goal.

Now the overgrown trail is shrouded in thick shadow. I come upon a small side trail that I missed on the way up, leading to an amphitheater and cedar grove. Upon turning onto this new trail, I realize the paved stone path is etched with writing.

There is poetry beneath my feet.

I pause to read the Chinook blessing carved in stone:

WE CALL UPON THE MOUNTAINS, the Cascades and the Olympics, the high green valleys and meadows filled with wildflowers, the snows that never melt, the summits of intense silence, and we ask that they
    Teach us, and show us the Way.

AGAIN I WEEP.

It's over. I am at the end not just of the hiking goal, this project, this year, but of a chapter in my life.

I stand here on the other side of it all, watching it recede into the past. I know that I've done the damned work to get to a better place. None of what I've been through matters anymore. I made it here.

The stone-etched poetry continues:

WE CALL UPON THE FORESTS, the great trees reaching strongly to the sky with the earth in their roots and the heavens in their branches, the fir and the pine and the cedar, and we ask them to
    Teach us, and show us the Way.

    And lastly, we call upon all that we hold most sacred, the presence and power of the Great Spirit of love and truth which flows through all the Universe, to be with us to
    Teach us, and show us the Way.

THERE IS nothing to do but go.

———

JENN JOSLIN (SHE/HER)

Portland, Oregon—traditional village sites of the Multnomah, Wasco, Cowlitz, Kathlamet, Clackamas, Bands of Chinook, Tualatin, Kalapuya, Molalla, and many other tribes who made their homes along the Columbia River

Jenn has a BS in conservation biology, has worked as an environmental educator and freelance artist, and has written about her experiences getting to know the natural world after a childhood spent very much apart from it. She has numerous illustration credits and has written helpful family-friendly articles about outdoor adventure in the Pacific Northwest for the blog *Embrace Someplace*. Despite feeling wholly out of her element when she began exploring, she found she could still benefit from being on the trail in any capacity. She especially enjoys being out with her beloved senior pup, Charlie, who has been with her through fifteen wild years of adventure and hundreds of beautiful hikes. She has come to realize that nature is accessible to everybody and that our lives can be greatly enriched by learning to connect with the outdoors and with ourselves in the process.

She can be found on Instagram @jennjoslinart and at www.jennjoslin.com.

roadkill

SEVEN HUNDRED MILES INTO A NORTHBOUND THRU-HIKE OF the Pacific Crest Trail, you reach one of the more coveted and well-documented moments of the trail system. Kennedy Meadows marks where the desert ends and the High Sierra begins. This is where you collect your mandated bear canister, eat your body weight in pancakes at Grumpy Bear's, and shoot the shit with your new friends as you strategize how to approach the next couple hundred miles. It's a time to welcome broad, breezy meadows and sources of water that don't have uranium in them.

In June of 2018, I sat picking at my share of pancakes—an island of Brown femininity in a sea of decidedly ultra-light, white outdoorsmen. A cloud of exhaustion from days of nauseous desert hiking in the baking hundred-degree heat separated me from their endless talk of gear and beer. Unable to best even two full pancakes, I was beginning to wonder: *What the fuck am I doing here?*

While I'd been recovering at Kennedy Meadows for two days, I knew that my current state wasn't the only thing separating me from my hiking peers. I seemed to lack the careless or carefree gall of many of my comrades. I'd started thru-hiking as an outdoors newcomer relying on my dancer's legs to propel me along the trail. I had been enticed by the romantic promise of solitude, beauty, adventure, physical challenge, and a chance to explore my home state of California. Now here I was, four weeks in, hiking thirty-mile days and running away from a perpetual stream of northbound men, all in the hopes of finding that freedom. God forbid I would have to pass the same person twice.

I mitigated my isolation by surrounding myself with a choice few of these men—all amusing late-start speedsters. With them came a feeling of safety and a superficial sense that I was in with "real" outdoorsy people. Through the miles, we became each other's makeshift support. I aimed to play the role of future "lifelong friend," which everyone knows is an integral part of the thru-hiking experience. Every time I tried to remind myself that my goal was to hike to Canada and that the social aspect was extracurricular, I was thwarted. The PCT was more social than I had anticipated. My attempts to masquerade as an outdoorsy person only made me feel more at odds with the other hikers.

Physically, my body was holding up well to trail life. I cried a lot those first 700 miles, but not a single tear was from a blister. I cried when I plugged in my headphones for the first time after a knee-grinding ten-mile descent and music sounded extra-sweet; I cried feeling alone in my tent at night; I cried when, at the end of a long day, I had to run away from a swarm of bees and a sunning rattlesnake blocked my path to freedom; I cried when I puked for 100 miles in the desert. Generally, these were all acceptable cries.

MY FIRST UNACCEPTABLE cry was walking toward me and my half-eaten pancakes at that table at Grumpy Bear's. As a solo thru-hiker, I'd been pink-blazed (trail-followed and trail-courted) for hundreds of miles, but Caesar Salad was, unfortunately, my first trail romance. Three hundred miles ago, a misguided gut feeling had led to thirty seconds of disappointing sex, at the end of which he came on my freshly laundered shirt and threw it at me, right before I was meant to head back on trail. I had wanted to rip him apart right then. And again, soon after, when he only maybe jokingly called me "exotic." And then also when his East Coast ass said, "I don't get what the hype is about burritos"—in a family-owned Mexican restaurant in Southern California. Ignoring my misgivings, I let this fool plop his pack down across the table from me.

"There are so many different kinds of people on trail."

After a moment's consideration, I said, "Um, I guess this is maybe a diverse group of white people." Nearly everyone I had met so far fit the same generic thru-hiker description.

"I mean I think this is just a diverse group of people. There are so many people from different countries."

"I don't see anyone here who looks like me."

"Well, I just think Black and Brown people are really, really lazy." He looked me dead in the eye, nothing but brazen self-assuredness to back up his claim. "That's why you never see them outside. I talk about this all the time with my family, but it's like you never really see them doing anything physical or trying to explore nature, and I think it's because they are just lazy."

Now, I was no stranger to rich white people recreating outside in ways that immigrants, the poor, and BIPOC in the USA would never even consider, but I had never heard such blatant white ownership of the outdoors in casual conversation. Did his my-parents-paid-my-way-through-grad-school ass just say that skin color and laziness were linked? Why would he say that to me?

At this point, two of my other man friends in short shorts sat down at the adjacent table and started listening in. I was about to rip this motherfucker's head off for his incredible ignorance, and I was happy to have two witnesses to vent with later.

"Wait, what are you talking about?" my two dudes chimed in.

"Well, Caesar Salad here was just saying you never see Black and Brown people on trail because they are lazy," I explained, ready to finish this man. "I don't think he realizes that Black and Brown people are also the ones more likely to be working with their hands and working outside, both historically and today, both here and all over the world. If you and your family spent all day working outside in a field or on other people's land, why would you want to spend your leisure time pretending you are poor, getting dirty, being in physical pain, and walking two thousand miles for shits and giggles. That's not 'fun,' that's just their fucking life. Not everyone can afford to eat-pray-love their way to finding themselves outside."

The seconds dragged as silence rang on. My voice had remained steady, but my hands were trembling.

"That's interesting, thank you for sharing your take on it, and I'm sure there are many sides to that conversation." An indictment from one of my blond-haired, blue-eyed friends.

My brain glitched as the conversation teetered ungracefully to other subjects. I gnashed my teeth in silence for a moment longer before pushing my chair back and wandering to my tent in the yard. There, I had my first real messy cry on the PCT. I want to say I cried at the social injustice and went back to the trail spreading a decolonizing gospel. But my tears were entirely personal. I was really crying because I wasn't a tall pale man whose dad taught me how to pitch a tent and make a fire, and in that moment, it fucking sucked. I came out here to challenge myself, and now if I didn't fully hike this trail, I knew at least a few people would think I was a lazy failure, representative of the lazy failure of all melanated peoples.

My tears were made of anger, too, not just sadness. I was pissed that the outdoors could not be a reprieve for me, just one more place where I would have to work harder than everyone around me to prove my worth. I was pissed that I would have to mold myself to yet another social script.

First, I would whitewash myself—feigning interest in mountain worship, boozy nights, country songs, burgers, and saying "howdy." Then, I would mute myself as I passed through small-town America. I would wear apoliticization like a shield around other hikers and the gun-toting, Jesus-fearing townsfolk. Despite vastly different politics, both groups seemed to get along with each other on the basis of whiteness alone. I didn't have that privilege.

Next, I learned about the perceived weaknesses of my femininity. In the endless gear chatter, I was rarely, if ever, asked for my opinion. I was thought of as slow, even when I was fast. I quietly ignored men who hiked behind me, openly staring at my ass. Most annoyingly, I was still expected to care for the physical and emotional needs of everyone around me. And I had to look and smell cute doing it.

White women I passed on trail seemed to feel some of these things too. They sometimes fought for "other" people because they were also "other," but eventually, they hit their groove. There were other white women who could show them how. My choices for navigating the social script felt more limited. I was never going to fully feel a part of things, and I never did find another person who looked like me on the PCT.

As I lay in my tent that night, mulling over these thoughts, I half-considered departing from Kennedy Meadows and walking into the Sierra then and there. I wondered if I was using a too-close magnifying lens on social politics and identity. Maybe I was too affected by my surroundings and unwilling to just show up and send it, hike my own hike, and have a happy trail. Very Gen Z of me.

THE NEXT DAY, I practically bolted out of Kennedy Meadows, a full day ahead of my trail family, determined to keep going and to go on my own. Miles over smiles became the antidote to the social intricacies of trail. Fuck if I was lazy, I was going to get to the end first. I didn't want to sit around and eat and drink in town. I wanted to see what I was made of, and I wanted to go harder, better, faster, stronger than the rest of them.

As I wound through the high passes of the Sierra and on to the rest of the trail, however, the tears still came, and I found myself code-switching to match the trail.

> I cried in Chester, California, the midpoint of the trail. I was sleeping at a church, one of two women in a large group of men. Some of those men started talking, with profound obscenity and degradation, about whether they would rather be fucking white or black pussy. No one told them to stop. I didn't feel safe enough to.

I cried out of tired frustration on the side of a fast, deep river crossing. All the long-legged, risk-taking men happily skipped over the wet rocks. I cried again with laughter and joy after one of my femme friends came up behind me, and together we rolled boulders down the steep banks to create our own river crossing.

I cried during my first forty- and fifty-mile days. I peppered these big days between my usual thirty-milers to beat boredom and to prove that I had a place outside.

I cried on my first sixty-mile day in ninety-seven-degree heat, on the second day of my period. I threw up 3,000 calories of milk products from town and rolled my ankle on volcanic rock. I would feel the effects of that day for the next 1,000 miles.

I cried numerous times my last four days on trail, when I was taking twelve Advil per day to hike with an injured Achilles, just to get to the finish line.

I cried when I didn't know how to fix my tent pole, and realized I was dependent on the men I was hiking with to help me. I cried out of gratitude for the men I was hiking with when they helped me.

I cried in gratitude for everyone I hiked with and all of the laughter they provided, the long downhills we skipped and ran together, and the binge eating that bonded us in town.

I DIDN'T, however, cry when I reached the northern terminus. I didn't even care. Objectively, I had emerged successful in this experience. I wasn't one of the lazy ones. I had achieved something in the grand world of outdoor recreation. There were hundreds of cute outdoor influencers posting their version of this moment, feeling that it was the greatest achievement of their life. If they had done something, I had probably done something too. That I didn't care about the achievement didn't matter. That I was bored for months on trail didn't matter. Neither the macro- nor micro-views of the trail mattered, so long as I put one foot forward and completed my goal, or so I was told.

The only thing that seemed to break through my apathy was that I had made it as an outsider in a space I didn't belong. I had planted myself in the thru-hiking community in spite of my own and others' assessments of my abilities. I had given those expectations the middle finger and proved them all wrong. That felt good.

The achievement of it all caught up to me when I realized that I could be the first South Asian person to Triple Crown, completing all three long-distance trails in the US. It didn't take me long to start fantasizing about the PCT's longer, harder cousin, the Continental Divide Trail. Post-COVID, in a changed world, I would attempt the CDT.

I would start in July and hike southbound, through hard miles in Glacier National Park and the Bob Marshall Wilderness. From there, it would be a race against the cold to Colorado. I was more experienced in the outdoors, but I had never decided that I actually liked thru-hiking. Even before arriving at the northern terminus of the CDT, I was worried about entering back into that world. Spending the pandemic in Colorado Springs only served to ramp up my social anxiety and racial fatigue. I didn't know if I was ready to enter into a space where I had to act like I could conquer all nature and disregard the people living in the places I passed. Plus, eight close-range black bear and mountain lion sightings on the PCT had proved that animals loved me, and I didn't want to meet too many grizzly bears.

On the other hand, I was starting to see more opportunities for BIPOC hikers on social media. I was curious to see whether, in this changing landscape, I would finally find my place on the trail.

———

I landed in Kalispell, Montana, with another thru-hiking friend, ready for four hours of hitchhiking to the Canadian border. Again, I was the only Brown person in sight. On my third hitch, the driver of an "om"-adorned, but otherwise clinical RV began telling me all about how he loves Indian people, especially his spiritual Indian yogi girlfriend/mistress. They'd spent many nights together in the bed I was sitting on. I lasted under three weeks on the CDT.

I cried on the first day, when I met a woman with long, dark hair and medium-brown skin. I said to her, "Wow, I'm so excited to meet you, I did not expect to see another Brown person out here, I've never met another Brown person on trail!" And she said, "Neither have I, especially on day one." We spent the night camping together. I thought that meeting her first must signify some change in the hiking demographic. In 2023, she would go on to finish her Triple Crown.

That night, we were camped out by a lake in Glacier National Park when we met two old Montana cowboys. After "watering their horses" in the lake, the cowboys got to drinking and guffawing. They yelled out to our group of hikers, "Hey! What's all y'alls name?" When I said "Ankita," I hoped they'd just gloss over it and not spend too much time asking what it is and where it is from. Unsurprisingly, one went, "Anika, or did she say Anita? I'm just going to call her Anita." Classic. I hoped they would move on. Instead, the other said, "No, man, that's racist! You can't just call her that!" His friend responded, "Well, I ain't tryna be racist, I just don't know what her name is!" So they continued laughing, and I started laughing too. I laughed so hard I cried.

I also cried one night in my tent after sitting around a fire in a large hiker bubble. The other hikers were making fun of the fact that they were all white guys with beards, wearing the same thing. But then they talked about how sad it was that there was no diversity on trail. That started a long conversation about how to get more people involved outside. No one said anything about laziness then. There was nothing but care.

Another time, someone asked about my trail name, Roadkill. I launched into the story of how I got it: some man terrorizing PCT hikers threw a machete at me in the Angeles National Forest. Normally people are surprised and impressed by that story, but this time everyone just looked at me in silence. Someone finally whispered, "I'm sorry you were assaulted on trail."

My biggest tears on the CDT, however, came in Lincoln, Montana. I spent my zero day listening to music at a biker rally, being shown guns by the local townspeople, and looking at "tipi burners" at Blackfoot Pathways—a sculpture park in the name of the Blackfeet Nation that was filled with only white-made art. That was enough.

LINCOLN WAS where I chose to leave the CDT. I was tired. I didn't care about reaching Mexico, or even Wyoming. Dreams of a Triple Crown felt distant. Unlike on the PCT, my miles stopped when I stopped smiling. Hiking across arbitrary state lines felt less monumental than ever before, and any perceived burden of shouldering representation outside didn't feel worth it.

In some ways, leaving the CDT felt like freedom. It would have been impossible for me to feel good about the accomplishment, and it felt good for me to abandon the attempt. I don't think that acquisition is meant for the land, and I don't think it is how I want to experience this country—like I am racing against time, needing to seize more and more of it. I don't think it's brave to be walking trails on stolen land, like we aren't all imparting traces of harm for fun or accomplishment or peace or whatever our gain is. The little hurts and microaggressions, sometimes macroaggressions, of the trail feel reflective of how we treat our planet and people.

At the same time, the social fabric of the CDT made me hopeful. The white people were starting to get it. Being a Brown person outside meant something, even if just on an interpersonal level, and that did not need to be proved. Problems with outdoor inaccessibility did not need to be proved. Enjoyment of landscapes and seasons and novelty as a shared resource—that did not need to be proved. And, in celebration of these new facts alone, I'll still take a long hike. But as I climb, spend time with wildlife, sharpen my homesteading skills, and make environmental art, I find that my own relationship with recreating is finally meandering outside lines.

ANKITA SHARMA (THEY/SHE)

Currently based in Brooklyn, New York—Munsee, Lenape, and Canarsie land. Originally from Fremont, California—Ohlone and Muwekma land.

Ankita is a backpacker, a climber, an aspiring adventure photographer, and a choreographer interested in environmental art. They hold a BA in dance and a BA in anthropology and have previously published academic work on the topics of decolonizing wildlife rehabilitation and primatology. They completed the Pacific Crest Trail in 2018, started the Continental Divide Trail in 2021, and completed the Pyrenees High Route in 2021. They have their sights set on the Sierra High Route in 2024. They want to see more Black, Brown, and Queer representation in the outdoors, not just with outdoor recreation, but in thinking about who belongs to and occupies land, how we care for the natural world, and whether land is accessible. They are excited to share thru-hiking stories with the world.

They can be found on Instagram @nki.creates and at www.anki tacreates.space.

hiking on empty

ON A BRISK, EARLY AUGUST MORNING, I WOKE UP AT 4 A.M. and drove toward the North Mount Elbert trailhead at 10,040 feet, just outside of Leadville, Colorado. The protein shake I was nursing sloshed in its bottle with every bump and pothole in the gravel road. By the time I rolled in, the parking lot was almost full of serious, die-hard hiker-athlete types with tiny hydration vests and trekking poles. The air buzzed with talk of past 14er trips, punctuated by the sharp clicks of pack buckles snapping together. As someone born insecure, I couldn't help but feel out of place in my Walmart base layers and the battered Patagonia Nano Puff I'd purchased heavily discounted from the gear shop I worked at in Missouri. Nevertheless, I stood at the bottom of the same mountain as these other hikers, knowing that when we were all done today, I would be on their level. I had come here to prove, once and for all, that I was a real hiker—a hiker good enough to climb to 14,000 feet and taste the glory of high-altitude adventure. After today, I would finally feel like I belonged in this community.

I reached down and touched the soft parts of my thighs, furtively pinching and pulling what I thought should be muscle. Thinner hikers stretched beside their Subarus, flexing lean calves and stuffing energy gels into the little compartments of their packs. Dozens of flat waist belts cradled taut cores, while mine dug viciously into the sides of my belly. The chalky vanilla protein shake was suddenly unappetizing, so I left it in the console and hurried to the trail, avoiding eye contact.

Once upon a time, I ran wild and barefoot through the Appalachian hills where I grew up. With soft soil between my toes, I danced on narrow deer paths. I once belonged to myself, my joy. I was unfettered by what others thought of me, never wondering whether I belonged outdoors.

Now, comparison was as natural to me as breathing. Since my early teenage years, feelings of inferiority around smaller bodies had bled into my daily life like a cut that would never heal. The vibrance of girlhood had been lost to a raging eating disorder that forced me to drop out of college my first semester. For two years I wove in and out of treatment centers, lying about the food I hadn't eaten and obsessing over every bite logged in calorie-counter apps. Finally, the fundamentals of recovery sank in enough for me to hear the therapists who were trying to help me get better. Even so, five years later, I still struggled to eat enough to sustain the active lifestyle I wanted. Intrusive thoughts still found their way in, often leaving me feeling powerless.

In the days leading up to this hike, I tried to acclimate to the altitude by doing short hikes and runs around Leadville. It was my first time in Colorado, and I'd made the biggest plans I could think of. Not only is Mount Elbert the tallest peak in the state, it's also the second-highest point in the contiguous United States, standing only sixty-five feet shy of Mount Whitney in California. While hiking and backpacking have always been my happy place, today's hike would be very different from the rolling Ozark hills I was used to. Now, at 11,000 feet, I was nearly eye level with the surrounding mountains. When the trail split from the overlapping Colorado Trail and Continental Divide Trail, things became much more difficult. Soon, I was crawling up steep grades, and yet I was still below the tree line.

Before the towering pines turned to miniature shrubs, I glanced upward through a break in the leaves. Far ahead of me appeared a massive, dome-shaped curve in the mountain made of sharp rocks. If I squinted, I could see hikers, like tiny ants, making their way up the trail. I wanted that dome to be the top of Mount Elbert, but I knew from my map that this was the first of two false summits. Even though I'd known about them ahead of time, seeing them in person was demoralizing and soul-crushing. At the rate I was moving, the remaining three miles to the summit would take forever.

Two hours into the climb, deep pangs of hunger reverberated through my rib cage and into my throat. Nausea from the lack of an adequate breakfast was so overwhelming, I could have gagged as my body stubbornly revolted from its emptiness. Runners and hikers glided past as I reached around into my backpack pocket for a granola bar. They tamed the mountain with each step, pushing it down with the soles of their shoes. Their agile bodies were strong against a beast I only dreamed of fighting. They were born for this. My fingers fiddled with the granola bar wrapper. I told myself that I didn't need those 250 calories. I didn't deserve them. So, I crammed the bar back into my pack and kept hiking.

Being above the tree line was like stepping foot onto an entirely new planet. The sky opened up, the land was vast, and rocks replaced the soft, dirt-beaten path. I pulled my gaze from the ground to look behind me and couldn't believe what I saw. From the shoulder of Elbert, all the other mountains looked like the stiff peaks in home-made frosting after it's whipped into formation. The crisp air felt like fall, but the sun was heavy on my back. If I leaned far enough out, I thought I could have tumbled into a different universe. One where I climbed mountains without bringing the eating disorder with me. One where I wasn't at war with the foods that helped me achieve my goals. One where I hiked and fell in love with the body that has carried me all this way.

Now switchbacks seemed to stop altogether, and the trail became especially precarious. I barely made any progress with each calculated step, as loose rock slid out from underneath my boots. I made my way, inch by inch, to the top of the first false summit, but getting there was a short victory as I knew that I had 1,500 feet still to climb. The tops of my thighs became numb and tired. I pulled myself slowly forward, tapping into my already dangerously low motivation reservoir. This was by far the hardest, most frustrating hike I had ever done. Other hikers passed me on their way back down the mountain, with smiling faces and breezy words of encouragement. It would be so easy to turn around and follow them down. I clenched my fists and fought back tears. I did *not* come all this way to quit.

"Just get there," I huffed under my breath.

At 13,500 feet, I was over the second false summit and crawling toward the actual top of Mount Elbert. Even with the end in sight, I stopped every five feet to gasp for air, gripping the same thighs I'd pinched with disdain at the trailhead, asking them for their support. The mountain's icy breath chilled the sweat on my face and back. Eventually, snotty-faced, chapped-lipped, and limping, I made it to the top of Colorado.

Several hikers milled around the summit, enjoying the view, and catching their breath before their descent. I lumbered over to the edge of the crowd and plopped down, feeling lightheaded and delirious. As I sipped from the bite valve of my water bladder, I stared out at the deep sea of pine and lime-green aspen filling the valley below. The clouds kissed the surrounding peaks, some just barely snowcapped, and the sun felt closer, its presence much more intimate than it had ever been in my life. Its rays soaked the landscape, basking this day in a fresh radiance that made me forget about the bottomless hunger and exhaustion I was experiencing, if only for a moment.

Everything around me should have been breathtaking. The taste of alpine atmosphere should have turned me instantly into a dirtbag obsessed with chasing "vert." I should have been dreaming up my next adventure before this one had even ended. I tried to tap into the feelings of awe that had been described to me by customers I helped at the gear shop in Missouri when they talked about Colorado. They had felt awe standing right where I stood, but all I felt was lost.

After taking a few pictures, I started walking back to the trailhead. If I thought climbing up the mountain was hard, going down was a fresh hell I couldn't have imagined. Coming from the Midwest, I had never needed trekking poles, so I hadn't bothered bringing any. At this point in the hike, I realized that had been a rookie mistake. I slowly retraced my steps, rocks sputtering down the trail with each shift of my weight. Plenty of hikers who had passed me on the way up and had taken their time at the summit were now slipping by me on the way down. Each time someone zipped up from behind, the tape and glue keeping me tenuously held together detached a little more. The tedious and slow descent, coupled with the painful cries of my empty stomach, short-circuited my brain. I needed to get off this godforsaken mountain.

Back below the tree line, I stepped off the trail, gripping the shoulder straps of my backpack in my hands and panting. I couldn't seem to catch my breath. Before today, I had been convinced that hiking a 14er would change my life. I had thought coming to Colorado and climbing the most monstrous mountain I had ever seen would make me a real hiker. This trip was supposed to prove that I belonged in the outdoors even if I didn't look like the badass endurance athletes I saw on Instagram. When I thought of a "real" hiker, images of women jaunting up these trails in brightly colored two-inch shorts and nothing but a bra under their hydration vests flooded my mind. Their hair was always pulled back into two French braids, and they would grind up the hillside with lean muscles engaged. I looked down at my body and realized that would never be me.

With just two miles to the trailhead, I closed my eyes and felt myself start to unravel. The air sucked from my chest, and I fell to the dirt gasping. Little shards of earth dug into my knees like glass. I grabbed handful after handful of rocks and pelted the trees around me. I'm pretty sure I missed every single trunk, which only made me more furious with myself. My body ached, my mind was bruised, and I wailed, but my stomach wailed louder, begging for anything to satisfy the hunger.

"God, just shut up," I sputtered. "Just stop. What more do you want from me?"

I had really lost it now. There I was, full-on ugly-crying and shouting at my own body. My body, which probably just needed a Clif Bar and a nap. I didn't want to give her that. She didn't deserve it. I wanted to leave her stranded, starving and crying, on that mountain. My anxious hands felt over the curves I never wanted and the ripples in my stomach where I demanded stillness. They paused on my heaving chest before traveling farther up. My breathing steadied with hands clutched around my neck.

I could feel her. I hadn't been looking for her, but still, I saw her so clearly. Tangled within the mess of pure hate and disgust, she was there. The girl who'd woken up with the whippoorwills. She was everything I used to be. She was fearless—an invincible force of nature with curls like crescent moons and a confidence that could stoke fires.

Before my body became something I didn't recognize, I was starry night skies and twigs for hair. She had been lost to the tough rubber plastered on my hips, the thick chunks of mold growing underneath my arms, and the knots of flour dough stuck onto my frame like the extra butter my grandmother adds to her apple pie recipes. To the alien way it felt to be in a woman's body. To the eating disorder and the depression and the moment when I thought I might be better off dead than to gain one more pound on the body I longed to escape. I could never go back in time and be that girl again, but for a moment, she was there.

Banging my hands into the Colorado dirt, I wished I was anyone else on the planet but myself. Howling like a wounded animal, I regained my feet and continued down the mountain. The twists and turns didn't matter much since I couldn't see the beauty of the land through my tears. When I finally reached the trailhead, my car was one of only a few left in the gravel lot. I pulled my boots off and sank into the driver's seat, my body feeling more splintered by the climb down than the hike up.

I had completed my first 14er. I felt the pain and false sense of glory rip through me like a knife. And I still hated myself.

On the side of Mount Elbert, I realized that the brokenness I felt inside had nothing to do with what I could accomplish in the outdoors. For so long, hiking and running long-distance trails had been a way for me to escape the parts of myself that I resented most. I had climbed that mountain looking for someone else. For a version of myself that fit into the mold I'd seen on social media, a version of myself that deserved love. But instead, I ran into my past self. I realized that nature was the only place where I could catch a glimpse of the girl I once was.

Today, I hike into the flowing Ozark hills surrounding my home in St. Louis. Her feral spirit seeps into me when I walk through the woods. On long hikes, I inhale the ghost of her and for a moment, I can breathe. Every now and again, someone much smaller than me runs past or effortlessly strolls up the steep climbs like they were born for that. I stop at the side of the trail and reach into my backpack to grab a granola bar. In one fluid motion, I tear into the wrapper with my teeth and take a bite. After a few swallows, I keep on hiking.

––––––

CALLIE LEISURE (SHE/HER)

St. Louis, Missouri—traditional territory of the Osage Nation and Illini Tribe

Callie is a hiker, backpacker, and trail runner. She has completed the Foothills Trail and many sections of the Ozark Trail in her backyard, and she aspires to thru-hike the Appalachian Trail. She is a psychology student at Saint Louis University and is on the equestrian team. She's passionate about animal rights and adores her rescue dog, Honey. She acknowledges her own complicated relationship with her female body and believes that mental health, body image, and feminine topics aren't talked about as often as they should be; she doesn't want anyone to have to struggle in silence.

She can be found on Instagram @callie.hikes and on Substack at calliehikes.substack.com.

red sky at morning

I thought that it would be easy, and that I wouldn't feel much when I found him, but it was the hardest thing I'd ever done. He broke me into a million little pieces, and most of them will stay forever out there in the snow.

He was a member of the Wyoming Range mule deer herd, arguably the largest and most celebrated in the world. It is renowned for its high-quality bucks—male specimens that defy imagination, rendering anyone who gets to behold them speechless with the simple awe that only a wild animal can strike in a human being. To many, they represent power and masculinity. To me, they embody a wild elegance that is almost painful to witness.

I was, and still am, the PhD student in charge of the Wyoming Range Mule Deer Project, a one-of-a-kind research project led by the Monteith Shop at the University of Wyoming, in collaboration with the Wyoming Game and Fish Department, the Bureau of Land Management, and the Forest Service. Our mission is to reveal the environmental processes that regulate the herd. Our research focuses mainly on females and their offspring, but we added a male component to the project in 2018 to better understand male ecology. Once we collar animals, we monitor them until death. One of the most critical components of my job is to go to them when they die and determine the cause of death, so that we might understand how mortality shapes the population.

I'd received the mortality email for M037 the previous afternoon. At first, I didn't believe it. Survival of adult males is typically very high, and we had not lost a mature buck during winter since I started running the project in late 2021. I packed up my truck right away and drove west from my home in Laramie across the state of Wyoming, so I could be ready to start snowshoeing at dawn. I was dimly aware that a lot of snow had come down over the holidays, but I hadn't been out to the field in several weeks. Nothing could have prepared me for what waited for me on the moonscape of the sagebrush steppe.

When I parked the truck at 8 a.m., blue twilight bathed a landscape mounded with chest-deep pillows of snow. Morning broke crimson on the ridgeline to the west while I readied my pack and strapped on snowshoes. With my first step off the snowplowed pavement of the highway, the reality of the snow conditions slammed into me, and I stopped. Fear bloomed an adrenaline-induced tingle through my veins as the sunrise stained the path before me red.

I took a deep breath and I kept going, staring down in disbelief as wet, heavy snow piled over the edges of my snowshoes. I owed it to him to get as close as I could, to understand and tell his story, even though I would never truly know who he was, or what happened in the moment his spark went out. But there was so much beauty in trying.

It took over three hours for me to walk just over a mile to where I knew he lay. The snow covered entire sagebrush and mountain mahogany. I sank to my knees even in snowshoes. Without them, I would have sunk to my hips or my chest. With each upward step, I lifted the wet, heavy snow that had filled in atop my snowshoes. I fell often—tripping on a hidden sagebrush branch, or simply losing my balance. Pouring sweat, a quarter mile in, I peeled off all of my outer layers, but kept my base layer on to protect my skin from the burning cold of the snow each time I fell. A half mile in, the tendon on the front of my left hip began a subtle but persistent complaint that soon began echoing around my head. Four hundred yards from him, I collapsed in frustration and pain. My heart pounded furiously in my chest, my body burned, my breath huffed thick clouds into the chilled air. But I got up again. I had to.

Along the way, I sensed that others were dead all around me. Magpies and ravens took off from concealed places as I passed, rejoicing in their winter meals.

Thirty yards from him, I intersected a deeply carved deer trail, a trench in the snow that animals had made with their passing and then used over and over to save themselves a little energy. I turned east to travel along it, joining my path with possibly thousands of deer that came before me. I knew he wouldn't be far from it.

Mule deer blend into their winter landscape like spirits on the wind. Or a wild crown of antlers soaring above the snow among the sagebrush—my first glimpse of him somewhat uncertain as my mind slowly distinguished the tell-tale pattern of his pointed tines from the sagebrush branches that wreathed them. A few minutes later, I was upon him—a huge form curled in a gentle ball in the deer trail, head bowed as though in sleep, body fully shrouded in last night's fresh snow, like the landscape and the winter and the storm wanted to keep him as a treasured secret forever.

The final hours of his life were clearly painted for me. I could almost see the rise and fall of his body in peaceful sleep, his letting go, the last burst of his hot breath rising.

This is when I fell apart. I do not know if we are meant to see these things, to learn such wild secrets. Grief and joy went to war with one another inside me, wrapped their claws tenderly around my neck, and drew me to my knees before him. The salt of silent tears mixed with the hot sweat on my cheeks and dripped in a steady stream from my chin down into the snow. Death and beauty go together in wild places. They always have and they always will. In his death, M037 was the most beautiful thing I had ever seen.

In my exhaustion, I considered crawling in to lie against his soft belly and join him in sleep. I imagined that my own end would not be very different from what he experienced. But this day was not my day.

And it was my responsibility to know what happened, to learn how he died. So I did the only thing I regret having to do that day and pulled him from his resting place. But the image, no, the *feeling* of him the way I found him, the whisper of his gentle ghost in passing—it will haunt me for the rest of my life.

I would not mar him. It is incredibly rare for a mature male to die in his prime coat and antlers, and rarer still for his body to be unopened by predators or scavengers. I knew that I must carry what pieces of him I could home with me. That I must confirm the cause of his death but preserve him as I went. Preserve him because he was whole and unsoiled and unfrozen. Because he could help us teach, and others learn, about the power that nature can wreak. The power that was ending lives out there. The power that would ultimately kill three-quarters of the Wyoming Range mule deer population over the next three and a half months during a winter that will forever be memorialized as a historic disaster. The power that was threatening my life.

I had never skinned anything for preservation before. *You must be careful. You must cut with knowledge and intent and respect.* I knew how to do it, conceptually. But I was on my own. I would do it as well as I could.

Blade up, I slide my Havalon knife into the hide of his right side, applying steady pressure to pierce his skin. Once the blade is in, it slides easily, and I cut around the full barrel of his body at roughly the third rib. I slice from the back of each front knee up the back of each leg to meet my main cut around his body. *Don't lose the armpit skin— cut behind and around it.* I cut around each knee fully, then gently peel his leg skin up toward his chest. I peel the whole front hide toward his head, as far as I can go up his neck, then cut off his head. This will make a cape for a shoulder mount.

Go slow. Pay attention. Cut well. Replace your Havalon blades before they start to dull, not after. Know where you are going. Stay present.

As I skin, I notice how delicate he is. How there is no fat anywhere on his body. How his hide hangs loosely over a bony frame. I can see his rib bones shining white through pink muscle once I've skinned his sides. He barely has anything left.

I cut a large chunk out of his hind quarter to expose the femur and crack it open with my hatchet. I know what I will see before I look. The marrow inside is light-brown and translucent and jiggles in a slimy way like rotten jelly. This last reserve of fat bereaved of its final stores as the energy required to survive the elements burned past all that he had.

His is the story of many. It isn't always red in tooth and claw at the end. Often it is white and cold and dark and all alone—the product of hunger and exertion, our reminder that the landscape giveth and the landscape taketh away.

I didn't know then that the winter of 2023 would quickly develop into a catastrophe—an ecological disturbance the likes of which few alive today in western Wyoming have ever seen. I didn't know that, when all was said and done, the winter would claim more than 18,000 lives, and I would kneel before hundreds more of the dead—60 percent of our adult males, 70 percent of our adult females, and every fawn that we'd collared last year—when I was called to meet them out there, beyond the end.

M037 was a warning. *Your tears will shatter over their wasted bodies like frozen glass.*

I roll up his hind cape and can just fit it into my pack. His head is going to be a problem. I forgot cordage, and the straps on my pack are not long enough to attach around him, which has never been an issue before. It isn't until this moment, when I realize that I must carry him in my arms, that I understand how big he is. How broad and large his skull. How thick and heavy his antlers, how far their tines are flung up and out from his ears.

My body is spent. Done. I barely have anything left. I am alive, but I am only halfway through my journey, I am injured, and only four hours of daylight remain. I wonder briefly about his decision to go to sleep. Was it conscious? Or, when it came down to it, was it simply the only thing he could possibly do?

STOP. Clear your mind.

Pick up his head and cape. Hold him with the back of his head against your chest so his antlers are pointing away from you.

Now, go.

Take ten steps until your body fails. Drop him at your feet. Heave, catch your breath. Let the fire in your burning muscles flee. Lament how the snow is many pounds heavier now than early this morning. Worship the trail you made on your way in. Now, gather yourself. Gather your buck. Take ten more steps.

A mile later. Three hours later. You fall. Your legs won't lift. Your arms won't lift. You lie curled around him in the snow, your head resting atop his, his antlers extending far past your plane of vision ahead and up and out. Cry a little. Scream into the back of his head. Breathe his warm, musky scent. Tremble. Now, get up. Get. Up.

Drink some water. Take ten more steps. You can only take five. Stop. Gasp. Roar. To the ridgetops. To the sky. You aren't even hot anymore. Your muscles are failing long before they can generate any heat. Take five more steps. Shake with every one. Grit your teeth. Fill your belly deep with breath. Let it go. Slowly, deliberately. Your body is failing, but you can still control your breath. Settle your mind. Quit thinking about how unbelievable this snow is. How you weren't prepared for it. How you are not as strong as you thought you were. How nobody would be strong enough for this. How much the animals that live out here must be struggling. Set your intention. You will make it out of here alive.

Drink some more water. Take five more steps. You can only take three. Stop. Be calm.

You can take one more step forever. And you must. And you will. And you do.

When you reach the truck, there is nothing left of you. You summon an ounce of energy that doesn't exist to lift him into the bed. Then, pause. Notice how much space he occupies. How his tines extend all the way up the sides of the truck bed. Rest your hand on his dark brow. Just for a moment. Now, get your snowshoes off. Fire up the truck. Get the heat going. Get your wet clothes off. Get yourself to the Flying J. Chug two yellow Gatorades. Devour four chicken tenders, plunged deep into ranch dressing and sweet-and-sour sauce. Drive home through the long cold dark. Fall into bed.

———

IN THE MORNING, I bring him to my boss, Kevin, for the next phase of his preservation into a shoulder mount for outreach and education. Kevin nearly falls over when he sees him. The look on his face says it all—*this animal is magnificent*. Kevin skins the rest of the cape from his skull. We find an infection in the right side of his face, where a wound in his mouth had created a space between his gums and his cheek, where food packed in and festered. It must have hurt him. It must have made it difficult for him to eat.

HERE IS how he is recorded in our database:
Animal ID: M037
End Date: 01/05/2023
Age: 9 ½
Cause of Death: Malnutrition
Antler Score: 194.125

———

REBEKAH RAFFERTY (SHE/HER)
Laramie, Wyoming—traditional territory of the Cheyenne and Arapaho peoples
Rebekah is working on her PhD in the Monteith Shop at the University of Wyoming, studying the ecology of mule deer in the iconic Wyoming Range herd. She loves making good food, writing, and being outside with her husband and corgi-mutt. She wants to share the celebration of both the bodies and lives of the mule deer she studies.
She can be found on Instagram @tudorraff.

and so, i run

MY LEGS ARE HEAVY, MY LUNGS BEG FOR MORE AIR, MY FEET scramble to find footing on roots and rocks and the muddy banks of cold streams. I will myself up a steep hill where the trail has become a washed-out trench. I try to gain time on the downhill stretches while they pound my knees and hips. I talk to myself: "Pick up your feet!" "Jump that log." "Duck that limb." "What am I doing?" "Why am I here?" I keep running.

In 2021, at age fifty-three, I connected the signs that I was and had been on the path of perimenopause. Like the scattered pieces of a jigsaw puzzle, I began fitting together the odd, subtle, and not-so-subtle symptoms that my body was increasingly losing estrogen. The gnawing cravings for certain salty or sweet foods were similar to those I'd gotten in the days leading up to a menstrual cycle, but now the cravings appeared day after day. Monthly migraines that had lessened as I got older crept back in. Once-solid muscle diminished, giving way to loose, wrinkled skin that revealed itself each time I folded into a downward dog. And heightened anxiety filled my mind with mostly imagined impending dangers. The racing thoughts felt like a raging river with banks too steep to climb out.

Though I knew that these feelings of anxiousness, frustration, anger, loss, and even peace and joy would not be permanent, and that downstream I might feel exactly the way I had before the rolling rapids carried me, I had reached a breaking point. I needed something new and adventurous.

I'd retired in 2018 after twenty-seven years in public education. My husband and I became full-time travelers living in our van, seeking out sublime places in an effort to genuinely connect with nature. I loved the freedom of and immersion in various landscapes. We were extremely active and planned a thru-hike of the Appalachian Trail in 2020. Of all the things that could take us off trail 300 miles into our hike, we never envisioned it would be a pandemic. That August, after three years on the road, we made the decision to purchase a house in Franklin, North Carolina, a small mountain town near the Appalachian Trail. We called the house "base camp" and began using it as a launching point for our hiking and backpacking trips.

Without the constant movement of living on the road, I soon began to feel trapped. I was far from participating in longevity training at the local gym, and the idea of taking up knitting or similar endeavors made me cringe. I didn't see myself aging into the old woman in a rocking chair waving a fan at the latest hot flash. I did not want to submit to the idea that these things happen and so be it. Then, I noticed a flyer outside our local gear store, Outdoor 76, announcing the Naturalist Race, a 25K/50K trail run. As an avid hiker, I knew I could hike 15.5 miles, but I'd never run longer than a 5K before. It seemed like just the kind of challenge that would allow me—a former college athlete—to stay curious and discover who I was and what I could be capable of as a woman in my fifties. After contemplating for a few months, I formally registered for the 25K.

The racecourse consisted of 5,500 feet of steep, rocky, rooty climbing on the Bartram Trail to one of North Carolina's natural bald mountains, Wayah Bald. The race instructions clearly stated that all runners had to reach the first aid station at Harrison Gap, 9.6 miles into the race, within three hours to continue the run. I became obsessed with training to meet that cutoff, constantly visualizing myself running into Harrison Gap with time to spare. From there I could fall back on my hiking skills.

The race became my sole focus. I hoped that it would push me out of my comfort zone. I hoped to combat the increasing anxiety coursing through my body, the spikes in appetite, the decreasing muscle mass, and the tight tendons that needed extra recovery time. I was trying to decide what my path to menopause would look like, would feel like, and how I would handle the hormonal changes in my body. I needed to run to feel my breath, my beating heart, my fatigue.

I would have loved to engage with other women—even my mother—about their experiences and advice. But there seemed to be no campfire stories around menopause, no women sharing their stories publicly, or even in hushed tones. Even if my reserved mother had shared her menopause story, my own health and body were so different from hers that I'm not sure I would have gathered many answers. When my mother was my age, her health was already in decline. She'd lost most of her eyesight to type 2 diabetes and her kidney function to high blood pressure. By seventy, she'd begun to show signs of Parkinson's syndrome—rigidity, slowing mobility, and depth perception challenges. Now that she was seventy-seven, Parkinson's syndrome affected her entire being—her mobility, her speech, her ability to swallow, her cognitive processing. Her once-tender hands were now clenched and rigid, unable to grasp a fork or move food to her own mouth.

I sought my own knowledge through podcasts as I embarked on my own private journey on the menopause continuum. I learned that my symptoms were only a small subset of the multitude that women experience during perimenopause. I was able to mitigate much of my discomfort by taking natural supplements, decreasing my caffeine intake, increasing the amount of protein I consumed at each meal, and adding vigorous running and heavy weightlifting to my weekly exercise schedule.

While working to keep my health in check and stay in tune to my body and its needs, I was also learning how to navigate my parents' aging. Each time I drove away from my parents' house, I wondered if I was visiting my mother for the last time. I had witnessed her slow decline over time, like watching the decay of a fallen tree in the woods. I wondered what it felt like, looked like, sounded like, and tasted like to be inside a failing body. My mother was aware and supportive through my training. She asked questions about the race and, true to her personality, rolled her eyes when I explained that a 25K is over fifteen miles. She always thought I was a little *too* adventurous and didn't understand the need to push limits.

The main training block for the race coincided with a commitment my husband and I had made to the National Park Service. We were volunteering for two months as camp hosts at Lewis Mountain Campground in Shenandoah National Park—fifty feet from the AT. This was my training ground for two-thirds of my race preparations.

In Shenandoah National Park, streams are called "runs." Runs flow down the canyons into the hollows, where they connect with rivers. Mossy-covered obstacles block the way. Sometimes, the racing water takes a breath in deep-blue pools before continuing on its path, flowing always down and onward. Water seeking its course. I trained to find my flow. To make the three-hour cutoff time to complete the first 9.6 miles. At the same time, I was learning to adapt to the natural changes occurring in my own body. I found that I needed more recovery time between strenuous runs. I had to fuel my body with quality protein and carbs before and after each run, or with the occasional motivational running reward of a package of powdered donuts and chocolate milk. I also focused on my rest and recovery by settling into the van by eight o'clock each night to read before eight to nine hours of sleep.

From the outset of my first ten-mile training run, my mind and body were both recovered and relaxed to have a great run. I thanked my lungs and my legs for supporting me and my blood for coursing through my veins as I glided along the trail. The nagging tendinitis in my left Achilles was behaving for once. The gentle morning air sighed a cool mountain breeze inviting me further into the run. About twenty minutes in, a kaleidoscope of light sliced through the mosaic of trees ahead of me and I glanced out toward a rocky opening on my right with a view of the Shenandoah Valley. I was entranced, distracted, when I hit a rocky patch and fell forward, landing hard on both of my palms and knees. Stunned by the fall, I rolled over and sat. The impact had jarred me from my headspace, leaving me frustrated and angry. Blood dripped down my leg and blood blisters quickly formed on both palms. I realized I was not hurt beyond repair, and no bone seemed broken. I thought to myself that I could call my husband and try this run again tomorrow. Or, I could not call him. I stood up, took a deep breath, and started to run again. It took another twenty minutes to shake the fall. The knowledge that I could fall again hovered in my mind. But I also knew that each run—good or bad—had a purpose.

With about a month of training left before the race, my husband and I returned home to "base camp." I was excited and nervous about finishing my training. The weeks ticked by, marked by ever-increasing long runs as the race approached.

A week prior to the race, Hurricane Ian, a deadly and powerful Category 5 storm, was brewing in the Atlantic. Communication from the run sponsor began early in the week. The storm was a possible threat, and the race was in danger of being canceled. My mind was all over the place as I decreased my mileage in the taper phase of training. Frustration. Acceptance. Anxiousness. Peace. I watched the weather. Ian was leaving a trail of devastation. Guilt. I was worried about a race while people were losing their homes and lives.

Two days before the race, I read the notification from the race sponsor that the Naturalist 25K/50K race would go on. The course would be altered to a 30K out-and-back for both the 25K and 50K participants due to safety concerns about wind at the higher elevations. For some, the race would be shorter; for the rest, it would be longer. I fretted over the extra 5K and considered postponing to 2023. Months of training, falling and getting back up, making the miles, climbing the hills, doing speed workouts in the heat and humidity, observing my mother's declining health and mobility—it all came back to me. I decided to run.

After my final training run the day before the race, I picked up my credentials, prepared my pre-race meal of pasta, set my clothes out, filled the water bladder in my running vest, and settled into bed. I woke at all hours of the night in anticipation. After a year's preparation, race day dawned. I had my coffee and peanut butter sandwich. My husband and I drove the short distance to Outdoor 76 to mingle with fifty-nine other runners. I did not mingle. I stood to the side observing. I did not feel part of the trail running community yet. I was a novice. I felt overwhelmed.

At 8 a.m., the race sponsor thanked everyone for attending and started a countdown to start the clock. Immediately, the majority of the runners were ahead of me as I tried to maintain focus on my own run. I knew from my training runs that I needed to start slow and that I would increase my speed and settle into the run as I warmed up. My husband cheered me on at the one-mile mark. I took a deep breath when I saw him and laughed. "Only seventeen more miles to go."

I celebrated when my feet finally touched the softer surface of the dirt trail after running the first three miles on the road. The forest wrapped around me, and I immediately felt more at home with roots and rocks under my feet. I crossed over the first bridge into the first climb. I glanced at my watch. I was on pace to make the cutoff. I continued forward and found my flow.

I knew that faster runners would pass me on their way back to the finish since the course was an out-and-back single-track. I set a new goal for myself not to be passed by another runner until I reached William's Pulpit, the first overlook on the trail, about five miles in. I navigated smoothly over rocks strewn like an obstacle course and over roots that were like veins and arteries reaching out of the forest floor. I settled into the run and my brain and body coordinated to simultaneously see and move over the uneven terrain. I witnessed another runner stumble and fall. I stopped only long enough to ask if he was okay. I continued to move forward.

"Yessss," I whispered, pumping my fist, as I passed William's Pulpit—no one had crossed my path yet. About ten minutes later, a beautiful runner flew down the hill toward a first-place finish. He was swift and flawless. I yelled to him, "Awesome job!" I continued forward into an unfamiliar section of the trail, which energized the wanderer and adventurer in me. I noticed a runner in front of me stooped over at the base of a steep incline. She was bent over to catch her breath. As I passed her, I encouraged her to keep moving forward.

I gagged down an energy gel at the six-mile mark. I was in my own head, focusing on my form and my breathing, trying to stay present and willing myself to push forward. I summited the next hill and found refuge in the fact that a ridge or downhill would be nearby. I knew I did not look like the gliding runner who had passed me on his way to the finish line—but I felt like him. There were more ups and downs. More pain and suffering to come. More ridges and roots and rocks.

I willed my body into a recovery run, not allowing myself to stop or just hike. When the mountain was winning and my suffering was growing, I thought of my mother and her labored gait and inability to walk without assistance. I thought about my dad, the sole caregiver for my mother, and his tireless routine of assisting her day after day. I focused on my feet hitting the trail and my legs striding.

I thought about my two grandsons who'd recently hiked a portion of this trail with me. I knew part of my motivation for running such a tough race was to be a role model for health and adventure for my stepchildren and grandchildren. I would top a hill and go into recovery mode and then run. There were times I felt like I was floating and times when I had to remind myself that hills are not infinite.

At 10:30 a.m., two and half hours into the race, I neared the turn-around point at the only aid station to cheers from volunteers. A young boy was on the trail with a bullhorn. He shouted that another runner was coming into the gap. That runner was me. As I entered Harrison Gap, tears filled my eyes. No time to celebrate, I was only halfway through. But this gap had been the sole focus of my training. I'd made it. The cheers, clapping, and support from the volunteers motivated me to make my stop quick. I peed, resupplied my water, and snagged a pack of peanut butter from the aid station. I was still choking it down with a swig of water when I ran back out of the gap.

The immediate steep climb out of Harrison Gap brought my

attention back to my body. I cycled through all my checks—my breathing, my posture, my gait. I kept going. At some point, I gagged down the remainder of the first energy gel. I saw a runner ahead who had stopped to catch his breath. Later, I learned his legs were giving out, but he too would finish. I willed my body to continue. I pushed through each mile of the course. My body and mind were an engine moving forward—no stopping.

As I topped William's Pulpit for the second time, I felt a surge of new energy. I was back to familiar territory. From my training, I knew the next two-mile section was all downhill. My feet floated over the trail as I dashed downhill, feeling a soft breeze touching my face. It was on this portion of the trail that I knew I would finish the course. I smiled. I had already run a half-marathon, the most I had ever run continuously.

My husband met me at the Wallace Branch trailhead before the last three-mile section of road back to the finish. He yelled and cheered, "You can do this! Keep going." I looked at him and said, "I am doing this shit."

Back on the narrow two-lane road, I felt like I was playing dodgeball with cars. I threw my hands up in the air like a crazy lady and yelled, "I am here!" It all seemed quite dangerous. Finally, I made it to the safety of the sidewalk. I felt empowered. My legs were tired. I kept running. I passed the familiar sights of Franklin's downtown and started the final climb past the Ace Hardware and the Lazy Hiker Brewery to the finish. I visualized how I wanted to finish. I pumped my arms and lifted my heavy legs.

I ran across the finish line with tears of joy on my cheeks. I, at fifty-four years old, had done a *big* thing—a massive run. I had set a goal and completed it. I was excited to see a few runners I had met on the trail. I was proud of them for finishing too. Now, I mingled. I was part of the trail running community.

I AM BACK AT SHENANDOAH, a year since I trained here to run the Naturalist Race. I am training again, and camp-hosting. I hike and run. I'm working on climbing steep inclines at a faster pace. My next race is a half-marathon in December in Helen, Georgia, that I am running with my stepdaughter. I rest with my back against a decaying oak, which lies perpendicular to Cedar Run. I listen to the orchestra of birds and water as it traverses and weaves through the rock; a canyon cut by water. A run. I see light reflecting, trickling water as it crests and turns kinetic. It falls downward, then surfaces to form a deep blue-green pool. Downstream, I notice the summer green of a basswood reflecting on its surface. I breathe. I let my thoughts float like clouds. *Be here. Be calm. This moment. This is sublime.* At any second the water will disappear down its course to the pool below, where it pauses for a time, then charges forward again toward the river where sometimes the rapids are fast and uncertain and the obstacles are many and where, sometimes, the water finds its way to a resting spot of tranquility.

And so, I continue to run.

I approach the last interval to the title of postmenopausal. I run to keep my body, mind, and soul connected so I can continue to move forward with goals, with purpose, and seek hope and happiness. And I run to take the grief and joy of life moment by moment. And I seek moments like the recent family hike when my four-year-old grandson looked at me with his daring and adventurous eyes and pronounced, "I have an idea."

He reached for my hand. We clambered up and over loose soil on a steep embankment. I held on to barely visible tree roots with one hand and held tightly to his hand with the other as we moved toward a rock overhanging the stream. And there we sat together.

———

Anne McArthur Jobe (she/her)

Franklin, North Carolina—ancestral territories of the Cherokee (East), Yuchi, and Miccosukee peoples

Anne is a trail runner and hiker who seeks peace in nature. She has backpacked 400 miles on the Appalachian Trail and is a camp host at

Lewis Mountain in Shenandoah National Park during peak thru-hiking months. She holds an EdS in educational leadership K–12 and spent 27 years in public education in Huntsville, Alabama. In addition to the outdoors, she is passionate about educating students, spending time with family, volunteering, reading, and traveling.

She can be found on Instagram @Seeking_the_Sublime.

from gold ridge to happiness

ON A CHILLY DECEMBER MORNING IN 2019, MY HUSBAND, Chad, and I pulled into a dark desert parking lot. The running group was already congregating around the Gold Ridge trailhead sign. A nagging headache prickled just behind my eyelids, and it had taken a herculean effort to get out of bed at five o'clock. By the time we had dropped our son off at my dad's, we were running late. I fidgeted with my gear, going through a mental checklist of everything I needed, while my husband parked. We had never run this trail, and other than finding the trailhead, I'd done no research. I took a long, slow pull from my coffee and one deep, centering breath before getting out of the car. *Thirteen miles. I can do thirteen miles.*

I knew that I could run thirteen miles because I'd done it several times that year.

The problem now was that we had registered for the Antelope Canyon 55K ultramarathon, a mere three months away, and we had committed very little effort so far to preparing for it. It felt imperative that we make the full thirteen miles with the group. I was starting to get acquainted with the core group that ran every Wednesday, but I hadn't done any of the long runs on Sundays yet. The route was an out-and-back, so the local running-store manager, and coordinator of the group, said anyone was welcome. *Go as far as you want and turn around.* I was bound and determined to go the full distance.

The group set off at an easy pace. Hikers in the back, seasoned runners in the lead. I somehow ended up near the front of the group, and the steady incline immediately tore at my legs and shot my heart rate up. For our previous races, Chad and I had trained on the road, finding it easier to push our young son in a stroller than to find a babysitter so we could go run trails. I hadn't yet learned one of the best things about trail running: you get to hike. I was under the delusion that if you didn't run the whole thing, you weren't a real runner.

A mile in, my heartbeat was a death knell in my throat and the trail showed no signs of leveling off. I was fairly certain my calf muscles were going to rip through my skin and completely separate from my body. Had I researched the trail, I would have known about the 3,000 feet of elevation gain—2,000 feet of which is in the first three miles.

Finally, we reached a gate, and I stepped to the side to take off my jacket. The runners behind me politely waited for me to step back into the lead and proceed up the mountain. I shook my head and made an excuse about needing to fix my pack so they would head off without me.

It was a straight shot to my pride. *At least keep up with them. If you can't run it, you shouldn't be out here.* My head pounded an acute reminder that I'd had more to drink than I meant to the night before. I took a deep breath and started jogging again.

The beginning had been a steady incline that gradually got steeper, but now the trail resembled the tail end of a dragon, and I was in the spines. Some sections were so steep I could have put my hands down and crawled. The trail abruptly peaked and then fell into a steep descent, before immediately turning back into another incline. I couldn't run it. I hiked slowly, looking at my Garmin the whole time. My pace was twenty-two minutes per mile. At this rate, the hikers were going to catch me. *Come on, just move your damn feet.* I topped out one section, only to see the trail go straight up again from there. Endless spines for as far as I could see. My heart landed in my stomach like a large stone and then rose up into my throat, stealing my air. I could see the group in the distance getting farther and farther away. I couldn't find Chad's distinctive gait among them, so I put my head down and kept climbing.

Halfway up the next incline, my foot slipped on loose shale. I slid down a few feet. My Garmin said I was moving at a twenty-five-minute-per-mile pace. The mountain seemed to have no end. I couldn't climb any faster. My legs were on fire, and I had completely forgotten how to breathe. Fuming, I sat down, picked up a rock, and chucked it as hard as I could over the edge. *God, this is humiliating. I am never drinking again.* I tucked my head between my knees and cried. It felt like the mountain had caved in on top of me. I don't quit, but I couldn't stomach taking another step up that goddamn mountain.

If I couldn't run thirteen miles, I wasn't going to be able to run thirty-four.

My head hurt. My heartbeat pulsated behind my eyes. My whole body felt heavy like it wanted to sink into the cool dirt beneath the thorny manzanita bushes and never rise again.

I knew my biggest problem was that I was hungover. Like so many times before, I'd promised to stop after two drinks. But the next thing I knew, I was six beers deeper. And now I was paying the price. It wasn't just the hangover, though. It was also everything else.

I'm a bad mom.

I shouldn't be out here wasting my time trying to run when clearly, I can't do it.

I should be home with my baby.

I should be getting ready for the school week.

I have grading to do and midterms to plan.

I have standardized tests and growth meetings to prepare for.

The sun rose higher into the sky over my curled, sobbing form. The mental laundry list of every cruel thing I could say about myself began to coalesce into a series of deep truths.

I don't want to be a teacher.

I don't want to drink so much.

I'm not the type of parent I want to be.

I want to do well at Antelope.

I miss my mom.

Chad's favorite quote popped into my head: "You are only one decision away from a completely different life."

Running had been one of those decisions, and up until this moment, it had been the single thing in my life I felt like I had any control over.

Eleven months before Gold Ridge, I had started running for the same reason I think a lot of people start running: I wanted to lose weight. When my son was eleven months old, I was done breastfeeding, and I wanted my body back. Motherhood is beautiful, but it is also hard. You lose pieces of yourself along the way, and I didn't feel entirely human anymore. For better or worse, losing the baby weight had felt like a good first step in rediscovering who I was, so I told Chad that it was my New Year's resolution. He had offered to join me in the endeavor—having gained quite a bit of weight in solidarity. In fact, he had taken my resolution one step further and suggested we sign up for a marathon. I negotiated down to a half-marathon.

On New Year's Eve, we had tipsily registered for the Tucson Shamrock Half Marathon. It was three months away, leaving us no time to procrastinate on training. I googled, "What is a good half-marathon time?" If I was going to do the thing, I was going to do it right. I decided I would run it in two hours. The internet also suggested that a person be able to run three consecutive miles before beginning a half-marathon training plan. I decided that was doable, even though I hadn't done it. I then searched, "How to run a two-hour half-marathon." I downloaded a training plan from *Runner's World* and stuck it on the fridge, then went to bed well ahead of midnight.

The next day, January 1, 2019, Chad and I put Kyler in the stroller and ran the road behind our house. As a novice runner, I didn't have a smartwatch or Fitbit, no way to track any of it. The training plan called for a two-mile run, so we took the short loop. (I now know that loop is about a half-mile.) I threw up when we made it back to the house. It's a miracle we didn't quit right then and there. It was a wake-up call, though.

In our former, pre-child lives, Chad and I had been athletic. We had both played varsity sports in high school, traveled on competitive club teams, and remained active into adulthood. Post-baby, we mountain biked, hiked, and snowboarded occasionally, though we were far from avid enthusiasts about any of it. Chad had been smoking a pack of cigarettes a day, and I was pretty well steeped in mommy wine culture at that point. That's the crux of being a former athlete. A part of you will always believe you are in shape, even when you are not. But I had already spent my money, registered for that race, and roped my husband into running with me. We were committed.

Chad and I did not miss a single training day. We ran in the rain; we ran in the snow. When we didn't have time during the day, we ran in the middle of the night. It was hard. The whole time. I ran in the wrong shoes and got shin splints. I ran every run too fast because I had no idea what an easy run was. But thanks to our diligence, the miles built up. I bought a Fitbit so I could keep track. I remember being amazed that I ran 250 miles in three months.

I completed the race in 2:00:49. Chad finished in 2:03:29. It felt absolutely liberating to set a goal—a goal that had felt impossible and one I had attempted to talk myself out of multiple times—and reach it. I may have technically "missed it" by forty-nine seconds, but to me, I had succeeded.

In three months, we had gone from puking in the backyard after a very slow half-mile to finishing a half-marathon in two hours. I loved it. I felt more like myself training and racing that half-marathon than I think I ever had. The adaptability of the human body amazed me.

On the drive home, I told Chad I was sad it was over. I had enjoyed adhering to a training regime, adapting, and trying new gear, and having something to work toward. Chad is a simple man with simple solutions. He said, "Sign up for another one."

So I did.

A great thing about signing up for races, and researching all things running, is your feed changes on social media. Instead of offers for wine club subscriptions, I was getting ads for Vacation Races with tagline: *Destination Races in Breathtaking Places.* The pictures of Antelope Canyon stuck out to me in those ads. The half-marathon distance went past Horseshoe Bend but didn't run through the slot canyons. I really wanted to run through the slot canyons. So, I called my husband.

Something to know about Chad: if he has limits, he doesn't know he has them. So he didn't hesitate. If we were going to drive all the way to Page and figure out how to bring a babysitter with us and all the logistics it takes to travel with a two-year-old, we might as well make it worthwhile. "Sign us up for the 55K."

And that's how I'd arrived here, sitting on the side of Gold Ridge, crying and feeling defeated. I wondered if it had been a mistake. The difficulty of the trail and my unpreparedness for it unfurled every difficulty in my life, bringing all my mistakes to light.

I watched the trail below me for what felt like hours, the dirt turning copper, white minerals in the rocks glittering in the rising sun. Eventually, I stood up and climbed to the top of that spine. I was nowhere near the actual top of the Mazatzals, but I faked some semblance of achievement by making it to the top of that section. I had run (or hiked) almost three miles, with 2,000 feet of elevation gain, and thankfully, Chad was standing at the top looking exasperated. He had turned around at three miles. We had to go pick Kyler up, and he'd realized that we weren't going to make the thirteen-mile goal at this pace.

"This is a fucking horrible trail," he said. "You can't even run it."

I shrugged, too raw to speak.

"Do you want to keep going?" he asked. "Or should we go back? Should be faster going back. We have some time before we have to get Kyler."

"Let's just head back. I'm done."

Chad started down the trail ahead of me, sliding and jumping between rocks.

"We aren't going to make it at Antelope," I said. It was easier to talk to his back, moving down the trail.

"Why?"

"We can't even do thirteen miles, and it's three months away."

Chad snorted. "Antelope isn't going to be like this. I bet we climbed more today than we will for that entire race."

He was almost right. I looked it up later, and we did climb almost as much in three miles on Gold Ridge as we would over the entire thirty-four-mile course at Antelope. The total elevation gain for Antelope Canyon would be 2,700 feet.

Chad kept bouncing down the trail, shaking his head and scoffing at how awful it was to run, but was otherwise in great spirits.

I felt better after crying myself out. As we headed back toward the trailhead, I realized that I had spent the whole climb staring at my feet. Now I could appreciate the view. It was surprisingly green for the desert, brush-covered hills rising all around us. In the distance, layers of blue mountains as far as I could see. I wondered how much better the vista would've been if I'd made it to the top.

———

I DIDN'T GIVE up on Antelope Canyon. Gold Ridge was the kick in the pants I needed to get going on training. We managed to sneak in a few more long runs on local trails but fell back to what I was most comfortable with, running loops around my small town. The road felt gentler on my legs and soul than the rocky, steep trails. I knew I'd get there, eventually.

I started seriously considering that my life might be better without alcohol. Giving it up felt like an impossible task, though. Parent-teacher conferences without wine after? Being the only one on holidays, birthdays, and Friday nights without a beer in my hand? Girls' night out without margaritas? The cognitive dissonance was dizzying. On the one hand, I had tangible evidence that drinking was making my goals harder to achieve, and on the other, I had near daily social reminders that life isn't livable without alcohol. Surely, I could just moderate. I'd set rules and follow them, no excuses.

No drinking before long runs.

No drinking during the workweek.
No drinking before five in the afternoon.
One glass of water between every alcoholic drink.

It worked, until it didn't. No drinking before long runs, except if it was my mom's birthday, then I deserved to drink with a childhood friend who had loved her too. Horrendously hungover, I ran eighteen agonizing miles the next day, swearing with every step that I was done. I'd never be hungover again. *Follow the rules. No excuses.*

The Thursday before Antelope Canyon, my best friend and I went out to celebrate the end of my mom's three-and-a-half-year medical malpractice lawsuit. It had touched every aspect of my life. Lawyers wanted pictures from my wedding, especially the one of me leaving my bridal bouquet on my mom's grave. They wanted pictures of me pregnant with my son, to show the jury the moments that had been stolen from us. It had made my grief feel staged. The decisions I had made to survive the loss felt inauthentic because they were being documented for a lawsuit. But finally it was over. We could all move on.

We sang karaoke and drank beer after beer while I spilled the relief I felt. In an alcohol-fueled haze, I felt that it was fate to close this chapter only a few days before my biggest run yet. It never crossed my mind that with each beer, I was sabotaging the race I was so excited for. The rule of drinking water between each beer was long forgotten. The bar emptied out, we finished our drinks, and my friend's husband stole my keys and gave me a ride home.

We drove to Page the following day. I sat in the back of the minivan with my son, thankful that my in-laws were driving and I could sleep it off. Of course Kyler decided he would not nap for the entire four-hour drive, so neither did I. I kept looking at the stress sensors on my Garmin, begging them to go down as alcohol seeped out of my pores. I was supposed to run thirty-four miles the next day, and I felt like sticky, nauseous death.

Between consuming gallons of electrolytes and vitamin supplements and going to bed as early as Kyler would allow, I woke up feeling okay on race day. The endorphins and adrenaline coursing through my body at the starting line worked miracles.

Once the race started, I didn't think about my hangover anymore. I didn't worry about whether we would finish. We were here. We were doing it. The miles of sand I had dreaded didn't feel so deep or so exhausting. Chad and I took a selfie in front of Horseshoe Bend. The mossy blue-green water contrasted starkly with the sunlit canyon walls below us. It was everything I'd hoped it would be.

The slot canyons were mesmerizing. The bright blue sky looked like a river above our heads surrounded by orange waves frozen in time. I soaked it in. As I hiked, I barely registered the other racers passing me. Who cared how fast I could run? This was amazing. This was why we were here. Not to see how fast we could push through fifty-five kilometers, but to see this, a spectacular underground canyon carved from years of floods and harsh elements and made more beautiful by time. Trail running isn't all about speed and precision. Sometimes it's about slowing down and taking in exactly where you are and how you made it there. We finished Antelope Canyon in eight hard, beautiful, blissful hours. I learned that day, and many times over since then, that ultramarathons are like a washing machine for the soul; you walk away feeling wrung out but clean.

Since my mom's death in 2016, I had been living my life in fast-forward. I had gotten married and had a baby before even a year had passed. Life events I was not on track for at all. I had felt like I needed to do all the things that mattered the most *right now*, because time is a finite resource, and I had been wasting a lot of mine. I started to prioritize the people and things I cared about and learned to say no to things that I didn't. I stepped back from a lot of my obligations at school that were making me miserable but that I had felt, as a new teacher, I had to do. My mom and I were extremely close, and she taught me a lot, but sometimes I think I learned the hardest, most important lessons about life when she died. I was forced to reexamine every life choice I had ever made.

In my rush to live life to the fullest, I never really grieved. I didn't have time for it, didn't want to feel it, so I stuffed it down and drowned it in alcohol. That was really the most ironic part. I wanted to live my best life, my fullest life, because my mom's was cut short, but I muted my whole world with alcohol because I didn't want to miss her. I have learned that you cannot selectively numb. I lost the good with the bad.

Gold Ridge was the first time in a long time that I had let myself feel her loss and what it meant for my son and the choices I was making as a parent. She would have been the world's best grandma. He is exactly the kind of little boy, ornery and full of energy, that she would have cherished and spoiled rotten. I had finally stopped for a moment to really feel that. Antelope Canyon was the first time I acknowledged that the best moments are the moments you stop pushing, stop comparing, and just let it be. It was only then that I could finally give up alcohol.

Immediately after finishing Antelope Canyon, I resigned myself to the fact that moderation was a trap. Despite my best intentions, there would always be moments when I couldn't moderate. I started with thirty-day challenges. During the thirty days, my alcohol-free body functioned better. I ran and played with my son and got through my days feeling strong and capable. At the end of a successful thirty days, I would give alcohol another chance. I quickly stopped sleeping as well, my anxiety spiked, and it became a chore to do the things I liked to do, especially running. Another thirty-day challenge would begin.

Over the course of two years, I read every book I could find about women's (particularly mothers') journeys to quit drinking. I found camaraderie and hope in these stories. I journaled relentlessly; pages and pages on why I no longer wanted to drink. I researched alcohol and its effects on the mind and the body, horrifying my subconscious into finally accepting that alcohol is in fact a poison. I even convinced my husband to quit with me. It was a slow process, and when someone asks me—usually in reference to how far I run—what's the hardest thing I have ever done, my response is still quitting alcohol.

Alcohol is a weird substance. It is the only drug you have to justify not taking. I think, hearing my story or discovering I don't drink anymore, some people assume I must have hit rock bottom. That I'm an alcoholic who needed AA to get my life back. But that's not it. I wasn't blacking out on a nightly basis, neglecting my family, or getting DUIs. By society's standards, I'd say I was a fairly average drinker, but I could see where I was headed if I didn't stop. My life was permanently muted. The colors weren't as bright. Now I know that parenting, running, living are all so much better in full color and sound. I've never woken up at 5 a.m. to run and wished I was hungover. I've never felt like a milestone in my son's life would have been more special if I had had a drink. Life is simpler and more vibrant without it.

———

A YEAR AFTER ANTELOPE CANYON, I went back to Gold Ridge and made it to the top with two running friends. We were training together for a 42K trail race, and neither of them had been before. I warned them that this trail had defeated me in spectacular fashion. It quickly became a joke and the theme of the day. I pointed out the spot where I had stopped previously, and Jamie agreed it was a particularly soul-crushing spot. We had a good laugh when we realized that if I had just pushed over the next ridge, the worst of the climbing would have been over, and the whole mountain range would have opened up.

Gold Ridge is always a tough run, but that day the burning in my legs didn't feel sinister. During the harder climbs, our conversations grew quiet, but I could still breathe and take in the changing landscape as we climbed higher. Scrub bushes turned to manzanitas, and manzanitas turned to pine trees. The lower green hills gave way to craggy rock ridges that rose defiantly against a bright blue sky.

The view was spectacular.

Gold Ridge has become one of my favorite routes during the winter months. Every time I run there, I can't help comparing where I am now to where I was that first time. I don't drink. I quit teaching. I own my own business and set my own schedule. Parenting is hard, but it's the best kind of hard. I run ultramarathons for fun. I like who I am, which is not something I was able to say before.

SKYE LAMMERS (SHE/HER)

Payson, Arizona—traditional territory of the Pueblos, Western Apache, and Hohokam peoples

Skye developed a love of trail running after a childhood exploring rugged Arizona terrain on horseback and on foot. She has completed the Whiskey Basin 92K and Black Canyon 100K. She's been published twice in *High Country Hunter: Hunting in Rim Country & the White Mountains*. She thinks that nature heals and the world would be a better place if more people attempted to do hard things out in the middle of nowhere.

She can be found on Instagram @SkyeLammers.

in the name of being present

I AWOKE TO A SHARP PAIN RADIATING FROM THE CENTER OF my being and sat upright in my tent before a wave of nausea sent me swimming for safety back under the warmth of my quilt. My mouth watered as I rolled over and reached for the zipper.

Air. I needed air.

It was day fourteen of my twenty-one-day thru-hike on the 211-mile Nüümü Poyo, also known as the John Muir Trail. My friends and I had been fortunate enough to score a permit on our second try. It felt like we had won the lottery, and now I was terrified that I would be the reason it all came to a screeching halt.

I cursed under my breath as I slowly poked my head out of the tent. The pain in my stomach convinced me I must have messed up somehow—contaminated my water, mixed up my clean and dirty bottles, broken my filter, done *something* terribly wrong—and given myself giardia.

I pulled on my fleece hat, climbed out of the tent, and slipped into my camp shoes before promptly sitting back down onto a rock. Nausea twisted my insides. I shivered, even though I was wearing all of my layers. My mouth tasted sour, and the idea of eating breakfast was repulsive. I took deep breaths as my best friend, Arms, sat down close beside me. We huddled together for warmth.

"Something must be wrong," I whispered to her. The sun hadn't yet peeked above the steep edges of the Sierra Nevada. The valley where we sat was in the shadows, a dusk-like space between light and dark. Just beyond the edges of what we could see, alpenglow bathed the mountains in a rich pink light. Camp was quiet with no signs of movement from the other tents scattered around the lake. I watched each exhale become tendrils of mist in the early morning light. In that moment, all we could hear was the sound of our breaths.

Arms's soft voice broke the silence. "I fell coming down the hill from using the bathroom earlier."

"Oh shit," I whispered. "Are you okay?"

"I don't know, it hurts. I'm going to keep hiking though," she said, pulling up the leg of her pants to show me her ankle, wrapped neatly in a bandage.

I hoped that our other hiking partner, Pig's Ear, was having a better morning than we were, and that our misfortune wouldn't stick to the "bad things come in threes" rule.

Eventually, the sky became bluer and hikers retrieved bear cans and made coffee over tiny stoves. My nausea gradually passed, but I was left with the deep pain churning my stomach.

My heart pounded harder than it should have as I climbed a small hill and squatted to pee behind a stand of scrubby conifers. Facing back toward camp, I would know if anyone approached, not that there was much I could do about it with my pants around my ankles and pee sprinkled on my shoes.

I wiped myself with my pee cloth and pulled my pants back up before stumbling back down the hill. Eventually, I choked down a few bites of breakfast before leaving camp around 7 a.m. It was the same time we'd left on other mornings, but half an hour later than we'd meant to be on trail that day.

As we climbed toward Mather Pass, my stomach remained tied in knots. It was too painful to tighten the hip belt of my pack; all thirty-five pounds sagged on my shoulders. My heart felt as heavy as my pack.

The day before I had left home in Maine for the Eastern Sierra, my relationship with my girlfriend, Chris, had felt like it was crumbling in front of me. She'd been avoiding spending one-on-one time with me in the weeks leading up to my thru-hike; my pleas for connection were cut short. Then the day before I was scheduled to fly to California, when we were finally together, she was called into the hospital where she worked.

"I'll just be a couple hours," she'd said as she rushed out the door. Three hours later, I needed to go home, and she still hadn't returned.

Swing by the hospital on your way out, she texted. *I'll get a break soon. I'll come down and say goodbye.*

Our kiss goodbye in the short-term parking lot of the hospital was punctuated by my own poorly timed attempt to seek reassurance that she'd still be there when I returned.

"Are you sure you won't find someone cooler to be with while I'm gone?" I asked, half-joking. It was a question I had asked more seriously the year before when I left on my first thru-hike, and I'd had more fear then that it would actually happen. This time, she responded to my energetic leaning in with a push away that sent me reeling.

"You know I won't. But one of these days I'm going to want to see other people too. That fear is something you'll eventually need to work on," she said, a cold edge to her tone.

"I know, babe, I was only joking," I managed through my tears. She wasn't wrong; despite being polyamorous myself, the idea of her finding someone else still brought up deep fears of being replaced. The timing of this conversation, however, was terrible. I sobbed the entire drive home.

Four days later, Arms, Pig's Ear, and I picked up our backcountry permit. That night at our campsite we shared what we wanted to leave behind as we set out on this adventure.

Arms and Pig's Ear both set intentions about leaving behind distractions and being more present. I wanted to leave behind my fears about my relationship with Chris. I swore to them and to myself that I wouldn't carry that heartache for 211 miles. But now, two-thirds of the way through our hike, there I was, crumpling under the load.

In the first few days of the trip, I'd called both my girlfriend, Chris, and my wife, Katrina, whenever I had service on trail. Cell service slowly tapered off as we ventured deeper into the wilderness. In those early calls and text messages, I'd learned that despite my being on the opposite side of the country and far from civilization, Chris wanted more space.

Pig's Ear walked directly ahead of me as we crawled up the switchbacks toward Mather Pass. I kept my head down, and when there weren't other hikers nearby, Pig's Ear played music on her phone to break up the monotony of the climb. I hardly noticed the scrubby trees giving way to towering rock faces and creamy clusters of white columbine flowers.

Arms opted to hike ahead for a bit. She needed alone time and planned to wait for us at the top of the pass. She was the least experienced in our group but easily cruised away from us. I admired the way her long legs covered ground uphill and thought about how often we must be holding her back.

As we pushed on, I wondered if the sick feeling in my stomach was partially a result of the punch in the gut I'd gotten from reading Chris's messages the night before in my tent. She had said she felt like our attachment styles were incompatible. She wanted to spend more time taking travel nursing assignments in other parts of the country, and she worried about how I struggled when one of us left for a period of time. It felt like she was looking for an easy out, something that I'd noticed in the year and a half we'd been dating. I couldn't understand why it seemed our relationship wasn't worth fighting for, or why she didn't want to commit to being with me when I tried to be the best partner I could be. I had gone to sleep hungry and heartsick, her words playing over in my head.

In reality, my acute stomachache was probably due to a combination of things, giardia the least likely among them. Though I'd planned for my caloric needs based on my experience thru-hiking Vermont's Long Trail the summer before, I'd never hiked at high elevation. None of us had taken into consideration that exertion at altitude would require our bodies to work harder and burn more calories. I'd been going to bed hungry for days. It was likely that my body had finally reached the end of its calorie-deficient rope.

I appreciated Pig's Ear's music. It covered up my barely contained sniffles as I alternated between focusing on the sheer weight of the pack on my shoulders and thinking about Chris's messages. I tried to focus on just putting one foot in front of the other. I thought of all the things I had ever wished I could say to Chris but hadn't—and still wouldn't for fear of causing the end of a relationship that I cherished.

I wanted to tell her how unfair it felt every time she did something reassuring and then turned around and did the opposite: sending me a love song that made her think of me, then choosing a friend over me; asking me to be there for her on a hard day, then telling me she just wasn't sure whether this would work out. Some days I felt like she was giving me false hope that our relationship was becoming more secure and stable. But the next day, it was like she had one foot out the door, ready to walk away at a moment's notice. I couldn't stop thinking about the ways she'd avoided being with me before I left, or how she'd somehow requested the wrong vacation time and would be gone on a trip when I came home from the trail.

Of course I'd had a hard time leaving for the trail—I felt completely disconnected from her.

Each time Pig's Ear and I paused to talk, I sipped water and pushed my sunglasses up my nose, hoping she wouldn't notice the tears continually threatening to fall. When we neared the top of Mather Pass and saw Arms waiting for us, I couldn't hold the sadness inside my body anymore.

"What's wrong?" she asked.

"I feel so sick." I gasped for breath. "My pack is so heavy without the hip belt tight. And the climb was hard. And I'm just so sad."

She held me until my tears slowed. From there, the descent was much easier than the climb. I tried to admire the way the smooth rock faces transitioned gently into the grassy spaces and surrounded the tiny blue lakes dotting the basin below. But the trail was narrow and steep and required most of my attention. I wore braces on both of my knees every day, a result of patellas that had preferred to dislocate rather than stay in place for years now.

Thanks to Pig's Ear's outgoing nature and a couple of weekend hikers who had overpacked, we secured some additional food later that afternoon. The extra rations were enough to boost our morale, and they would get us through more comfortably until our final resupply.

For the better part of a week, rain had fallen daily in the Sierra Nevada. A light sprinkle often turned to a total downpour for hours a day and the locals were calling the weather pattern unprecedented. The rain had done so much damage that two days earlier we'd nearly had to hike out after learning that the road to our next resupply was closed. There was no known reopening date, and more rain was forecast every day. As a hiker from New England, I could begrudgingly handle hiking in the rain, but I was concerned about our ability to access our next resupply or exit safely if we needed to.

I used my GPS device to text the motel we'd be staying at for our final resupply in Independence. They told me that they had been able to shuttle hikers despite the road closure, so we continued on, taking some extra precautions to camp away from creeks that could swell beyond their limits overnight.

My mental state deteriorated from the rain, much like the trail. After falling asleep to the sound of raindrops on my tent nearly every night, I pulled on damp clothes again each morning. One night I cried and broke my own rule about not eating inside my tent. It felt like the rain was never going to end. I wiped the tears from my eyes as I slowly chewed a Snickers bar, hoping the chocolate would help both my growling stomach and my sadness. I'd been hungry since we arrived in camp but decided to hide out in hopes that the rain would pass so we could make dinner without crowding together under Pig's Ear's sun umbrella.

At the top of one particularly chilly, rainy pass on day sixteen, Arms whispered, "Guys, I'm really cold." She sounded exhausted and struggled to get her snack bar out of its wrapper. She shivered violently as Pig's Ear and I rushed to help her put on more layers. I tore open an emergency packet of hand warmers with my teeth and handed them to her. Icy rain pelted our exposed faces and fingers. Arms and Pig's Ear had both brought thin polyester gloves, but they weren't waterproof and were no match for the rain. I'd made a rookie mistake and had not brought anything for my hands. I would buy a pair of gloves in Independence.

The trail was hard to find in spots, probably due to rockslides and all the rain. As we picked our way down the steep switchbacks, climbing over and around boulders, Arms's teeth stopped chattering. She warmed up and became more sure of her footing. By lunchtime she was feeling much better.

Communication with both of my partners continued to be spotty. I tried to give Chris the distance she wanted. When we finally hitched into Independence and got to our motel, I wondered if maybe Chris and I shouldn't talk. When I got service on the descent to the trailhead, an excited *Hi!!!!* made me think she wanted to catch up. But I didn't want to face the text conversation we'd had or address everything that was leaving me hurt and frustrated. I don't remember who called whom, but when we talked in the morning, we followed an unspoken agreement not to discuss how hard things had been between us. In some ways, it felt reassuring—a sign that things might be able to go back to normal when I went home, even though "normal," that back-and-forth dance we'd been doing for well over a year now, hadn't been quite right. At the very least, it let me set out on my last few days of the hike with less fear that Chris would break up with me before I made it home.

I set out from Independence on day seventeen feeling hopeful. Sun shone down on our faces when we reached the top of Kearsarge Pass. It lifted my mood, leaving me with a subtle sense of promise that this challenge in my relationship with Chris would be just another bump in the road, and that we'd be okay.

I caught my breath and turned a full 360 degrees, panoramic views as far as I could see. The valley we'd just climbed up from lay below on one side, its winding road cutting a ribbon through the open desert beneath the thick green band of conifer trees. I turned around again, facing toward the trail. Sun illuminated the sandy descent into the trees and grassy meadows surrounding Bullfrog Lake. Wind blew across the surface of the water, making it dance and sparkle like glitter.

Weather on trail improved for a couple of days, aside from a near miss with a hail and lightning storm that left us drenched and terrified on top of 13,200-foot Forester Pass on day eighteen. But day nineteen rolled in with overcast skies.

I had learned that if there were any clouds in the sky when I left my tent in the morning, it was going to rain at some point that day. A sky full of clouds, their bellies swollen and heavy with rain, was bad news. We had ten miles to our next campsite, just beyond Guitar Lake, where we would stage for our ascent of Tumangaya, or Mount Whitney, at sunrise the following morning. Reaching the summit would signify the official end of the John Muir Trail, though we would still have another night at camp, followed by half a day's hiking to reach the trailhead at Whitney Portal and the end of our journey.

I had two main goals that day. The first was to keep my clothes dry for our ascent the next morning. Tumangaya is the tallest mountain in the Lower 48, standing at 14,505 feet. Conditions at that elevation can be unpredictable, but the forecast called for below-freezing temperatures and wind, which would make it feel even colder. My second goal was to be present in the beauty of the Sierra Nevada. I wanted to enjoy this time with my friends, to create memories that would become a core part of our friendship. I wanted to fully celebrate the journey we'd been on together.

It rained off and on all day, the drenching interrupted by brief periods of humid sunshine. I hiked in a merino wool bra and underwear under my raincoat and pants. My rain pants were made of a nonwoven, lightweight fabric, and with so much wear over the past three weeks, they were literally falling apart at the seams. I'd patched the butt with duct tape, but the waterproof top layer flaked off as I walked.

Sweat rolled down my body, unable to evaporate through my rain gear. I watched Pig's Ear struggle with her puffy coat. It had gotten soaked in the hail and lightning storm on Forester Pass and hadn't had an opportunity to dry out. With the rain and humidity, it wouldn't dry today either; she would be wearing a damp, non-insulating layer for our climb in the morning. I decided I would tolerate the sweat and leave my clothes safe inside the waterproof liner of my pack.

Another friend we had made, Barn Dawg, planned to camp with us that night, so we could all summit together the next morning. He messaged me on my GPS to let us know that there were campsites available, with access to water, but they were very exposed, and the wind was increasing. He wondered if we might want to stop sooner. We were limited on campsite options (everything nearby was well above tree line), so we stuck to our plan and continued on to meet him.

My knees screamed at me. The braces helped, but the hike was taking its toll, and my body was reaching its limit for the day. Tears filled my eyes—and I tried my hardest not to let them fall—as a sharp pain grabbed at the insides of my kneecaps with every step. I was used to a constant dull ache, but this pain took my breath away.

I swallowed a couple extra ibuprofen with a swig of electrolyte water. My friends suggested I lead the final half-mile push so I could set a pace that was comfortable for me. The trail was a stream of water from the downpour, all uphill with no relief. I was tired, cold, and sore, and now it was raining again. Somehow the last half mile always feels the longest.

We arrived, picked out tent pads, and started sorting our gear. The rain graciously paused long enough for us to set up our tents. The ground was so rocky and hard-packed, the stakes for my rain fly would not go into the earth. Instead, I did the same thing others had done and used rocks left behind to hold down the guy lines and corners of my rain fly and tent.

We groaned when the rain returned before we'd eaten dinner. Pig's Ear and Barn Dawg had already retreated to their tents with their food, but Arms and I sat in the downpour, filtering water and waiting for our slower solid fuel stove to boil. We huddled together and ate dinner as the sky continued to dump on our heads. I'd saved one of my favorite backpacking meals for the night before our big climb. I affectionately called it "Thanksgiving Dinner in a Bag." Inside the quart-sized Ziplock bag were layers of instant mashed potatoes, instant stuffing, powdered gravy, freeze-dried chicken, and a handful of dried cranberries. All I had to do was add boiling water, stir it up, and enjoy. Even as I shivered, rain dripping off my hood, I scraped the inside of the bag with my spork. I was going to savor every last calorie.

After dinner, I unzipped my rain fly and tried to peel off my saturated layers while squeezed into the tiny vestibule outside my tent. I'd been carrying a small trash bag with me to help keep my clothes dry when they were outside my pack liner. For the first few days I'd wondered if I really needed to be carrying the weight. Through the rainy stretch, though, it had become a priceless piece of gear.

I stuffed the disintegrating pieces of my rain gear into the trash bag to keep my quilt and everything else inside from getting wet. I knelt on the bare floor of my tent, hard from the packed ground underneath. Wearing my bra, underwear, and soaking wet socks, I pulled my quilt out of the bottom of my bag and up over my body like a turtle shell. I rested my forehead on my sleeping pad, which was still rolled up and neatly contained within its bag.

I shivered uncontrollably underneath the quilt and began to cry. Earlier in the day, Arms had told me that we'd been hiking in the rain for eleven straight days. In town we'd learned that the same storm systems that had been passing over us, dumping water, had caused catastrophic and unprecedented flooding in Death Valley, eighty-five miles to the east, the driest place in the United States.

The harder I shook, the more the sobs overtook me. As the wind whipped the rain against the sides of my tent, I couldn't hold back anymore. I was sick of the rain, frustrated with my knees, and sad about Chris. I had tried to give her the space she wanted over the last several days on trail, only texting here and there to see how her day was, and giving her my location in camp every night. But the enormity of how far away she felt had worn me down, just like the endless rain.

The wind rattled the poles of my tent, and the rain fly came loose at the bottom of the vestibule, pulling away from the pile of rocks that had been anchoring it. The rain-soaked fly flapped against the mesh wall of my tent, and water started sprinkling the top of my head. I knew I only had moments to fix it before the water would be pouring through the mesh onto my belongings inside.

I unzipped the door and crawled out, slipping into my camp shoes while still wearing just my bra and underwear. The rain and my tears combined to form tributaries that streaked down my face in tiny rivers. With numb, shaking hands, I wedged the fly's zipper pull back between two rocks, praying it would hold.

I dove headfirst back inside my tent, kicking off my camp shoes as I went, and quickly zipped the vestibule and door behind me. I pulled my quilt over myself again to try to get warm. I had hoped the tears would subside, but a few minutes later they were still washing over me, rolling relentless waves that somehow kept pulling me under.

The next morning, we planned to summit. It should have been a moment of antsy anticipation, excitement, joy, and camaraderie among my hiker family. It should have been a celebration of all we'd accomplished, and eagerness for the final push together. But instead, I was lying on the hard ground in my tent, crying alone.

I wanted to be home, curled up on the couch between Katrina and Chris, watching movies and eating snacks. I wanted to be warm and cozy and dry. I wanted to feel safe and held and loved. I don't usually consider myself a quitter, but right then I would have given anything to be done, to give up and be teleported away from the mountains.

I had cried plenty on this trip, but it was my determination—and failure—to *not* be the heartbroken woman running away on a thru-hike that had led to this full-blown breakdown. I used my GPS to text Katrina and Chris separately. I gave in to my sadness and told them both how I was feeling. They both sent their love, and Katrina sent reassurance that she'd been watching the forecast and radar for Tumangaya. She was always my steadfast supporter, but I could feel her helplessness at my situation. She promised that the rain would stop any minute now, and we should have clear skies for our predawn climb.

With swollen eyes and blurry vision, I peeled my forehead off my rolled-up sleeping pad. I was warm enough now to strip my wet bra and underwear off and pull dry base layers on. Once clothed, I laid out my sleeping pad and inflated it, pulling on the elastic straps for my quilt with a familiar ease. I slipped under the comfort of my quilt, wrote in my journal, and set an alarm for 11:30 p.m. We had agreed to leave camp at 1 a.m. Finally, I took Benadryl and melatonin, in the hopes that sleep would come even though the darkness wouldn't arrive for several hours.

At 11 p.m. I awoke to Barn Dawg and Pig's Ear stirring nearby. I dozed for a few minutes before pulling on the rest of my clothes and stepping out of my tent. With tremendous relief and gratitude, I looked up at the cloudless, star-filled sky. The moon was nearly full and still high, and the Big Dipper rested low over the mountains. I spent a few minutes taking photos and admiring the dark beauty of the night.

Our group of four began the ascent just after our scheduled start time of 1 a.m. We were slow and steady as a team, carefully climbing the countless rows of switchbacks by headlamp. I had hand warmers in my new gloves, my hat pulled down over my ears, and my puffy zipped all the way up. The higher we climbed, the colder it got, and I was grateful for my dry layers and the suffering I had endured to keep them that way.

As we stopped for water breaks, I admired the silhouette of the mountains against the sinking moon. When the moon finally disappeared behind the shadow of the peaks, the stars became brighter, more vibrant in the sky. It was the height of the Perseid meteor shower, and I counted shooting stars streaking across the sky, one after another, until I couldn't keep track anymore. Though the sky was filled with stars, it was also incredibly dark, a backdrop for the spectacular light show above us. Our distance from civilization meant that there was no light pollution from cities. Far below I could see other headlamps bobbing their way up the trail, little specks of light in the distance.

We were well above 13,000 feet now, higher than I'd ever been before. I felt a change in the air. The breeze shifted and the air smelled cold, the way it does in the hours before a snowstorm. My poles stuck in the wet sand as it began to freeze.

I was reminded of my first-ever pre-sunrise hike years before, and a night that had felt so dark that I had questioned for a moment if the sun would rise. When dawn finally came, I had remembered that the sun always returned—I just needed to have a little trust and patience. Climbing Tumangaya with my friends, I didn't have any doubts that the sun would rise. I'd already walked through the darkest part of this hike. My heart soared as Chris and Katrina each texted me, despite the early hour, without me reaching out first. This was the first time on my hike that Chris had sent me a message of gentle encouragement, and I wondered if maybe we would be okay after all.

We moved with caution as the trail maneuvered across rocky, narrow ledges, with small gaps that could easily trap an unsuspecting ankle. The frost-slicked rocks sparkled in our headlamps. When the path leveled out through a boulder field, I could sense we were getting close, though it was still too dark to see.

And then, all at once, there we were, climbing up to the summit of Tumangaya and the stone hut with no door. We piled inside the tiny room to get out of the wind. It was 4:50 a.m. and we had reached the official end of the John Muir Trail. We signed the register, smiles wide across our faces. We were the first ones to arrive at the summit that day.

We perched on the frozen rocks wrapped in our quilts and watched as the sky began to lighten. Soft pastels filled the rounded edges of the earth and wisps of clouds blew over us, leaving my quilt covered in droplets that quickly froze. The clouds swirled, dancing in front of my eyes, rising and falling like the earth's breath between the peaks and valleys of the spires below.

I watched the sky in awe, filled with gratitude for my body that felt just as good now at 14,500 feet as it had at 12,000 feet the day before. I could hardly believe that a few hours earlier I had been ready to give up.

It was as if a key had unlocked my mind. I understood now that no matter how much I tried to leave the heaviness behind in the name of being "present," I would never succeed. The harder I tried to avoid being the girl crying in the wilderness, the more impossible it was to be immersed in the beauty around me. When I was able to make space for and honor what I was experiencing, I was also able to be more present in the magic of the Sierra Nevada. Whether it was endless rain, a heavy pack, a sore knee, or an aching heart, there was no running away—there was only accepting what was.

As the sun crested the horizon, I turned over a small heart-shaped rock between my fingers. I breathed the morning air deep into my lungs, and for the first time in three weeks, I held my own heart in my hands.

———

Meaghan "Rapunzel" Martin (she/her)
Standish, Maine—ancestral territories of the Wabanaki Dawnland Confederacy

Meaghan has loved the forest as a friend since childhood, but the mountains and trails have challenged her to grow in ways she didn't know were possible. She has thru-hiked the Long Trail and the Nüümü Poyo (John Muir Trail), and she is slowly chipping away at climbing New Hampshire's forty-eight 4,000-foot peaks. She has a BA in English with a minor in creative writing, as well as an MA in social work. She has been published in *Horses with a Mission: Extraordinary True Stories of Equine Service* and *Animals and the Kids Who Love Them: Extraordinary True Stories of Hope, Healing, and Compassion*. She believes there is great power that can be found in lending our voices to discussion about the things we are told we aren't supposed to talk about.

She can be found on Instagram and TikTok @meaghan_adventures.

if i can do this

THE FIRST TIME I EVER SHIT IN THE WOODS, I CRIED. I WAS twenty-four years old. It was a one-night backpacking trip. One of only two that I went on as practice for the Appalachian Trail. I probably could have held it until we returned to the parking lot on the second day if I hadn't drunk so much premixed margarita the first night at the campfire. But first thing that morning, my insides were roiling. Angry. My head ached and tears threatened as I tried to talk my stomach down. In my pack was the collapsible pooping trowel my mom had bought for me for my future hike of the AT. It was sort of cute, silver and turquoise with a little button that slid the handle into the head. I had placed it into the side pocket of my pack with the sincerity of an amateur who knows this item is on the packing list— but hasn't given any thought to the reality of its use.

Throughout my childhood I had avoided public restrooms like they were contaminated with the plague. I once almost peed my pants on a class trip to Disney's Animal Kingdom rather than brave the horrors of a theme park restroom without my mother there to check the stall before I went in. At Girl Scout camp, I called my dad to come pick me up because the idea of pooping in a porta-potty had me so distressed that I actually vomited.

In college, my girlfriends would sometimes duck behind a car and pop a squat in a parking lot after a night out drinking. A habit I found horrific and fascinating. They would just pee. On the ground. Wasn't pee getting on their shoes? They didn't seem to care about being seen. By my early twenties, I had mostly conquered my fear of public bathrooms, so long as they were clean and didn't have gaping holes between the door and the wall. But squatting in a parking lot? No way. It just wasn't natural. Humans were meant to pee in toilets.

As I rummaged through my pack for the trowel, the heat of my insides burned my cheeks. The rest of the group went about their morning chores—breaking camp, packing their gear, disappearing into the bushes with their own trowels and coming back as if nothing decidedly unnatural had just happened. I tried to hide my face as I left camp with a plastic baggie of toilet paper and my shame shovel. I was planning to hike the Appalachian Trail. If I couldn't do this, there was no way I could do that.

I looked behind the first row of bushes—not nearly far enough from camp. Someone might walk up on me or, worse, be able to see me from their tent. I walked a bit farther, and then a bit farther. For ten minutes, I wove through bushes and trees, searching for the perfect spot. Somewhere secluded, flat, not too prickly, no sign of critters. As much as I searched, I secretly hoped the feeling would subside and I wouldn't have to go through with it. I could wait it out.

But I couldn't. The liquor shits wait for no man. Or woman.

I knelt before my fate. Poking halfheartedly at the dry earth with the tiny trowel, I realized that digging a six-to-eight-inch-deep cathole was more of a task than I had bargained for. As the churning of my stomach increased, I frantically stabbed and gouged at the earth. It was like chipping away stone. I tried to use my hands to pull up the dirt, to no effect. I looked around for some other tool—but nothing seemed more appropriate than the literal shovel I held. That's when the tears welled up. A feeling of hopelessness gripped me. There I was, a grown-ass woman, stabbing at the stubborn ground with a miniature shovel, only a few miles from a perfectly good pit toilet. My face contorted into the hideous grimace of a squalling child. My stomach tightened. A dramatic sob caught in my throat. I was pitiful. Pathetic.

The sun had risen on a crisp October day in California. We had slept just around the corner from Horseshoe Lake and would head there to swim as soon as we were packed. As everyone else rolled their tents and ate their breakfasts, I sat alone in the bushes crying. And I was the one who was supposedly preparing for a six-month thru-hike. I was the one who had come here to practice for something bigger. To hone my skills. And this was a skill in desperate need of honing. Nobody was going to waltz up to my super-secret perfect pooping spot and rescue me. I had to figure it out.

I wiped my eyes and snotty nose on the sleeve of my wool base layer before reassessing the area. Nearby, a promising patch of grass stuck up from the dirt. It couldn't be as dry and hard as the spot where I had been digging if grass was growing there. I moved. I dug. I shimmied my pants down to my ankles and scurried into an uncomfortable squatting position. I released the demons from within. I wept. I buried the evidence.

The relief that flooded me was almost powerful enough to extinguish the waves of nausea that had been breaking all morning. Wiping my clammy hands on my pants, I extricated myself from the bushes and wobbled back to my tent. My breath steadied as I resumed packing up my belongings.

I wondered if the others could see the change in me.

There are defining moments in a person's life. For me—there is before I shit in the woods and after.

EIGHT YEARS and a hundred or so shits in the woods later, I found myself 1,700 miles from the hole I had left in the earth near Horseshoe Lake in California. I now walked through the Ouachita Mountains in eastern Oklahoma, approaching the Arkansas state line. My attempt to set a speed record on the 223-mile Ouachita Trail was in the process of going completely off the rails.

Pins and needles prickled the soles of my feet, forcing them to curl away from the earth in protest. The four hours of sleep I had promised my mind and body had been a lie. Unintentionally undelivered. I hadn't realized that the fudge brownie–flavored endurance goo I'd eaten, complete with slow-burning fats and fast-burning carbs, also delivered a punch of caffeine. For most people this wouldn't have been of much concern, but for someone with a dysfunctional autonomic nervous system, who has never really developed an affinity for the bounding heart rate and panicked interior monologue that accompany dosing with our most socially acceptable drug, it was ruinous. After a thirty-six-mile first day on the trail, I had lain staring up at the pitch blackness of the inside of my lime-green tent. The Ouachita National Forest was so dark and silent, my surroundings no longer existed. All that was real in that moment was the thunderous pulsing of blood in my veins, my heart, my eardrums, the bottoms of my feet.

If I had a chance in hell of finishing this thing, I needed to rest. I closed my eyes, but they peeled themselves back open. My brain buzzed with thought loops that started and ended with *I should be sleeping now.* The aggressive desire to be unconscious ratcheted up my anxiety against the frenetic circles that seemed to be physically swirling in the giant cavity where my brain should have been. I wondered why I was even out here. Was it supposed to be fun? Hell no. But why force suffering on myself? Why was I a person who must always move through the world with something to prove? Perhaps it stemmed from my entirely defiant existence on this earth. From birth I have been a medical miracle, operated on hours after being surgically removed from the womb, to tuck my wandering insides back into my body. The same body I have fought against ever since. The same body I was now forcing in a death march down another long trail, just to prove that this body was worthy of existence. That my mounting list of diagnoses was not sufficient to keep me from the mountains.

If I can do this, then . . .

These are the words that push me ever onward. That keep me coming back. The target is always moving, growing, increasingly outlandish and far-fetched. Each finish line I cross reveals another, only going to show that my work here is never done. Suggesting perhaps that this body's worth cannot be earned but must be given freely.

The wildlife could hear me lying awake for miles around and kept their distance.

I had risen after three hours and continued to walk. What else was there to do? What had started out as a solid 3-to-4-mile-per-hour pace slowed to a grueling 1.5. I checked my watch compulsively. Pace. Time. Miles. Pace. Time. Miles.

On the second day of my attempt, I had planned to hike only a mile or two farther than the first day—already the longest day I had ever put down. It hadn't seemed crazy on paper. I'd been training all season.

Now I dragged my feet through inches of leaf litter—the sound of my *crunch-crunching* itself a measure of my pace. I'd heard rumors that the first thirty miles of the trail were the hardest and rockiest. I had expected that. I hadn't considered the inches of dry, dead fallen leaves hiding the heaps of boulders from view, making every step a risky one. I also hadn't been forewarned that all those rumors were a lie. Now more than forty miles into the trail, I'd seen no significant decrease in the rocks. Even the elevation profile was misleading. The trail flattened out as it wound its way through the Kiamichi Valley, which might lead a hiker to think that they're in for a few cruisy miles. But no, rocky riverbeds broke up long stretches of thorny overgrowth that obscured, you guessed it, more rocks. This stretch also included the addition of hundreds of fat-bodied, brightly colored, poisonous-looking orb weaver spiders, notorious for weaving webs as fast as you can tear through them—always face-first, of course.

My only regret when reaching the other side of the valley was that I had to climb out of it. The ascent was grueling. My leaden legs rebelled against the limping gait I'd adopted in response to my screaming feet. My eyelids hung heavy, hindering my ability to navigate the rocks and leaves. I hadn't seen another human being all day. My cell phone's battery had been leached by my need to make some contact in my weakened state. I'd sent out messages:

My feet hurt.

I'm going too slow.
I don't know if I can do this.

The responses didn't matter. Only that somebody knew what I felt. That I wasn't alone out here. Even though I was completely alone out here. Nobody could take my pain away. Or do the hard work for me. Or make me into the person I wanted to be. I would have to walk through it. That's what I was trying to do. I wanted to be the kind of woman who could suffer in the name of becoming. But I hadn't known that that woman's feet were capable of hurting this badly.

I allowed myself to sit and rest. Again. Again. Minutes slipped past, much faster than I was able to walk by now. Around 4 p.m. the sun began to sink. November days were so short. I hadn't thought of that either when I planned this trip—the hours spent hiking in the dark.

I dragged my feet another twenty steps. Stopped. Sighed. Sniffled. I walked again. Twelve steps. The Ouachita Mountains are barely hills in many eyes, reaching elevations of less than 3,000 feet. But in that moment, they were the biggest mountains a molehill could make. I put one foot in front of the other, pressing into the earth with all my willpower. My mind battled my body. Pinks and purples colored the sky. My mind said, *Keep going, don't be weak, this is what you came for, this is what you trained for, this is where you prove something.* My body lay sprawled beside the trail. I wanted to curl in on myself, but it was too hot, and my muscles were too tired. I had moved fifteen miles in just under twelve hours. Records aren't set with paces like that.

I called my partner.

"Hey!" His voice was cheerful. He was proud of what I was doing. It was interesting and impressive. He loved to be in partnership with the woman I wanted to be.

"I want to come home," I choked.

A long silence followed. I tried not to let him hear my ragged, snotty breathing. He knew the battles I waged with myself. He knew the very real limitations of my chronically ill body. He knew, but didn't truly understand, why this was so important to me. He'd been my biggest cheerleader, but also the voice of reason. Sometimes, it seemed, he wasn't sure which one to be.

"Why?" he asked.

"The pain in my feet is excruciating. I'm moving way too slowly. I just don't think it's possible to make up the lost time. Resting isn't helping. And I don't think they're going to recover unless I stop hiking."

"Okay. Then come home."

Sometimes I wasn't sure whether I needed a cheerleader or a voice of reason either.

I got up and kept walking. Whether or not I was quitting, I couldn't stop here—miles from the nearest road, lying on the side of the trail, embraced by the detritus of the surrounding oak trees. If I planned to give up, I would have five more miles to think about it.

Tears came in waves as the trail wound its way through the Ouachita Mountains. I spoke to myself. I justified. I bargained. I scolded. I pep-talked. I considered spending a night at Queen Wilhelmina Lodge to see if I might feel up for another big day after a proper sleep. However, I knew that the pain in my feet would not, could not, resolve with just one night of rest.

When I reached the lodge and called my dad to come pick me up, the relief of quitting washed over me. I thought about what real athletes endure in the name of fastest known time records, the absolute body-breaking mental fortitude that they exhibit in these attempts. I have read the stories, seen the pictures of feet that will turn your stomach, and heard of the sleep-deprived hallucinations. People in this sport show a level of resilience and perseverance that often crosses the line into legitimate self-endangerment. I wasn't out here to compete with those athletes. My dream of putting my name on the board was only possible because there are many hundreds of trails where women's records are not only noncompetitive, but nonexistent. This was only a competition between me and my body.

———

JUST A FEW DAYS shy of one year later, I walk through the same stretch of fallen leaves and heaped boulders. The first twenty-five or so miles seem to go on forever, because I'm not hurrying along the trail, trying to set a record. The next twenty-five go much faster, because I'm not limping along on feet that cry out with every step. I told myself that this wasn't about speed. That I just wanted to experience this trail. To enjoy the hike. To go at my own pace. To remember why I first fell in love with hiking.

As I approach the fifty-mile mark, I keep watch alongside the trail for the place where I collapsed last year. I try to remember the specific trees who watched over my tears. I try to identify a section of the climb that was more crushing than the rest, which might have been the final straw that broke me mentally—that made me give up entirely. But the trail only meanders through the forest, turning this way and that, steadily, but not aggressively, climbing up to the ridgeline.

The sun sets in pinks and oranges tonight, and a wind howls over the ridgeline, bending the walls of my tent. I wake up the next day and hike on. I finish the trail in fifteen days, including a zero day in the only town along the way. I put my hands on the crumbling wooden sign in Pinnacle Mountain State Park at the eastern terminus in Little Rock, Arkansas. I've reached the finish line. Tears blur the leaves and trees and trail.

If I can do this, then . . .

———

CHRISTINE REED (SHE/HER)
Editor of *Blood Sweat Tears.*

acknowledgments

A million thanks to all the writers who share of themselves fully and vulnerably in this collection. I have so much admiration for the work you put in and the stories you told. And I am eternally grateful for your patience with me, the process, the inevitable delays, and the occasional long silences as we all poured our blood, sweat, and tears into these pages.

To Sarah, Laura, and Marina for your invaluable contributions. It was my mission to make this project a full collaboration of outdoorsy women+, and being able to extend that to the designer and editors was an important alignment.

To every single person who submitted a story for the collection. Storytelling is an act of bravery and connection. Opening yourself up to rejection is another. I hope those of you whose stories were not chosen will share them elsewhere and continue submitting in the future. Your story matters.

To the Rugged Outdoors Women+ Write Group. You keep me honest, keep me working, keep me showing up. And graciously allow me to step away when needed. So much love to you all, and here's to many more years of friendship and community.

To Jasmyn and Maggie, who reached out to offer financial support completely of their own volition. I cannot explain how intensely appreciated that is.

To Nancy for being there at the birth of the movement. This idea had been brewing in different forms for a long time, but our conversation at the Authors' Table at Trail Days in 2023 was the catalyst that made it all start moving forward.

To Lindy, who spent an entire day reading not even half of the submissions aloud with me to kick things off. For helping me keep a clear head and plow on as I quickly realized what I'd gotten myself into. And for always offering some wild story to distract me during eight months of angst.

To my dad, who stretches himself to understand my passions and what I have to offer the world. Who is always a safe place to land, and somebody to get snappy at when I'm stressed out. And who I know is proud because he tells all his friends that I'm a "free spirit."

To Ryan, who has been my biggest emotional and practical support through the four years of our partnership and beyond. Who rises above the call of duty and continues to be my warehouse and distribution manager as our relationship shifts and evolves.

To Austin for your intense energetic investment during the first five months of the project. When I had nothing left to give, you reminded me of my why.

To John for the camaraderie and literal shoulder to cry on in the homestretch. Having another writer around is magic. I don't know what I would have done without you.

To everyone who is reading these words, thank you for that.

rugged
outdoorswoman
publishing

Please leave a review to help others find these words.

For other books by Rugged Outdoorswoman Publishing –
visit www.ruggedoutdoorswoman.com